HARRIET TUBMAN

HARRIET TUBMAN

M.W. Taylor

Senior Consulting Editor
Nathan Irvin Huggins
Director
W.E.B. Du Bois Institute for Afro-American Research
Harvard University

CHELSEA HOUSE PUBLISHERS
New York   Philadelphia

Chelsea House Publishers
Editor-in-Chief Remmel Nunn
Managing Editor Karyn Gullen Browne
Copy Chief Juliann Barbato
Picture Editor Adrian G. Allen
Art Director Maria Epes
Deputy Copy Chief Mark Rifkin
Assistant Art Director Loraine Machlin
Manufacturing Manager Gerald Levine
Systems Manager Rachel Vigier
Production Manager Joseph Romano
Production Coordinator Marie Claire Cebrián

Black Americans of Achievement
Senior Editor Richard Rennert

Staff for HARRIET TUBMAN
Copy Editor Philip Koslow
Editorial Assistant Leigh Hope Wood
Picture Researcher Nisa Rauschenberg
Designer Ghila Krajzman
Cover Illustration Vilma Ortiz

9

Library of Congress Cataloging-in-Publication Data

Taylor, M. W.
    Harriet Tubman: antislavery activist/by M. W. Taylor
        p.   cm.—(Black Americans of achievement)
    Includes bibliographical references.
    Summary: Describes the life of the energetic abolitionist, including
her origins as a slave in Maryland, her role as a "conductor" for the
Underground Railroad, her service to the Union during the Civil
War, and her role in establishing an old-age home for Afro-Americans.
    ISBN 1-55546-612-5
        0-7910-0249-7 (pbk.)
    1. Tubman, Harriet, 1820?–1913—Juvenile literature.   2.
Slaves—United States—Biography—Juvenile literature.   3. Afro-
Americans—Biography—Juvenile literature.   4. Underground railroad—Juvenile literature.   5. Slavery—United States—Antislavery
movements—Juvenile literature. [1. Tubman, Harriet, 1820?–
1913.   2. Slaves.   3. Underground railroad.   4. Afro-Americans—
Biography.] I. Title.   II. Series.
E444.T82B57 1990
305.5'67'092—dc20   89-77281
[B]   CIP
[92]   AC

Frontispiece: *Harriet Tubman*
(far left) poses with a group of
former slaves in the North.

CONTENTS

————— ❦ —————

BLACK AMERICANS OF ACHIEVEMENT

RALPH ABERNATHY
civil rights leader

MUHAMMAD ALI
heavyweight champion

RICHARD ALLEN
religious leader and social activist

LOUIS ARMSTRONG
musician

ARTHUR ASHE
tennis great

JOSEPHINE BAKER
entertainer

JAMES BALDWIN
author

BENJAMIN BANNEKER
scientist and mathematician

AMIRI BARAKA
poet and playwright

COUNT BASIE
bandleader and composer

ROMARE BEARDEN
artist

JAMES BECKWOURTH
frontiersman

MARY MCLEOD
BETHUNE
educator

BLANCHE BRUCE
politician

RALPH BUNCHE
diplomat

GEORGE WASHINGTON
CARVER
botanist

CHARLES CHESNUTT
author

BILL COSBY
entertainer

PAUL CUFFE
merchant and abolitionist

FATHER DIVINE
religious leader

FREDERICK DOUGLASS
abolitionist editor

CHARLES DREW
physician

W.E.B. DU BOIS
scholar and activist

PAUL LAURENCE DUNBAR
poet

KATHERINE DUNHAM
dancer and choreographer

MARIAN WRIGHT EDELMAN
civil rights leader and lawyer

DUKE ELLINGTON
bandleader and composer

RALPH ELLISON
author

JULIUS ERVING
basketball great

JAMES FARMER
civil rights leader

ELLA FITZGERALD
singer

MARCUS GARVEY
black-nationalist leader

DIZZY GILLESPIE
musician

PRINCE HALL
social reformer

W. C. HANDY
father of the blues

WILLIAM HASTIE
educator and politician

MATTHEW HENSON
explorer

CHESTER HIMES
author

BILLIE HOLIDAY
singer

JOHN HOPE
educator

LENA HORNE
entertainer

LANGSTON HUGHES
poet

ZORA NEALE HURSTON
author

JESSE JACKSON
civil rights leader and politician

JACK JOHNSON
heavyweight champion

JAMES WELDON JOHNSON
author

SCOTT JOPLIN
composer

BARBARA JORDAN
politician

MARTIN LUTHER KING, JR.
civil rights leader

ALAIN LOCKE
scholar and educator

JOE LOUIS
heavyweight champion

RONALD MCNAIR
astronaut

MALCOLM X
militant black leader

THURGOOD MARSHALL
Supreme Court justice

ELIJAH MUHAMMAD
religious leader

JESSE OWENS
champion athlete

CHARLIE PARKER
musician

GORDON PARKS
photographer

SIDNEY POITIER
actor

ADAM CLAYTON POWELL, JR.
political leader

LEONTYNE PRICE
opera singer

A. PHILIP RANDOLPH
labor leader

PAUL ROBESON
singer and actor

JACKIE ROBINSON
baseball great

BILL RUSSELL
basketball great

JOHN RUSSWURM
publisher

SOJOURNER TRUTH
antislavery activist

HARRIET TUBMAN
antislavery activist

NAT TURNER
slave revolt leader

DENMARK VESEY
slave revolt leader

MADAM C. J. WALKER
entrepreneur

BOOKER T. WASHINGTON
educator

HAROLD WASHINGTON
politician

WALTER WHITE
civil rights leader and author

RICHARD WRIGHT
author

ON
ACHIEVEMENT

Coretta Scott King

Before you begin this book, I hope you will ask yourself what the word excellence means to you. I think that it's a question we should all ask, and keep asking as we grow older and change. Because the truest answer to it should never change. When you think of excellence, perhaps you think of success at work; or of becoming wealthy; or meeting the right person, getting married, and having a good family life.

Those important goals are worth striving for, but there is a better way to look at excellence. As Martin Luther King, Jr., said in one of his last sermons, "I want you to be first in love. I want you to be first in moral excellence. I want you to be first in generosity. If you want to be important, wonderful. If you want to be great, wonderful. But recognize that he who is greatest among you shall be your servant."

My husband, Martin Luther King, Jr., knew that the true meaning of achievement is service. When I met him, in 1952, he was already ordained as a Baptist preacher and was working towards a doctoral degree at Boston University. I was studying at the New England Conservatory and dreamed of accomplishments in music. We married a year later, and after I graduated the following year we moved to Montgomery, Alabama. We didn't know it then, but our notions of achievement were about to undergo a dramatic change.

You may have read or heard about what happened next. What began with the boycott of a local bus line grew into a national movement, and by the time he was assassinated in 1968 my husband had fashioned a black movement powerful enough to shatter forever the practice of racial segregation. What you may not have read about is where he got his method for resisting injustice without compromising his religious beliefs.

He adopted the strategy of nonviolence from a man of a different race, who lived in a distant country, and even practiced a different religion. The man was Mahatma Gandhi, the great leader of India, who devoted his life to serving humanity in the spirit of love and nonviolence. It was in these principles that Martin discovered his method for social reform. More than anything else, those two principles were the key to his achievements.

This book is about black Americans who served society through the excellence of their achievements. It forms a part of the rich history of black men and women in America—a history of stunning accomplishments in every field of human endeavor, from literature and art to science, industry, education, diplomacy, athletics, jurisprudence, even polar exploration.

Not all of the people in this history had the same ideals, but I think you will find something that all of them have in common. Like Martin Luther King, Jr., they all decided to become "drum majors" and serve humanity. In that principle—whether it was expressed in books, inventions, or song—they found something outside themselves to use as a goal and a guide. Something that showed them a way to serve others, instead of living only for themselves.

Reading the stories of these courageous men and women not only helps us discover the principles that we will use to guide our own lives but also teaches us about our black heritage and about America itself. It is crucial for us to know the heroes and heroines of our history and to realize that the price we paid in our struggle for equality in America was dear. But we must also understand that we have gotten as far as we have partly because America's democratic system and ideals made it possible.

We are still struggling with racism and prejudice. But the great men and women in this series are a tribute to the spirit of our democratic ideals and the system in which they have flourished. And that makes their stories special and worth knowing. ⬧

HARRIET TUBMAN

1

A WOMAN CALLED MOSES

Tubman escaped from slavery in 1849, then returned to the South at least 19 times during the next 10 years to lead more than 300 blacks to freedom in the North. According to one historian, "No fugitive was ever captured who had [her] for a leader."

On THE AFTERNOON of April 27, 1860, a tall black man named Charles Nalle stood defiantly before United States Commissioner Miles Beach in a courthouse in Troy, New York. A runaway slave, Nalle was being watched closely by an assortment of attorneys, court officers, and armed U.S. marshals, as well as Henry J. Wall, a plantation agent from Virginia. The marshals and Wall had just finished giving evidence against Nalle in their effort to send him back into slavery. Two years earlier, he had escaped from Virginia and made his way north to freedom.

But on this spring afternoon, 500 miles from the nearest slave state, Nalle faced the prospect of being told he was still a slave. According to the Fugitive Slave Act, federal legislation that was passed in 1850, he remained the property of his owner, even in a free state. The U.S. government was legally obliged to return a captured slave to bondage.

As the sounds of a crowd gathering outside the courthouse began to fill the second-floor room, Commissioner Beach disclosed his chilling decision to the court: Nalle must be turned over to Wall and returned to his southern master. Nalle edged toward the window. Below, on First and State streets, their eyes fixed on him, stood more than 1,000 people, black and white, women and men. Nalle knew that Troy, like most other northern cities, was home to many opponents of slavery. Some of these abolitionists favored ending slavery peacefully and lawfully. Others were ready and willing to help a slave escape any way they could.

Nalle lunged for the window. He almost made it through, but marshals seized his arms and dragged him back into the courtroom. At that moment, freedom must have seemed like a dream to Nalle. Even if the people outside the courthouse had wanted to come to his aid, how could they do it? He was now closely guarded by armed men, and he had no friends or allies nearby. The only black face in sight belonged to a spectator, a bent old woman wearing a shawl and bonnet and carrying a basket. The guards had probably let her in because they felt sorry for her. What could one old woman do, anyway?

A band of patrollers—white slave catchers—guns down a quartet of fleeing blacks in the mid-1800s. The passage of the Fugitive Slave Act in 1850 accelerated the South's relentless tracking of runaways.

Suddenly, a voice from the crowd below shouted a question that was heard in the courtroom: How much money would it take for the southern agent to free Nalle?

"Twelve hundred dollars," Wall replied.

Purses were opened and hats hastily passed. A few minutes later, the spectators announced that they had collected the price of Charles Nalle's freedom. Agent Wall responded by raising the figure to $1,500. A low, angry roar swept the crowd: The slave catcher was mocking them; he had no intention of releasing Nalle.

The abolitionists had tried to save Nalle and had failed. There was nothing else they could do. Now that the hearing was over, he would be put aboard a train and sent south, back into slavery.

Guards chained Nalle's hands and pushed him toward the stairs that led to the street. Near the landing, the guards brushed aside the old black woman, who was standing quietly, her head bowed. But as soon as they had passed her, she tore off her sunbonnet and raced to the window. "Here he comes," she shouted to the people below. "Take him!"

The crowd surged forward, meeting Nalle and his guards at the foot of the stairs. The marshals raised their clubs, yet the crowd continued to press in. Then down the stairs, like an avenging angel, charged the "old woman." Without her shawl, basket, and stooped pose, she revealed herself as a small, very dark-skinned woman of about 40. Her eyes were bright, even fierce; her arms were muscular, her fists clenched. The marshals ducked as she flew at them, punching furiously and shouting at the top of her lungs.

"Drag him to the river!" the woman cried. "Drown him! But don't let them have him!" Then, an eyewitness reported later, "like a wildcat" she

knocked down one of Nalle's guards and wrapped her arms around the manacled prisoner. Wrenching him away from a second guard, she pulled Nalle through the crowd toward the river. Marshals flailed at Nalle and his rescuer with fists and clubs, but the woman refused to let go. The crowd joined her.

The *Troy Whig* described the scene as "a regular battlefield." In the "surging mass" of people, said the newspaper, "the pulling, hauling, mauling, and shouting gave evidences of frantic efforts on the part of the rescuers, and a stern resistance from the conservators of the law." The street filled with screams, curses, and the smell of gunpowder.

"In the melee," a local attorney stated later, the small black woman "was repeatedly beaten over the

Slaves—men, women, and children—carry their harvest after a 16-hour day in the cotton fields. Escaping from such bondage in 1858, Virginian Charles Nalle was recaptured two years later in Troy, New York, but was eventually freed by Tubman and others.

head with policemen's clubs, but she never for a moment released her hold, but cheered Nalle and his friends with her voice, and struggled with the officers until they were literally worn out with their exertions, and Nalle was separated from them. True she had strong and earnest helpers in her struggle, some of whom had white faces as well as human hearts, and are now in Heaven. But she exposed herself to the fury of the sympathizers with slavery without fear, and suffered their blows without flinching."

Finally, the crowd managed to pull Nalle, chains and all, away from his captors. They rushed the bleeding, dazed fugitive to the riverbank and pushed him onto a waiting rowboat. As an oarsman pulled away from the shore, the black woman, along with some

400 allies, boarded a steam-powered ferryboat and followed the rowboat.

But more marshals, alerted by telegraph, awaited them across the river. They seized Nalle, locked him in a house, and placed armed guards at every window. Undeterred, the woman and her friends began to hurl rocks at the makeshift jail. The marshals responded with gunfire, and the crowd fell back. Then a man's voice shouted, "Who cares? They can only kill a dozen of us—come on!"

Eager to do his part, a huge black man emerged from the crowd, strode up to the house, and kicked down the door. Marshals swiftly felled him with an ax, but his body jammed the door open, and the abolitionists poured through. Strong hands picked up the battered Nalle, carried him outside, and put him into a wagon that rolled north, carrying the former slave toward Canada and freedom. Meanwhile, the crowd dispersed, and the black woman disappeared from view.

When the liberated slave revived, he asked about the woman who had engineered his rescue. Nalle's

A photographer in the mid-1800s created this powerful image of a slave on the run. In 1850 alone, more than 1,000 blacks fled their southern plantations for the free states of the North.

$100 REWARD.

Ran away from my farm, near Buena Vista P. O., Prince George's County, Maryland, on the first day of April, 1855, my servant MATHEW TURNER.

He is about five feet six or eight inches high; weighs from one hundred and sixty to one hundred and eighty pounds; he is very black, and has a remarkably thick upper lip and neck; looks as if his eyes are half closed; walks slow, and talks and laughs loud.

I will give One Hundred Dollars reward to whoever will secure him in jail, so that I get him again, no matter where taken.

MARCUS DU VAL.

BUENA VISTA P. O., MD.,
MAY 10, 1855.

Posted by a Maryland slave owner in 1855, a handbill offers $100 for the return of "servant" Mathew Turner. Notices about runaways, increasingly common in the decade before the Civil War, inspired widespread manhunts.

escorts told him she had gone into hiding because she carried a price on her head—she was wanted by authorities in both the North and the South for helping slaves escape from their masters. Her name was Harriet Tubman, they said, but she was better known as "Moses." A namesake of the biblical prophet who had brought his people out of bondage and into the Promised Land, Tubman had led more of her brethren out of Egypt—as she called the slaveholding South—than any other person, black or white, male or female, in American history. ☙

2

THE SHORT
CHILDHOOD OF
A SLAVE

◗◗◗

Harriet TUBMAN WAS born into slavery as Harriet Ross around 1820 on the Eastern Shore, a peninsula shared by the state of Delaware and parts of Maryland and Virginia. Bordered on the east by the Atlantic Ocean and on the west by the shallow, fish-filled waters of Chesapeake Bay, the area has a moderate climate. The Eastern Shore's flat, rich farmland is also known as the Tidewater because its countless inlets, swamps, and small rivers rise and fall with the tides of the nearby sea. Near the center of the peninsula, where Delaware and Maryland meet, is the nation's northernmost cypress swamp.

Although the Eastern Shore lies only a few miles from the industrial cities of Baltimore and Philadelphia, its atmosphere resembles that of the Deep South. Situated at the Confederacy's northernmost edge, it was the birthplace of some of the most renowned and valiant warriors in the battle against slavery, including Frederick Douglass and the woman who would be known as Moses.

Harriet Ross's birthdate is approximate because no one officially recorded it; few slaves could read or write, and slave owners kept no more precise data on

Facing a camera in the mid-1800s, a young slave embraces his little brother protectively. Tubman, like most children born into slavery, started work early; she was five years old when her master hired her out as a housemaid.

A southern planter barks out a command to his field slaves. As an adult, Tubman said of her cruel masters: "They didn't know any better. . . . They were brought up with the whip in their hand."

the lives of their slaves than they did on the lives of their pigs and chickens. Harriet was one of 11 children born to Harriet Green and Benjamin Ross, slaves belonging to Maryland planter Edward Brodas. Harriet's mother, known as Old Rit, gave her daughter the "cradle name" of Araminta. The little girl's family usually called her Minty.

Both Green and Ross were full-blooded Africans; their parents had been brought to the United States in chains. According to legend, the family came from the Ashanti, a West African warrior people who successfully battled the British during much of the 19th century. Harriet Tubman believed in this version of her roots; as an adult, she sometimes remarked that she was "one of those Ashantis." In any case, she would prove to be a formidable warrior herself.

On his plantation, situated on the Big Buckwater River in the Tidewater's Dorchester County, Edward

Brodas raised apples, wheat, rye, and corn. His land also included vast stands of trees, including oak, cypress, and poplar, which he sold to the Baltimore shipyards across the Chesapeake Bay. Harriet's father, Benjamin ("Old Ben") Ross, spent most of his days cutting timber for his master. Harriet's mother worked for the Brodas family in their elegant home, called "the big house" by the slaves.

Like many slave owners in the Upper South, Edward Brodas bred and raised blacks as a cash crop, renting and selling them to others. Georgia slave traders made frequent appearances in the neighborhood; by the time she was 13, Harriet Ross had seen sisters, brothers, and friends sold "down the river" to work on the vast cotton and sugar plantations of the Deep South.

The childhood of a slave was short. When Harriet was five years old, her master rented her to a local couple named Cook. At their home, the little girl slept on the kitchen floor, poking her feet under the fireplace ashes when the nights grew cold. For meals, she shared table scraps with the Cooks' dogs.

Mrs. Cook put Harriet to work winding yarn, but when the young slave proved slow at the job, her mistress turned her over to her husband. He assigned Harriet to watch his muskrat traps. Now she spent her days, barefoot and wearing only a thin shirt, wading in the edge of the icy river, looking for animals on James Cook's traplines. Before long, she developed a cough and a high fever, which her masters accused her of faking to escape work. Calling her useless, lazy, and stupid, the Cooks finally sent her back to the Brodas plantation. There, under her mother's care, Harriet recovered from a six-week bout of measles and bronchitis. Then Brodas rented her again, this time to a woman who wanted a housekeeper and baby nurse.

Many years after the experience, Harriet Tubman described it to a friend who recorded her account:

I was only seven years old when I was sent away to take care of a baby. I was so little that I had to sit on the floor and have the baby put on my lap. And that baby was always on my lap except when it was asleep or its mother was feeding it.

One morning, after breakfast, she had the baby, and I stood by the table waiting until I was to take it; near me was a bowl of lumps of white sugar. My mistress got into a great quarrel with her husband; she had an awful temper, and she would scold and storm and call him all kinds of names.

Now, you know, I never had anything good, no sweet, no sugar; and that sugar, right by me, did look so nice, and my mistress's back was turned to me while she was fighting with her husband, so I just put my fingers in the sugar bowl to take one lump and maybe she heard me for she turned and saw me.

The next minute she had the rawhide down. I gave one jump out of the door and I saw that they came after me, but I just flew and they didn't catch me. I ran and I ran and I passed many a house, but I didn't dare to stop for they all knew my mistress and they would send me back.

By and by when I was almost tuckered out, I came to a great big pigpen. There was an old sow there, and perhaps eight or ten little pigs. I tumbled over [the fence] and fell in . . . so beaten out that I could not stir.

And I stayed there from Friday until the next Tuesday, fighting with those little pigs for the potato peelings and the other scraps that came down in the trough. The old sow would push me away when I tried to get her children's food, and I was awfully afraid of her. By Tuesday I was so starved I knew I had to go back to my mistress. I didn't have anywhere else to go, even though I knew what was coming. So I went back.

The terrified little girl returned to her mistress, who gave her a savage whipping, then brought her back to the Brodas plantation. Harriet, said the woman who had rented her, "wasn't worth a six-pence." Once again, Old Rit nursed her child, salving the fresh wounds that overlay the scars from earlier beatings. And once again, as soon as Harriet was able to work, Brodas hired her out. This time, she was put to work splitting fence rails and loading timber on wagons. It was backbreaking labor, better suited to a brawny adult male than a little girl. Nevertheless, Harriet preferred it, she said later, to working in a house under the harsh scrutiny of a "lady."

By the time she was in her early teens, Harriet was known as a strong but surly laborer, unfit for indoor work but useful as a field hand. She never forgot her painful childhood, and she never had a good word for any of her masters. If they had any excuse for their cruelty, she asserted, it was ignorance. "They didn't know any better. It's the way they were brought up . . . with the whip in their hand," she said as an adult. "Now that wasn't the way on all plantations," she added. "There were good masters and mistresses, as I've heard tell. But I didn't happen to come across any of them."

In 1831, when Harriet was about 11, exciting but terrifying rumors swept the slave quarters of the Brodas estate. Nat Turner, a slave on a Virginia plantation—only 100 miles away, across the Chesapeake Bay—had led an army of 60 rebel slaves against their white masters. More than 50 whites, whispered the Brodas slaves to one another, had been killed in the uprising. True, Turner and his men had lost their battle, but their daring revolt offered proof that Africans were men, not animals, and that they would fight and die for their freedom.

Turner's was not the only black uprising in the 19th-century South. In 1800, a Virginia slave named Gabriel Prosser had tried and failed to establish an independent black state, and in 1822, Denmark Vesey had organized hundreds of blacks in a spectacular but futile bid for freedom in South Carolina. These rebellions sparked hope and elation among the South's blacks, terror among its whites.

Slaves found other ways, too, to establish some degree of independence. Some pretended to be stupid, "accidentally" destroying their masters' tools and

Nat Turner, the Virginia slave who led a revolt in 1831, surrenders after evading pursuers for two months. News of Turner's rebellion, in which more than 50 whites were killed, sent waves of fear—and pride—through the Brodas plantation's slaves.

Labeled like cattle, most slaves wore tags showing the name of their master. Free blacks carried medallions marked with the liberty cap (top), a token given to freed slaves in ancient Rome.

crops; others ran away when they saw their chance. Escape, however, was extremely difficult. When a planter reported a runaway slave, bands of mounted white men, known as patrollers ("patterollers" to the slave community), ranged through the countryside, tracking the fugitives with dogs. The standard punishment for runaways was whipping, branding with the letter *R*, and exile to the Deep South, where working conditions for slaves were more brutal than anywhere else. The slaves who trudged off in chains to Louisiana or Georgia never came back and rarely lived long.

During Harriet's childhood, even runaway slaves who managed to elude their pursuers had no place to go. Not until the mid-19th century, when the abolitionist movement began to develop in the North, was there any refuge for blacks fleeing their bonds.

It was an escaping slave who inadvertently brought disaster to 15-year-old Harriet. In the fall of 1835, she was shucking corn along with the rest of the plantation's workers when she noticed a tall black man sneaking away from the group. The overseer, carrying his snakeskin whip as usual, followed the black man. So did Harriet.

Catching up with the runaway at the crossroads store, the overseer prepared to whip him. He spotted Harriet and told her to hold the slave while he tied him up for the lashing. She refused. The black man bolted, and Harriet stationed herself in the doorway, blocking the overseer's way. Enraged, he grabbed a two-pound lead weight from the store counter and flung it after the running slave. The weight missed its mark and hit Harriet squarely in the head. She fell like a stone, blood pouring from a deep gash in her forehead.

When Harriet was carried home, her shocked mother dressed the wound, stopped the bleeding, and prayed. But the teenager remained in a coma for weeks, lying on a bed of rags in the corner of her

family's windowless wooden cabin. Not until the following spring was she able to get up and walk unaided.
Although her injury was never medically diagnosed
(doctors were rarely wasted on slaves), Harriet had
probably suffered a fractured skull and severe con-
cussion.

She would carry a scar and a dent in her forehead
for the rest of her life and, from that point on, would
suffer periodic "sleeping fits." Without warning,
wherever she might be, she would suddenly fall into
a deep sleep. Such attacks took place as often as three
or four times a day, even when Harriet was in the
middle of a conversation. Until she regained con-
sciousness by herself, nothing could rouse her.

While Harriet lay unconscious, the overseer who
had struck her appeared at the cabin door—not to
ask about her health but to see if she was fit enough
to sell. He clearly wanted to be rid of this stubborn
slave girl who had dared to defy him. Several times
while Harriet was recuperating, the overseer pushed
open the cabin door to give prospective buyers a look
at her. But, as she later recalled, "They wouldn't give
a sixpence for me."

Harriet had inherited her parents' strong religious
faith, and as she slowly recovered from her head

A slave auctioneer takes bids for
a black woman and her daughter.
Slaves were considered easier to
manage once they were separated
from their relatives and friends.

wound, she prayed hard—for the soul of plantation owner Edward Brodas. Years later, she told her first biographer, Sarah Bradford, about these days. "As I lay so sick on my bed, from Christmas till March, I was always praying for old master," she said. "Oh, dear Lord," she begged, "change that man's heart and make him a Christian." Although Brodas kept sending possible purchasers to look at her, she kept praying for him. "All I could say," she recalled, "was, 'Oh, Lord, convert old master.' "

Then more grim news swept the slave quarters: Brodas had decided to sell Harriet and two of her brothers and send them south in chains. At this point, Harriet recalled later, "I changed my prayer, and I said, 'Lord, if you're never going to change that man's heart, *kill him*, Lord, and take him out of the way, so he won't do more mischief.' "

Not long afterward, Brodas suddenly fell ill and died. Harriet, who never questioned the power of prayer, was horrified. What had she done? "I would [have given] the world full of silver and gold, if I had it," she said years later, "to bring that poor soul back, I would give *myself*; I would give everything! But he was gone."

Brodas's death left Harriet with a sense of deep guilt, but it also slightly improved her prospects. In his will, the plantation owner had left his estate to a young relative, directing that it be managed by Anthony Thompson, a local clergyman, until the heir came of age. Brodas's will also stipulated that none of his slaves be sold outside the state of Maryland after his death.

Thompson, however, continued Brodas's practice of hiring out the plantation's slaves. By this time, Harriet's head wound had healed, and although she suffered from violent headaches and sudden blackouts, she was once again able to work. Harriet was hired out to John Stewart, a local builder. At the same time, the estate manager rented Harriet's father, Ben Ross, to Stewart as a woodcutter. Her father, Harriet recalled later, was pleased by the assignment; he knew and respected Stewart, at least as much as any slave could respect a white southerner in those times.

At first, Harriet was assigned to work as a maid in the Stewart home. She hated every minute of it, much preferring heavy outdoor labor. At the end of three months, she begged Stewart to let her work outdoors along with the men. Aware of her unusual strength, he agreed to let her try.

Stewart soon realized Harriet Ross was worth much more as a field hand than as a domestic. She could plow, chop wood, and drive a team of oxen more efficiently than most men. Ben Ross had been put in charge of a gang of rented slaves who cut timber for the Baltimore shipyards. Harriet began working with the timber crew, swinging an ax alongside her father.

Stewart was so impressed with Harriet's energy and will to work that he allowed her a privilege given only to the most trusted slaves: When times were slack on his farm, he let her hire herself out. In return, she paid him about $50 per year; any money she earned above that was hers to keep. For the next five years, she cut timber for Stewart and, in her spare time, chopped and hauled wood for the neighbors. Gradually, she accumulated a small amount of money of her own.

Harriet Ross liked her strenuous outdoor work, and she liked the feeling of money in her pocket, no matter how little. Still, she lacked what she considered the most important thing in life. It was something mentioned only in whispers by the slaves of the South, but it was talked about more and more openly in the free states only 90 miles to the north. It was freedom. ❧

Slave women wash their master's linens. Despising domestic work, Tubman much preferred outdoor labor—chopping trees or loading wagons along with her father and other male slaves of the Brodas plantation.

3

"A GLORY OVER EVERYTHING"

IN THE MID-1840s, as millions of blacks toiled for their southern masters, a small but growing band of northerners worked toward ending more than two centuries of North American slavery.

The American colonies' first African slaves, a cargo of about 20 blacks, arrived at Jamestown, Virginia, in 1619. The number of slaves increased steadily; by 1763, the colonial population included about 230,000 blacks, most of them slaves. Of these, some 16,000 lived in New England, 29,000 in the Middle Colonies (New York, New Jersey, and Pennsylvania), and the remainder in the South.

Great Britain outlawed the slave trade in 1807, the United States a year later. But these moves only barred the importation of slaves; those already enslaved remained in bondage, as would their descendants. The British Empire, which included Canada, finally abolished slavery altogether in 1838. In the southern United States, however, the institution continued to flourish. Its strength rested largely on cotton.

In the late 18th century, the textile industry entered a period of rapid development in England and the northern United States. Its rise created a tre-

An Atlanta, Georgia, merchant advertises his wares: china, glass, and Negroes. Slave trading was big business in the prewar South; between 1850 and 1860 the average price of a slave increased by 70 percent.

Using inventor Eli Whitney's cotton gin, slaves rapidly remove the seeds from freshly picked cotton. Introduction of the machine vastly increased the South's cotton output; in 1860, the area produced 5 million bales.

mendous demand for southern cotton. But before it could be shipped to a textile mill, cotton had to be freed of its many sticky seeds. Seeding was a slow, labor-intensive process; even a skilled slave could clean only a few pounds of cotton per day. Then, in 1793, a Massachusetts-born inventor, Eli Whitney, developed a revolutionary new machine, the cotton engine. One slave using this engine, or "gin," as it came to be known, could clean as much cotton as four or five slaves working by hand.

Now the cultivation of cotton became hugely profitable; 10 years after Whitney invented his gin, southern cotton production had increased by 800 percent. Cotton became "king" not only in the Carolinas and Georgia but in the newly opened western lands of Alabama, Mississippi, and Louisiana. Needing more and more field hands, plantation owners turned to the long-established slave states of Virginia and Maryland. There, Edward Brodas and other slave owners began to breed and sell slaves as though they were livestock. The outlawed international slave trade was now replaced by an internal trade; thousands of blacks from the Upper South were sent to the Deep South to labor and die on the cotton plantations.

In 1860, 1 American family in 4 owned slaves; of a national population of almost 12 million, about 4 million were slaves, the vast majority of them in the South. Although a few voices were raised against slavery in the 18th century, most Americans seem to have taken the institution for granted. By the early 19th century, however, an increasing number of thoughtful people had come to see human bondage as a monstrous evil and its abolition as absolutely necessary.

In the South, slaves themselves were beginning to fight back, and in the North, free blacks took up the abolitionist cause with militant passion. Blacks and their white supporters had been deeply impressed by the actions of Toussaint L'Ouverture, a former slave who led a 1791 revolution in Haiti (then called St. Domingue). After freeing Haiti's black slaves, L'Ouverture had forced the departure of the British and the Spanish and then established the Western Hemisphere's first black republic. Another galvanic abolitionist was David Walker, a free black Bostonian. In 1829, he published *Appeal*, a fiery pamphlet that urged the slaves of the South to rise up and fight. Some historians credit Walker's powerful arguments with inspiring Nat Turner's revolt of 1831.

At the forefront of the abolitionist movement was William Lloyd Garrison, a white Massachusetts journalist and reformer. Garrison, who began publishing a journal called *The Liberator* in 1831, spoke a language that both blacks and whites could understand. "He that is with the slaveholder is against the slave," asserted Garrison. "He that is with the slave is against the slaveholder."

Most abolitionists favored gradual emancipation and payments to slave owners for their property, but Garrison demanded immediate abolition with no compensation. In the first issue of *The Liberator*, he announced that he would never compromise on slavery. "I am in earnest—I will not equivocate—I will not excuse—I will not retreat a single inch—AND I WILL BE HEARD," he thundered.

Frederick Douglass, another towering figure in the antislavery movement, was born a Maryland slave in about 1817. Escaping to Massachusetts in 1838, he became an agent of the Massachusetts Anti-Slavery Society and a tireless lecturer on abolition. In 1847, Douglass founded an abolitionist newspaper, the *North Star*, later retitled *Frederick Douglass's Paper*. As dedicated as Garrison but less radical, Douglass recruited thousands of conservative Americans to the abolitionist cause.

By 1840, about 200,000 Americans belonged to some 2,000 antislavery organizations. As their movement gained strength in the North, these people

Former slave Toussaint L'Ouverture headed a revolt in 1791 that drove British and French forces from the Caribbean island of St. Domingue. Thirteen years later, the island became Haiti, the New World's first black republic.

Publisher of the antislavery newspaper The Liberator, *William Lloyd Garrison was cofounder of the American Anti-Slavery Society and served as its president from 1843 to 1865. An uncompromising abolitionist, he urged the northern states to separate from the slaveholding South.*

began to look for practical ways to achieve their goal. Many otherwise law-abiding citizens proved willing to break the law in order to help runaway slaves escape. In the South, free blacks and other slaves were almost always willing to aid fugitive blacks. Thus was the Underground Railroad born.

According to one legend, this system of transport got its name during the 1831 pursuit of Tice Davids, a runaway Kentucky slave. When Davids reached the Ohio River, he plunged in and began a desperate swim for Ohio and freedom. His master followed closely in a boat, but when he reached the shore, his quarry had disappeared. Searching in vain, the frustrated slave owner reportedly cried, "He must have gone on an underground road!"

The Underground Railroad, of course, did not involve actual trains or tracks; it was a loose network of people willing to hide runaway slaves in their homes and "conduct" them to the next "station," or safe house. Slaves had always run away, but by the 1830s, they had allies willing to help them get out of the South and stay free. Word of these Good Samaritans began to spread through the slave quarters of the Upper South.

In 1839, news of a daring act at sea struck hope into the heart of all those who opposed slavery, black and white alike. A Spanish slave ship, the *Amistad*, was hijacked at sea by its captives, led by an African named Joseph Cinque. After killing most of the Spanish crew, the rebels sailed the ship to the coast of Long Island. There, they were arrested and jailed on charges of piracy and murder. Abolitionists across the country took up the cause of the mutineers, who eventually won their freedom in court and returned to Africa.

The *Amistad* case created a great furor. Harriet Ross and the other slaves at the Brodas plantation probably heard of it. Certainly, they were dreaming more and more of freedom.

Years afterward, Harriet Tubman told an interviewer about a recurring dream she had in those days: "I seemed to see a line, and on the other side of the line were green fields, and lovely flowers, and beautiful white ladies who stretched out their arms to me over the line, but I couldn't reach them. I always fell before I got to the line."

Such a line indeed existed. In 1767, a pair of English surveyors, Charles Mason and Jeremiah Dixon, had laid out the boundary between Pennsylvania and Maryland. That demarcation, later extended westward to mark the Pennsylvania-Virginia boundary as well, came to be known as the Mason-Dixon line. By the 1820s, the term was used to indicate the entire border between the free states of the North and the slave states of the South. Harriet Ross must have known that the line where freedom began was less than 100 miles from her home on the Eastern Shore.

In 1844, John Tubman, a free black man who lived in a cabin near the Brodas plantation, asked 24-year-old Harriet Ross to marry him. Already old for marriage by local standards, she agreed. Because his slave parents had been freed at their master's death, John Tubman had been born free. Marriage to a free man, however, did not change Harriet Tubman's slave status; it only meant that she was free to share her husband's cabin at night. Her children, if she had any, would belong to the Brodas estate.

Ironically, Harriet Tubman's husband used the slave system to control his own wife. She later said that he refused to listen to her talk about freedom and that he once told her he would betray her if she ever tried to run away. Nevertheless, she seems to have loved him; at any rate, she remained by his side for the next five years. But she never forgot her dream of freedom.

It was while she was married that Harriet Tubman learned she was being held in slavery illegally. Her

One of the nation's leading abolitionists, Frederick Douglass escaped from slavery in 1838 and published a best-selling account of his life 18 years later. A wartime adviser to President Abraham Lincoln, Douglass also served as a District of Columbia official and ambassador to Haiti.

mother, Old Rit, had often said she had been promised freedom years earlier but had been cheated out of it. Over the years, Harriet Tubman had managed to save five dollars, and in 1845, she took it to a local lawyer and asked him to look into her mother's records.

The lawyer discovered that Old Rit's original owner had willed her to one of his young relatives, specifying that the slave be freed when she reached the age of 45. But the relative had died soon afterward, and Rit had been sold despite the will's provisions. The lawyer told Tubman that her mother—and therefore she herself—was legally free. However, he said, because so much time had passed and because the women had always lived as slaves, no judge would even consider their case. With regard to black people, it seemed that justice was truly blind.

Harriet Tubman continued to suffer from blackouts, during which she often had strange and frightening dreams. She described them later as scenes from the "middle passage," the Atlantic crossing that cost the life of millions of captured Africans en route to America. She said she dreamed of ships where blacks

Slave-ship crew members in Africa, preparing for a voyage across the Atlantic Ocean, stow their human cargo below deck. Raised on firsthand reports of the dreaded "middle passage," Tubman had frequent nightmares about such journeys.

and whites fought on decks stained red with blood. She dreamed of a mother clutching a baby to her breast and leaping to her death in the sea.

Even after her marriage, Tubman lived in terror of being "sold South." During those years, she said later, "I never closed my eyes that I did not imagine that I saw the horsemen coming and heard the screams of women and children as they were being dragged away to a far worse slavery than they were enduring there." These dreams were not without foundation. Harsh as it was in the Upper South, slavery was much worse in the cotton states of Georgia, Mississippi, Alabama, and Louisiana.

In 1849, Tubman's worst fears came true. The young heir to the Brodas estate died, and word spread that his guardian planned to settle the plantation's bills by selling some of its slaves. One afternoon, Tubman learned that two of her sisters had just been sold and were already in chains, heading south. She knew it was time to go, and she persuaded three of her brothers to go with her. She told them what she had heard of the Underground Railroad and of the people in the North who would help them. Her father had showed her the North Star at night and told her how to use it as a compass; she assured her brothers she could guide them by watching it.

Tubman was reluctant to leave her husband, but she knew better than to ask him to come along—or even let him know she was going. He had already promised to betray her. She left late at night with her brothers, but they soon began to drag their feet. Even though she urged them on, they went slower and slower, worrying about what would happen when they were missed. Signs would be posted everywhere; alarm bells would be rung; the dogs would be set loose; and mounted patrollers with whips would track them down. They had no food, no money, no friends, and they were heading for unfamiliar country. Slavery,

Kidnapped by Spanish slavers in 1839, Joseph Cinque led his fellow prisoners in a revolt at sea. After killing most of their captors, the Africans sailed the slave ship to New York, where they were jailed, tried, and eventually freed.

A column of southbound slaves, chained to each other at wrist and ankle, makes its way through Washington, D.C. Tubman and her fellow slaves lived in constant fear of being "sold south"—led in chains to the Deep South's plantations, where living and working conditions were unbearable.

bad as it was, was at least familiar. The brothers feared the unknown. They turned back and made their sister turn back with them.

She crept back into her sleeping husband's bed, bitterly disappointed. But she had learned an important lesson, one she would never forget: Freedom is only for those bold enough to take it.

Two days after the botched escape, a slave from a nearby plantation gave Tubman bad news: She had been sold and was scheduled to start south the next day. This time she knew she would have to run alone. Years later, she described her thoughts at that moment: "There was one of two things I had a *right* to, liberty or death; if I could not have one, I would have the other; for no man should take me alive; I should fight for my liberty as long as my strength lasted, and when the time came for me to go, the Lord would let them take me."

Tubman wanted someone in her family to know she was leaving on her own, that she was not on her way south. After her last experience, she would not tell her brothers. How could she relay the news safely? Legend has it that she made her way toward "the big house," where one of her sisters was working in the kitchen. Walking back and forth near the window, Tubman sang an old spiritual:

> I'll meet you in the morning,
> When I reach the Promised Land,
> On the other side of Jordan.
> For I'm bound for the Promised Land.

That night, after her husband was asleep, Harriet Tubman wrapped up a little cornbread and salt herring, then tucked her favorite patchwork quilt under her arm. Did she kiss John Tubman good-bye as he slept? Did she regret leaving him? No one will ever know, for she never said. But perhaps she hinted at her feelings in her choice of a name: For the rest of her life, she identified herself as "Mrs. Tubman."

Tubman had heard of a local white woman who was said to help runaways, and she made her way through the woods to the woman's house. When she saw Tubman at her door, the woman seemed to know what her visitor wanted. She invited her in, then gave her two slips of paper, explaining that each contained the name of a family on the road north. When Tubman presented the slips, said the woman, these people would give her food and tell her how to get to the next house. The slips of paper were Tubman's first "tickets" on the Underground Railroad. In gratitude, Tubman gave the woman her precious quilt, then started on her way.

Reaching the first house just after dawn, Tubman presented her slip of paper. The woman of the house responded by giving her a broom and telling her to sweep the walk. Tubman was shocked. Was this a betrayal? Was she now this woman's slave? But she soon realized the move was for camouflage. A black woman with a broom would hardly be noticed, certainly not suspected as a runaway.

As soon as night fell, the woman's husband put Tubman in the back of his farm wagon, covered her with vegetables, and drove her north to the next "station." In this way, sometimes helped by others, sometimes left to her own devices, Harriet Tubman made her way north, walking up the Eastern Shore peninsula toward Pennsylvania. She began to learn the route she was to use so often and so effectively in the future.

Traveling by night, hiding in the daylight, Tubman trudged through 90 miles of swamp and woodland. At last, many days after she started, she found herself across the magic line, on free soil. Years later, she said of that morning: "I looked at my hands to see if I was the same person now that I was free. There was such a glory over everything; the sun came like gold through the trees, and over the fields, and I felt like I was in heaven." ❧

4

"A FRIEND
WITH FRIENDS"

I WAS FREE but there was no one to welcome me to freedom," recalled Harriet Tubman. "I was a stranger in a strange land."

Years later, Tubman talked to biographer Sarah Bradford about her arrival in Pennsylvania in 1849. "To this solemn resolution I came," she said. "I was free, and [my parents, brothers, and sisters] should be free also; I would make a home for them in the North, and the Lord helping me, I would bring them all there. Oh, how I prayed then, lying all alone on the cold, damp ground. 'Oh, dear Lord,' I said, 'I ain't got no friend but you. Come to my help, Lord, for I'm in trouble!' "

Tubman, however, was no woman to wait for help to come to her. Making her way to Philadelphia, she managed to get a job in a hotel kitchen. She spent the winter cooking, washing dishes, saving her money, and thinking about how she could rescue her family from Maryland. At that time, Philadelphia was second only to Boston as a center of abolitionist sentiment; the city was home not only to many whites working toward emancipation but also to a large number of blacks, some of them legally free, some of them escaped slaves like Tubman.

Horse-drawn traffic rumbles through the cobbled streets of mid-19th-century Philadelphia. Tubman, who arrived in the bustling Pennsylvania city in 1849, wasted no time in finding herself a job; she signed on as a hotel cook and dishwasher.

39

The Philadelphia Vigilance Committee greets Henry "Box" Brown, a slave who escaped from Virginia in a wooden crate. Clergyman James Miller McKim stands at the far left; next to him is William Still, who kept a written record of the fugitive slaves who passed through Philadelphia.

Both blacks and whites in Philadelphia (and the rest of the North) had been galvanized by the passage of the Fugitive Slave Act of 1850. Under this federal legislation, any Negro accused of being a runaway could be brought before a federal judge or a special commissioner. Denied a jury trial or even the right to testify on his or her own behalf, the alleged runaway could easily be returned to slavery. All the law required was a sworn statement from a white individual who claimed to be the black person's owner. The law also provided heavy penalties for anyone who helped a slave escape. Many northerners, even some who were not abolitionists, believed that the Fugitive Slave Act violated both the Constitution and basic human rights.

Soon after Congress passed the infamous law, Harriet Tubman paid a call on the Philadelphia Vigilance Committee. This organization, formed to assist fugitive slaves, was managed by two of the Underground Railroad's busiest "station masters": white clergyman James Miller McKim and William Still, a freeborn black Pennsylvanian. Still managed to meet just about every escaping slave who passed through Philadelphia. He fed them, listened to their stories, and helped them plan the next stage of their journey, no matter what the danger to himself.

One celebrated incident in McKim and Still's career involved Henry Brown, a slave from Richmond, Virginia. Brown persuaded a sympathetic white friend to nail him into a wooden packing box and ship it to the Vigilance Committee's office. After 25 hours in the small, suffocating crate, a beaming Brown emerged to greet the astonished Still and McKim. For the rest of his life, the ingenious escapee was known as "Box" Brown.

Unlike most of the fugitive slaves he helped, Still could read and write, and he used his talents well. He interviewed the runaways who passed through and recorded their names and stories in a ledger. It was Still's hope that one day all slaves would be free, and that when that day came, families might be able to trace their relatives through his records. He kept his ledger hidden in a graveyard, but in 1872, when it was at last safe to make it public, he published it under the title *The Underground Rail Road*. Still's book, one of the few written records of the legendary slave-escape system, has proved a gold mine to students of American history.

Tubman took to making frequent visits to Still's office, where she met and talked with many fugitive slaves. Meanwhile, she saved her pennies to help finance the trip she planned, back to the Eastern Shore to bring her family across the Mason-Dixon line. As it turned out, her first trip as a conductor was not to the Eastern Shore but to Baltimore, across the Chesapeake Bay.

Author Ann Petry described Tubman's first return to the South in her 1955 book, *Harriet Tubman: Conductor on the Underground Railway*. One night, according to Petry, Tubman was paying a call on Still and McKim when a stranger appeared, asking for help. He wanted the Vigilance Committee's assistance in rescuing a black woman and her two children from Cambridge, Maryland. The woman's husband was a free man, said the visitor, but his wife and children were about to be auctioned off to slave traders from the Deep South.

The visiting abolitionist said a local Quaker (a member of the Religious Society of Friends, a pacifist Christian sect) might be able to get the family out of Cambridge; but they would need someone to pilot them across the dangerous stretch from Baltimore to Philadelphia. As he outlined the escape plan, he mentioned the name of the free husband: John Bowley. Tubman must have looked startled; Bowley was her brother-in-law, husband of her sister Mary.

Baltimore, shown here in an 1849 photograph, was known as a dangerous spot for fugitives. The Philadelphia Vigilance Committee's William Still tried to talk Tubman out of going to the Maryland city in 1850, but she knew she was needed there, and she went.

At once, Tubman announced that she herself would go to Baltimore and guide the Bowley family to safety. Still objected. Tubman, he noted, was still a fugitive herself, and Baltimore was a dangerous city for runaways. Travel, too, was extremely hazardous. Blacks who tried to board trains, even in the company of their masters, were weighed and measured like sacks of grain so they could be compared with the ever-growing list of runaways.

But Tubman insisted. She knew the land, she said; she had crossed it herself. And she could leave at once. Time was growing short, and the mission would have to be accomplished quickly. Reluctantly, Still agreed to let Tubman try.

On the day of the Cambridge auction, a black man claiming to belong to the auctioneer came to the slave pen during the noontime break. He gave the guard an official-looking letter, requesting him to turn the female captive and her children over to the bearer; the slaves, said the letter, were to be taken to the hotel where the auctioneer was having lunch.

The "auctioneer's slave" was John Bowley, and his official letter had been forged by his Quaker ally. Sensing nothing amiss, the guard unlocked the pen. Bowley marched his family through the streets of Cambridge to the home of his Quaker accomplice. The Quaker hid the fugitives in his attic until nightfall, then escorted them to the river. There, a small sailboat awaited them.

An experienced seaman, Bowley hustled his family aboard and set sail for the North. When he spotted the prearranged signal, one blue and one yellow lantern, he brought the boat ashore. A white woman met the fugitives, concealed them in a wagonload of potatoes, and took them to a brick house.

Bowley knocked on the door, and a voice from inside said, "Who's there?" He responded with the password: "A friend with friends." The door flew open, and Harriet Tubman rushed out to embrace her relatives. With her precious "shipment" in tow, Tubman made it back to Philadelphia safely, as indeed she was always to make it. "I never ran my train off the track," she proudly noted years later, "and I never lost a passenger."

Baltimore, as Still had pointed out, was a dangerous place for a fugitive slave, but the Eastern Shore was even more perilous. Nevertheless, it was there that Tubman's remaining family lived, and it was there she went. She made her first trip to Dorchester County in the spring of 1851. When she returned to Philadelphia, she brought one of her brothers and two other men, whom she entrusted to Still's care. She worked all that summer and fall, saving money for a trip she had dreamed of ever since the day she first left Maryland.

A slave pen, built to hold blacks designated for auction, stands ready to receive its human merchandise. It was from such an enclosure that Tubman's brother-in-law, John Bowley, spirited his wife and children out of Cambridge, Maryland, and into Tubman's arms.

Fugitive slave Thomas Sims (second row, center), after his 1851 arrest by Boston marshal Charles Devins, is escorted to the ship that will return him to Georgia. Boston's Vigilance Committee plastered the city with copies of a poster (opposite) warning all blacks to be wary of slave catchers after Sims was captured. (Despite a major attempt to rescue him, Sims was returned to Georgia. In 1863, he escaped again. In 1877, he showed up in Washington, D.C., where he was employed by the U.S. attorney general—Charles Devins, the man who had sent him back to slavery 26 years earlier.)

In December, Tubman made her way back down the peninsula to Dorchester County. She had to exercise extraordinary caution, because this was an area where she was well known. When she arrived at the Brodas plantation just after dark one evening, she went directly to her husband's cabin. Perhaps she hesitated before approaching his door. He had, after all, often ridiculed her dreams of freedom and had even threatened to betray her. What kind of welcome would she get? She knocked on the door. It swung open to reveal John Tubman—and a young, attractive black woman.

When Harriet Tubman told her husband she had come back for him, he laughed in her face. The young woman at his side, he said, was now his wife, and he had no interest in going anywhere. Late that night, Harriet Tubman left the plantation with several slaves and never looked back. She never laid eyes on John Tubman again and rarely spoke of him.

That was Tubman's third trip to the South. By now, she had developed the routes and techniques that would serve her so well as she conducted her people to freedom. Although every step was risky, Tubman's familiarity with the roads, the hiding places, and the "depots" allowed her to travel with increasing assurance.

On her rescue expeditions, Tubman usually traveled in Delaware as far as possible before crossing into Maryland. Delaware offered several advantages. First, it contained the headwaters of most of the rivers that drained the Eastern Shore, which meant she could use a small boat to reach almost any point. Even more important, Delaware was home to many more free black men and women than slaves. The state's black population in 1860 was 21,627, of whom only 1,798 were slaves. Delaware was, in fact, the only state in the South where a black person was assumed to be free unless proven to be a slave. Tubman could thus cross the state fairly openly, at least on the way down.

Tubman's return route took her past a number of Underground Railroad stations, or safe houses. When she approached one, she would hide her "passengers," then knock at the door. When someone responded from inside, she would answer with the magic words: "A friend with friends."

On most of Tubman's trips from the South, her last stop was Wilmington, Delaware, a city right on the Mason-Dixon line. Wilmington was the home of Quaker Thomas Garrett, a remarkable man who would become one of Tubman's closest friends. Garrett owned a large shoe store; when fleeing slaves arrived at his door, he hid them behind a false wall in his shop. He also provided each runaway with a pair of shoes, for many the first they had ever owned. According to William Still's records, Garrett helped some 2,700 slaves escape.

CAUTION!!

COLORED PEOPLE
OF BOSTON, ONE & ALL,
You are hereby respectfully CAUTIONED and advised, to avoid conversing with the
Watchmen and Police Officers
of Boston,
For since the recent ORDER OF THE MAYOR & ALDERMEN, they are empowered to act as
KIDNAPPERS
AND
Slave Catchers,
And they have already been actually employed in KIDNAPPING, CATCHING, AND KEEPING SLAVES. Therefore, if you value your LIBERTY, and the *Welfare of the Fugitives* among you, *Shun* them in every possible manner, as so many *HOUNDS* on the track of the most unfortunate of your race.
Keep a Sharp Look Out for KIDNAPPERS, and have TOP EYE open.
APRIL 24, 1851.
THEODORE PARKER'S PLACARD

Several times arrested, found guilty, and heavily fined for assisting runaways, Garrett finally lost both his shoe business and his sizable personal fortune. Undeterred, he went back to work at the age of 60 and continued to help fugitives. He was arrested and fined again; this time, the presiding judge said he hoped the experience would teach Garrett to stop interfering "with the cause of justice by helping off runaway Negroes." Garrett, who spoke in the Quakers' biblical phrases, rose, looked hard at the judge, and said, "Friend, thee hasn't left me a dollar, but I wish to say to thee . . . that if anyone knows of a fugitive who wants a shelter, and a friend, *send him to Thomas Garrett!*"

In an 1868 letter to Sarah Bradford, Garrett referred with awe to "the remarkable labors" of Tubman. "In truth, I never met with any person, of any color, who had more confidence in the voice of God, as spoken direct to her soul," he said. "She has declared to me that she felt no more fear of being arrested by her former master . . . when in his immediate neighborhood, than she did in the State of New York, or Canada, for she said she ventured only where God sent her."

A runaway black family arrives at an Underground Railroad station. Operated by a loosely organized network of abolitionists, the Railroad consisted of a series of way stations where fugitives could rest, eat, and get directions to the next stop. Some historians believe that as many as 75,000 blacks escaped to freedom via the U.G.R.R., as the system was sometimes called.

By 1851, the Fugitive Slave Act was taking a heavy toll of runaways. Tubman heard ominous news of fugitive slaves arrested and returned to the South from such previously safe cities as Boston and Syracuse, New York. Abolitionists were outraged. "The only way to make the Fugitive Slave Act a dead letter," said former slave Frederick Douglass, "is to make a half dozen or more dead kidnappers."

Free blacks and their allies in the North began to fight back. In Boston, 300 armed men were needed to send 1 fugitive back to the South. The Fugitive Slave Act backfired in the long run because it increased northern opposition to slavery; yet it succeeded in making life difficult for Harriet Tubman. No longer able to work safely in Philadelphia, she moved to St. Catharines, Canada, a small town near Niagara Falls where many free blacks and former slaves had settled.

Between 1851 and 1857, Tubman made two trips to the Eastern Shore each year, one in the fall and one in the spring. Now instead of 90 miles, she had to conduct her passengers on a grueling journey of almost 500 miles. But the trips brought her people to genuine freedom, and they gave her the chance to meet the leaders of the abolitionist movement, many of whom lived in New York State and New England. It was on these pilgrimages that she met and befriended such giants of the movement as Frederick Douglass, Gerrit Smith, J. W. Loguen, and John Brown, the man who would most inspire her. ◖◗

John Brown (seen here in an early portrait) was to leave an indelible imprint on American history—and on Tubman. Along with the rest of the nation, Tubman probably first heard of the fiery abolitionist in 1856, when he staged a series of spectacular raids on proslavery settlements in Kansas Territory.

5

"MOVE OR DIE!"

ALREADY, PEOPLE WERE calling her Moses. She traveled light and she traveled fast.

She knew the places where it was safe to hide: drainage ditches, hedges, and abandoned sheds or tobacco barns. Sometimes, she concealed her fugitives in potato holes, board-lined pits where farmers stored their winter vegetables. Once, she and her group hid in a manure pile and breathed through straws.

In addition to such hideouts, there were the more comfortable way stations, most of them operated by Quakers or free black people. Residents of the Cooper House in Camden, New Jersey, for example, regularly hid fugitives in a bunk-room over their kitchen. Another stopover for fleeing blacks was in Odessa, Delaware, where the Friends Meeting House (the Quaker version of a church) had a concealed loft over the sanctuary.

Tubman holds a musket in this engraving, but her choice of weapons was usually a pistol. Carrying her weapon—and willing to use it—the Underground Railroad conductor enforced iron discipline on the sometimes faint-hearted fugitives she escorted to freedom.

Harriet Tubman always carried a revolver on the Underground Railroad, and she was always ready to use it. "She could not read or write, but she had military genius," a contemporary said of her.

Tubman's standard procedure was to gather money and supplies in the North and then slip down the Eastern Shore, through Delaware and into Mary-

49

This clergyman's residence in Ripley, Ohio, was among the Underground Railroad's busiest stations. High on a bluff overlooking the Ohio River, the house could easily be seen by escaping Kentucky slaves on the river's opposite bank.

land. There, she would make contact with the slaves who were ready to escape. She usually led them away on Saturday night, hoping they would not be missed and pursued until Monday. Before heading out, she paid someone to take down the wanted posters that would be sure to appear across the countryside.

In a 1907 article, the New York *Herald* described Tubman's methods:

> On some darkly propitious night there would be breathed about the Negro quarters of a plantation word that she had come to lead them forth. At midnight, she would stand waiting in the depths of woodland or timbered swamp, and stealthily, one by one, her fugitives would creep to the rendezvous. She entrusted her plans to but few of the party. . . . She knew her path well by this time, and they followed her unerring guidance without question. She assumed the authority and enforced the discipline of a military despot.

Once the slaves had left, there was no turning back. Tubman knew too well what happened to runaways who returned: They were beaten until they revealed their escape plans and the names of the people who had aided them. She would allow no one to betray her routes and secrets.

More than once, a slave grew fainthearted and wanted to go back, just as her brothers had the first time she tried to run away. Sometimes they were men twice her size. But now she was prepared. The hesitant slave would feel the cold steel of a revolver at his head and hear Tubman's voice harsh in his ear: "Move or die!" They moved. None of her passengers ever turned back, and she never lost one. To keep babies from crying, Tubman sometimes drugged them with opium, then readily available. When their mothers grew tired, she carried the babies in a basket on her arm.

To raise the flagging spirits of her followers, Tubman often sang to them as they plodded through woods and swamps. Hearing her strong, husky voice, the weary fugitives often joined in. The spiritual they most often sang referred to the biblical Moses' delivery of his people from Egyptian bondage:

You may hinder me here, but you can't up there,
Let my people go.
He sits in the heavens and answers prayer,
Let my people go!

Oh go down, Moses,
Way down in Egypt land,
Tell old Pharaoh,
Let my people go.

Tubman's blackouts still came upon her at unexpected times. She would simply collapse by the side of the road, and her passengers could only watch and wait until she awakened; then they would be off again. Sometimes, Tubman would steal a slave owner's buggy for the first stage of the journey. She knew the neighbors would assume the slaves were out on an errand for their master. When the horses grew winded, Tubman would abandon the buggy and continue the trip on foot, by boat, or in a cart heaped with vegetables.

Conductor Tubman became an expert at disguise and deception. Once, when she had to enter the village where her former master lived, she disguised herself as an old slave bringing chickens to market. The New York *Herald* told the story 50 years later: "As she turned a corner she saw coming toward her none other than her old master. Lest he might see through her impersonation, and to make an excuse for flight, she loosed the cord that held the fowls and amid the laughter of the bystanders, gave chase to them as they flew squawking over a nearby fence." In her 1869 biography of Tubman, Sarah Bradford added, "And [the master] went on his way, little thinking that he was brushing the very garments of the woman who had dared to steal herself, and others of his belongings."

On another occasion, Tubman disguised herself by pretending to read a book—hoping she was holding it right side up. Soon she heard one man whisper to another: "This can't be the woman. The one we want can't read or write."

By 1854, the woman called Moses was well known throughout the Eastern Shore, a legend among the slaves and a demon to the slaveholders. Try as they might, the plantation owners never got so much as a glimpse of this mysterious figure who came to the slave cabins at night and spirited away their valuable property.

In late 1854, Tubman got word that three of her brothers, Benjamin, John, and William Henry Ross, were going to be sold south the day after Christmas. It was time for a trip to Dorchester County. Tubman had a friend write to Jacob Jackson, a literate black man who lived near the estate where her brothers worked as hired slaves. "Read my letter to the old folks [Old Ben and Rit], and give my love to them," said the letter. "Tell my brothers to be always watching unto prayer, and when the good old ship of Zion comes along, to be ready to step on board."

On Christmas Eve, Tubman arrived on the Eastern Shore. Collecting her brothers, 2 other men, and
a young woman, she headed for her parents' cabin,
some 40 miles to the north. She would not take Ben
and Rit this time; she knew that at their advanced
age they were unlikely to be sold and shipped south.
The group left in such a hurry that Tubman's brother
William Henry had to leave his wife and newborn
baby, promising to return for them soon. When it
was time to go, Tubman waited for no one.

When the party arrived at Ben and Rit's cabin,
they hid in an outbuilding where feed corn was stored.
The parents knew nothing of the escape plan. Tubman longed to see her mother, but she knew the old
woman was unable to keep a secret and would tell
the whole neighborhood. To make matters worse,
Rit had been expecting her sons all day and had killed
and cooked a pig for them. Tubman sent the two
extra men to the cabin; they called Old Ben out into

*Fugitives arrive at the Ohio farm
of Levi Coffin, a dedicated supporter of the Underground Railroad. Like his fellow Quaker
Thomas Garrett of Wilmington,
Coffin made no secret of the hos-
pitality, financial assistance, and
transportation he provided to
fleeing slaves.*

Louisiana runaways rest before heading north. Faced with immense distances through hostile country, fugitives from the cotton states were far more likely to be killed or captured than were those escaping from the Upper South.

the night and told him what was going on. He promised to keep the secret from Rit and said he would bring the hungry travelers some food.

Ben Ross, a slave for almost 50 years, had earned a widespread reputation for honesty. Indeed, he must have doubted his own ability to lie, for when he visited his children in the corncrib, he averted his eyes and never looked directly at them. And later, on Christmas Day, when he said good-bye to them, he tied a bandanna over his eyes.

Tubman and her passengers headed north toward freedom. A few days later, a team of slave chasers brought a report to the man who owned Ben and Rit. The men said they had questioned the fugitives' parents. They found the old woman heartbroken because she had been expecting her boys for Christmas. And the old man said he had not laid eyes on his children. The slaveholder accepted the story. He knew Ben Ross was no liar.

"Moses arrives with six passengers," noted the Vigilance Committee's William Still when Tubman brought her fugitives into Philadelphia. "Great fears were entertained for her safety, but she seemed wholly devoid of personal fear," wrote Still in his ledger. "The idea of being captured by slave-hunters or slave-holders, seemed never to enter her mind." Still added that he found it "obvious" that Tubman's "success in going into Maryland as she did was attributable to her adventurous spirit and utter disregard of consequences. Her like it is probable was never known before or since."

After escorting her brothers and their friends to Canada, Tubman prepared for her next mission. This one, undertaken in November 1856, involved a woman and three men. One of the men, Josiah Bailey, was the kind of slave every master wanted. Strong, healthy, and skilled as a farmer, he never talked back or gave any trouble. Bailey had been rented out by his master for six years to a planter named William Hughlett. In 1856, Hughlett decided to buy Bailey. He paid $2,000, a steep price but worth it to the purchaser, who planned to save money by making Bailey his overseer.

The day he bought him, Hughlett gave Bailey a savage whipping. The slave had done no wrong, said the master, but he needed to learn who owned him. Bailey submitted silently but, he later told Tubman, he said to himself, "This is the first and the last." That night he "borrowed" a rowboat and made his painful way down the river to Rit and Ben Ross's cabin. Speaking to Ross alone, he said, "The next time Moses comes, let me know."

Tubman arrived soon afterward. With Bailey and the other escapees, she headed north, closely followed by a small army of slave catchers. Because Bailey was so valuable, his master offered an unusually high reward for his capture. Hughlett posted signs all through the Eastern Shore. They showed the South's symbol of a runaway, a black figure with a knapsack and a walking stick. The signs read:

> Heavy Reward
> Two Thousand Six Hundred Dollars

After describing the runaways, the signs—which Bailey read to Tubman and the others—said that $1,500 was for Josiah Bailey alone; the rest was for the other slaves. Separate posters announced an even higher reward for a certain black woman. Harriet Tubman, "sometimes called Moses," was worth $12,000 to any person who delivered her to the authorities. The countryside swarmed with bounty hunters, but Tubman knew the Eastern Shore better than any of her pursuers. At one point, she led her shivering people across a deep creek, using a hidden ford that she said she had seen in a dream.

For the first time Tubman had a helper. Tough and courageous, Josiah Bailey pushed the group forward, singing in a low voice. Among his favorite verses was this one:

> Who comes yonder all dressed in red?
> I heard the angels singing—
> It's all the children Moses led,
> I heard the angels singing.

Keeping to the fields and hedges, the party made it as far as Wilmington, but they found the Delaware River bridge heavily guarded. Wanted posters were everywhere. Tubman scattered her group, placing them in the homes of sympathetic free blacks. She

believed her friend Thomas Garrett would find a way
to help, and she was right. Garrett sent a wagonload
of bricklayers across the bridge; when they returned
to Wilmington that night, seemingly drunk, they
carried five black fugitives hidden under the bricks.

From Wilmington, Tubman led the group to Philadelphia, then on to New York City. The trip had
gone as well it could have, but Bailey was growing
discouraged. He had thought they would be safe in
the North, but the wanted posters were on every wall
here, too. When the fugitives walked into the office
of the New York Anti-Slavery Society, its president,
Oliver Johnson, shook Bailey's hand and said jok-
ingly, "Well, Joe, I'm glad to see the man whose head
is worth $1,500!"

Bailey did not laugh. "How did you know me?"
he asked. Johnson showed him a copy of the poster
and said that anyone who read it would recognize
Bailey easily. That meant that anywhere between
New York and Canada—a distance of more than 300
miles—someone might pounce on him and drag him
off for the reward. Disheartened, Bailey begged Tubman and the others to go on to Canada without him.
With him along, he said, they were all bound to be
caught. Tubman, of course, refused.

The rest of the trip north was easier. Much of the
Underground Railroad's route through New York
State involved real trains; Tubman and her charges
traveled in a baggage car, watched over by a sympathetic trainman. But Bailey, Tubman later told
Sarah Bradford, "was silent. He talked no more. He
sang no more. He sat with his head on his hand, and
nobody could rouse him, or make him take any interest in anything."

When the train approached Niagara Falls, the
conductor took the group into a coach so they could
see Canada on the other side of the bridge. Even
there, they were still in danger. Until the train

*The figure of a fleeing black often
appeared on the South's wanted
posters, most of which offered rewards. Few escapees, however,
were worth as much to bounty
hunters as Tubman; the price on
her head was $12,000.*

Nineteenth-century painter Thomas Mason caught the sense of terror felt by blacks who braved storms, swamps, and snarling dogs in their quest for freedom. Tubman must also have known fear on her many rescue missions, but by all accounts, she never showed it.

reached the center of the bridge, any slave catcher could legally arrest them and drag them all back into slavery. But the train moved steadily across the great iron bridge. When it reached the center, Tubman gave Bailey a shake and shouted, "Joe, you're in Queen Victoria's dominions! You're a free man!"

Bailey used his voice for the first time in days. With tears streaming down his face, he looked up and began to sing, "Glory to God and Jesus too, One more soul is safe!" He kept on singing, even after the train had stopped on the Canadian shore. A crowd of curious white people gathered around him on the platform, staring as he bellowed, "There's only one more journey for me now, and that's to heaven."

Tubman tugged at his sleeve, trying to quiet him. "Well, you old fool," she joked. "You might have looked at the Falls first and gone to heaven afterwards!" ❧

6

"THE GREATEST HEROINE OF THE AGE"

T HE 1850s BEGAN with the passage of the infamous Fugitive Slave Act and ended with violence and bloodshed at Harpers Ferry, Virginia. In the years between, the storm clouds that had been gathering in the 1830s and 1840s grew darker. North and South eyed each other with increasing mistrust. The United States moved steadily toward division.

The abolitionist movement had been intensifying its crusade against slavery from the 1830s on. By the 1850s, a battalion of popular lecturers was sweeping through the North, driving home the message that slavery was a sin. Among the most effective speakers were such former slaves as Frederick Douglass and such white abolitionists as Wendell Phillips, an aristocratic Bostonian who later served as president of the Anti-Slavery Society. In Congress, Senator Charles Sumner of Massachusetts and other proabolition legislators made passionate speeches, which they transcribed and mailed to thousands of voters. Many northern newspapers, including the powerful New York *Tribune*, took an unreserved stand against slavery. Perhaps the most irresistible abolitionist message, however, was delivered by a remarkable book, *Uncle Tom's Cabin*.

Published by the American Anti-Slavery Society, an 1835 handbill shows an image widely used in abolitionist literature: a chained slave asking, "Am I not a man and a brother?" The Anti-Slavery Society, formed in 1833, flooded the North with such emotional appeals.

Abolitionist orator Wendell Phillips addresses an antislavery meeting on Boston Common. An admirer and good friend of Tubman's, Phillips served as president of the Anti-Slavery Society from 1865 to 1870.

Written by New Englander Harriet Beecher Stowe and published in 1852, *Uncle Tom's Cabin* struck America like a thunderbolt. Set in the plantation South, the novel tells the story of a devoutly Christian slave, Tom, and his friends and fellow slaves, George and Eliza Harris. George escapes from his cruel master, planning to buy his wife and son's freedom as soon as he can. Meanwhile, Eliza learns that circumstances have forced her kindhearted owner, Mr. Shelby, to sell both Tom and her son, Harry. Desperate, she flees with Harry.

Tom is shipped south, where he saves the life of Eva, a six-year-old white girl. Eva's grateful father, Augustine St. Clair, then buys Tom, but both St. Clair and his daughter soon die. Tom is bought by the sadistic Simon Legree, who viciously mistreats the patient old slave. Eliza and George Harris manage to escape with their boy to Canada, but Tom meets a grim fate. Just as George Shelby, the son of his former master, arrives to buy him back, Tom is beaten to death by Legree. Appalled, Shelby denounces slavery and becomes an abolitionist.

The first edition of *Uncle Tom's Cabin* sold out within a week of publication; little more than a year later, sales reached 1 million. The book, described by historian J. C. Furnas as "a verbal earthquake, an ink-and-paper tidal wave," sparked a wave of hatred against slavery, even among many previously neutral northerners. In the novel's wake came a flood of "Tom shows," popular dramatic portrayals of the horribly mistreated but always forgiving Uncle Tom.

According to Sarah Bradford, Tubman's friends once tried to persuade her to attend a Philadelphia performance of *Uncle Tom*. "I've heard *Uncle Tom's Cabin* read," she reportedly replied, "and I tell you, Mrs. Stowe's pen hasn't begun to paint what slavery is. . . . I've seen the *real thing*, and I don't want to see it on any stage."

The slavery issue continued to occupy the national stage as well, fanning ever-deeper anger between North and South. In 1857, the United States Supreme Court finally expressed its opinion on the issue, but instead of soothing the interregional quarrel, the Court's decision heightened it. The case involved Dred Scott, a Missouri slave whose master had taken him to the free territory of Minnesota and then back to the slave state of Missouri. Claiming that residence in free territory had made him a free man, Scott sued for freedom from his master. When the state supreme court decided against Scott, his abolitionist lawyers took his case to the U.S. Supreme Court.

After hearing lengthy arguments on both sides of the question, Chief Justice Roger B. Taney issued the Court's majority opinion. Scott, said Taney, was not a citizen and had no right to sue in a federal court. The Constitution had created a white man's government, and Negroes, "beings of an inferior order," had "no rights which a white man was bound to respect." Furthermore, stated the chief justice, Scott's resi-

Uncle Tom and Little Eva, *characters in Harriet Beecher Stowe's* Uncle Tom's Cabin, *appear on a 19th-century theatrical poster.* "Tom shows"—*stage versions of Stowe's best-selling novel about slavery—swept the nation in the 1860s, but Tubman refused to attend one.* "I've seen the real thing," *she said.*

dence in a free territory had not affected his status as a slave; he was property, and the Constitution forbade anyone to deprive a man of his property without "due process of law."

Meanwhile, a young Illinois politician named Abraham Lincoln was making a name for himself by engaging in public debates on the slavery issue. Like many Americans in the North and the Midwest, Lincoln—whose oratorical skills would help carry him to the White House—opposed slavery on moral, political, and ethical grounds. He did not, however, support social and political equality for blacks.

In Lincoln's view, slavery presented a threat to white Americans. If the United States accepted the idea that blacks were not created with equal rights, he said, it might next deny equal rights to other groups. "As a nation," Lincoln said in 1855, "we began by declaring that 'all men are created equal.' We now practically read it 'all men are created equal, except negroes.' " At that rate, continued the Illinois Republican, "it will [soon] read 'all men are created equal, except negroes and foreigners, and catholics.' "

Lincoln opposed the extension of slavery into the territories because, he said, white free labor would be unable to compete with black slave labor. Although his views would become less conservative over the years, in the 1850s Lincoln maintained that if slavery were confined to the South, it would eventually die of its own accord. Given enough time, he said, the "wrong" of human bondage would disappear from the United States.

As Lincoln addressed the citizens of Illinois about slavery, people were fighting and dying over the issue in the territory known as "bleeding Kansas." Soon after Kansas Territory was opened for settlement in 1854, large numbers of pioneers moved there. While most of the newcomers came to establish farms, many came to determine the status of slavery in the terri-

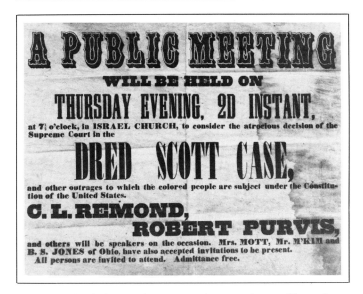

An 1857 poster advertises a meeting to protest "the atrocious decision of the Supreme Court in the Dred Scott case." The decision labeled blacks "an inferior order" and said they had "no rights which a white man was bound to respect."

tory. Both dedicated Free-Soilers and equally ardent supporters of slavery poured into Kansas, each side ready to fight for its beliefs.

In 1856, a band of proslavery adherents attacked the town of Lawrence, killing several antislavery residents. In revenge, John Brown, a fiercely dedicated white abolitionist who believed that God had appointed him to destroy slavery, attacked the proslavery settlement of Pottawatomie and killed five people. As a result of the 2 raids, civil conflict broke out in Kansas; more than 200 settlers died in the guerrilla warfare between the 2 factions.

In this climate of violence and turmoil, Harriet Tubman continued her work, traveling to the Eastern Shore, meeting with slaves who wanted to escape, and telling them about the North's abolition movement. During the mid-1850s, she began giving certain groups of runaways directions to Underground Railroad stations and sending them off on their own. In other cases, she escorted groups of escapees as far as Philadelphia or New York, left them in charge of friends there, then headed back south for more passengers. When Tubman felt unsure that a group of escaping slaves would be able to make the trip without her, she accompanied them all the way from Maryland to Canada. Tubman had now become a regular on the route that led north from New York City to Troy and Albany, then west across the Mohawk Valley to Niagara Falls and free Canada.

In 1855, journalist Benjamin Drew visited several Canadian towns where free blacks had settled. In the village of St. Catharines, Drew met and interviewed the celebrated woman known as Moses. He asked her to comment on slavery and recorded her response in his 1856 book, *The Refugee; or Narratives of Fugitive Slaves*:

> I grew up like a neglected weed—ignorant of liberty, having no experience of it. I was not happy or contented: Every time I saw a white man I was afraid of being carried away. . . . We were always uneasy. Now I've been free, I know what slavery is. . . . I think slavery is the next thing to hell. If a person would send another into bondage, he would, it appears to me, be bad enough to send him to hell if he could.

About a year after she talked to Drew, Tubman made her first visit to Boston, where she was invited to attend an antislavery meeting. Historian, playwright, and novelist William Wells Brown, a former slave who had become an ardent abolitionist and a popular speaker, noted her presence in one of his many books, *The Rising Son; or the Antecedents and Advancements of the Colored Race*:

> For eight or ten years previous to the breaking out of the Rebellion [the Civil War], all who frequented antislavery conventions, lectures, picnics, and fairs could not fail to have seen a black woman of medium size, upper front teeth gone, smiling countenance, attired in coarse, but neat apparel, with an old-fashioned reticule or bag suspended by her side, and who, on taking her seat, would at once drop off into a sound sleep.

Tubman, said Brown, became a frequent visitor at the homes of Boston's leading abolitionists. These highly educated, cultured men and women would listen spellbound as Tubman, who could neither read nor write, discussed slavery and abolition. Brown found himself awed by Tubman. "Men from Canada, who had made their escape years before, and whose families were still in the prison-house of slavery, would seek out Moses, and get her to go and bring their dear ones away," he wrote. "How strange! This woman—one of the most ordinary looking of her race; unlettered, no idea of geography, asleep half of the time. . . . No fugitive was ever captured who had Moses for a leader."

Tubman was resourceful, courageous, and dedicated to freedom. But like the rest of the human race, she was also capable of making human errors. Apparently very lonely in her midthirties, she committed one of the strangest acts of her life: She abducted a child. The episode began in 1855 or 1856, when she stopped at the Eastern Shore home of one of her brothers and became captivated by his daughter Margaret. More than 80 years later, Margaret's daughter, then Mrs. A. J. Brickler of Wilberforce, Ohio, recounted the story to an interviewer:

> My mother's life really began with Aunt Harriet kidnapping her from her home on Eastern Shore, Maryland, when she was a little girl eight or nine years old. Aunt Harriet fell in love with the little girl who was my mother. Maybe it was because in mother she saw the child she herself might have been if slavery had been less cruel. Maybe it was because she knew the joys of motherhood would never be hers and she longed for some little creature who would love her for her own self's sake. Certainly whatever her emotion, it was stronger than her better judgment, for when her visit was ended, she, secretly, and without so much as a by-your-leave, took the little girl with her to her Northern home.

Tubman, continued her grandniece, "must have regretted her act for she knew she had taken the child from a sheltered good home to a place where there was nobody to care for her." In any event, said Brick-

William Henry Seward was governor of New York (1839–43), U.S. senator (1849–61), and U.S. secretary of state (1861–69). He was also one of Tubman's staunchest admirers. "I have known her long," he once wrote, "and a nobler, higher spirit, or a truer, seldom dwells in the human form."

ler, not long after she had carried Margaret off, Tub-man "thought of her white friends . . . and decided to place her dearest possession in their hands." She brought Margaret to her friend Frances Seward, wife of U.S. senator William H. Seward. (A former governor of New York and a dedicated abolitionist, Seward would serve as U.S. secretary of state from 1861 until 1869.)

"This kindly lady," said Brickler, "brought up mother, not as a servant but as a guest within her home. She taught mother to speak properly, to read, write, sew, do housework, and act as a lady. Whenever Aunt Harriet came back, mother was dressed and sent in the Seward carriage to visit her. Strange to say, mother looked very much like Aunt Harriet."

In 1857, soon after her short-lived experience as a mother, Tubman settled down in a home of her own. She had always been forthright about asking supporters to help finance her rescue missions, but she never asked for personal funds. Now, however, her friend William Seward took a firm stand. According to biographer Bradford, he said, "Harriet, you have worked for others long enough," and presented her with the deed to a little house in Auburn, New York. To avoid any appearance of charity, Seward "sold" Tubman the house; he required no cash but asked her to make a regular series of small payments. Situated in the central part of the state, Auburn served as a major station on the Underground Railroad. The small town was to be Tubman's home for the rest of her life.

Not long after she moved to Auburn, Tubman received troubling news. Her father had been arrested and was awaiting trial for helping a fellow slave escape. In the eyes of the South, Ben Ross's crime was enormous; Tubman knew that even though he was more than 70 years old, he would be punished severely if found guilty. She made plans to head south immediately. Needing money for her trip, she stopped off at the New York City office of the Anti-Slavery Society and asked for $20, a sizable amount in 1857.

Tubman later told Sarah Bradford what happened next. The abolitionist official said, *"Twenty dollars! Who told you to come here for twenty dollars?"* Tubman replied, "The Lord told me, sir." "Well," countered the official, "I guess the Lord's mistaken this time." Tubman lifted her chin. "No, sir," she said, "the Lord's never mistaken! Anyhow, I'm going to sit here until I get it."

As good as her word, Tubman sat down and immediately went to sleep, probably suffering one of her frequent blackouts. As she slept and woke, then slept again, she was aware of visitors coming and going through the office. Many must have been sympathetic to her plight; when she awoke late in the afternoon, she found a pile of bills—amounting to $60—in her lap. Tubman set off for the Eastern Shore. Her father's trial was imminent, and there was no time to spare.

Tubman's rescue of her parents was a model of simplicity—and extraordinary daring. Slipping into Ben and Rit's cabin late one night, she told the as-

After rescuing her elderly parents from Maryland, Tubman brought them to this house in Auburn, New York. The building, purchased on easy terms from William Seward in 1857 and still standing today, was Tubman's home for more than 50 years.

tonished old people to prepare for a trip north. Next, she walked over to the plantation stable, found a horse, and hitched it to a rickety farm wagon. Then, wrote Quaker Thomas Garrett later, "She got her parents . . . on this rude vehicle . . . and drove to town in a style that no human being ever did before or since." Three days later, Tubman and her parents arrived in Wilmington. "I furnished her with money to take them all to Canada," wrote Garrett. "I afterward sold their horse and sent them the balance of the proceeds."

Tubman brought her parents first to Canada, then to Auburn. "Harriet's abduction of her parents was an event in Underground annals," observed biographer Earl Conrad in his 1943 account of Tubman. "It was significant, not only because rarely did aged folks take to the Road, but because Harriet carried them off with an audaciousness and an aplomb that represented complete mastery of the Railroad and perfect scorn of the white patrol. Her performance was that, at once, of the accomplished artist and the daring revolutionary."

Not everyone, however, applauded Tubman's courage. John Bell Robinson, a Philadelphia supporter of slavery, characterized the rescue of Ben and Rit as "a diabolical act of wickedness and cruelty." In his 1860 book, *Pictures of Slavery and Freedom*, Robinson called "the bringing away from ease and comfortable homes two old slaves over seventy years of age . . . as cruel an act as ever was performed by a child towards parents." To help elderly people to freedom was "a thousand times worse than to sell young ones away," insisted Robinson. Even "confinement in the penitentiary for life," he said, "would be inadequate to [Tubman's] crime." There is no indication that Tubman ever heard of Robinson or his opinions. If she did, perhaps she just looked at her parents and smiled.

By now, as Conrad observed, the Eastern Shore was being "plucked of slaves like a chicken of its feathers before roasting." And Harriet Tubman was the primary culprit. She began arming the runaways she sent north: In 1857, for example, she equipped a departing group of 28 men, women, and children with revolvers, pistols, and butcher knives. All of them made it safely to the home of Thomas Garrett and then to Canada. Frantic plantation owners hired more slave hunters and raised the price on Tubman's head. "It now came to pass," noted a contemporary northern account, "that . . . rewards were offered for the apprehension of the Negro woman who was denuding the fields of their laborers and the cabins of their human livestock."

In the late 1850s, Tubman agreed to speak at a few New England antislavery meetings. She had little time for such activities; between her trips south, she

Their stolen wagon hitched to a pair of oxen, a band of fugitives crosses Virginia's Rappahannock River. As Tubman brought more and more slaves out of the South, slave owners became increasingly eager to catch the woman who was "denuding the fields of their laborers."

"Fighting Minister" Thomas Higginson feared for the life of his friend Tubman, whom he called "the greatest heroine of the age." She "will probably be burned alive whenever she is caught," said Higginson, "which she probably will be, first or last, as she is going again [to the South]."

had to work hard to support herself and her parents. (Strange as it seems, this daring commando earned her living as a domestic, usually in hotels.) When she did find time to address conventions, Tubman enthralled her audiences.

Clergyman Thomas Wentworth Higginson, president of the Massachusetts Anti-Slavery Society, often praised Tubman's abilities as a speaker. A celebrated orator himself, he said he had learned the art from "the slave women who had been stripped and whipped and handled with insolent hands and sold to the highest bidder . . . or women who, having once escaped, had, like Harriet Tubman, gone back again and again into the land of bondage to bring away their kindred and friends. . . . [I] learned to speak," he added, "because their presence made silence impossible."

Higginson, who was known as the Fighting Minister, wrote a letter to his mother about Tubman in 1859:

> We have had the greatest heroine of the age here, Harriet Tubman, a black woman and a fugitive slave. . . . Her tales of adventure are beyond anything in fiction and her ingenuity and generalship are extraordinary. . . . The slaves call her Moses. She has had a reward of twelve thousand dollars offered for her in Maryland and will probably be burned alive whenever she is caught, which she probably will be, first or last, as she is going again.

Despite her friend's grim predictions, Tubman was never caught. Before she changed her antislavery strategy, she would have made 19 excursions into the South, "stealing" more than 300 human beings from the land that had tried—and failed—to keep her in bondage. **◄○►**

7

GENERAL TUBMAN
GOES TO WAR

Tubman, probably about 40 years old in this portrait, still bears a scar on her temple from the ferocious blow she had received as a teenager. She also continued to suffer from the unpredictable "sleeping fits" induced by her near-fatal head wound.

HARRIET TUBMAN'S WORK had always involved stealth and secrecy; she chose, as Frederick Douglass once put it, "to labor in a private way," her activities observed only by "the midnight sky and the silent stars." She addressed occasional meetings only because her abolitionist friends insisted; a few words from her, they said, helped the cause more than dozens of speeches by its educated, well-to-do supporters. After she caught the attention of John Brown, however, Tubman lost any chance for obscurity.

Convinced he was God's instrument to destroy slavery, Brown had already battled proslavery forces in Kansas. By the late 1850s, he had decided it was time to take arms and end slavery everywhere. For his starting point, he settled on a little town at the northernmost corner of the South. He would assemble an army of abolitionists, both black and white, and strike at Harpers Ferry, Virginia, where the Potomac River passes through a gap in the Blue Ridge Mountains.

Brown planned to bring weapons to Harpers Ferry, seize more arms from the town's large arsenal, then retreat to the mountains, where he expected thousands of rebellious slaves to join him. With these

John Brown, *who believed he had a divine mission to end slavery by force, became a national figure during the Kansas Territory slavery battles of the mid-1850s. By the end of the decade, he was ready to start a full-scale war.*

troops behind him, Brown expected to liberate all the slaves in the South, then establish a new national government. By late 1857, he had recruited a small band of free blacks and fugitive slaves. What he needed now was black leadership—charismatic figures who could inspire and lead these volunteers. He believed there were two such leaders in the United States: Harriet Tubman and Frederick Douglass. Brown would invite them both to join him in his great enterprise.

In the spring of 1858, Brown traveled through New England, rounding up support for his revolution among such leading abolitionists as Thomas Higginson and Franklin Sanborn of Massachusetts. From New England, Brown went on to New York State, meeting up with Frederick Douglass in Rochester. The celebrated orator, former slave, and abolitionist was apparently skeptical about Brown's plan, but he encouraged the fiery reformer to talk to Harriet Tubman, who had spent the winter working in St. Catharines. Accompanied by Tubman's friend, J. W. Loguen, the black clergyman and abolitionist, Brown accordingly headed for Canada. He arrived in April.

During the preceding winter, Tubman had had a recurring dream. Night after night, she recalled later, she dreamed of a "wilderness sort of place, all full of rocks and bushes." In the dream, a snake raised its head from among the rocks; as she watched, it turned into the head of an old man with a white beard and fierce, glittering eyes. He gazed at her, she said, "wishful like, just as if he was going to speak to me." Then, in the dream, two other heads, younger than the first, appeared. Finally, a crowd of men rushed in and struck down all three heads. Tubman told friends about the dream, which puzzled and disturbed her.

When she met John Brown, Tubman stared hard. His was the face—that of the old, bearded man with fire in his eyes—that she had seen in her dream. Still, the dream's meaning was unclear to her; maybe its message would reveal itself later. Meanwhile, Brown told Tubman of his planned revolution and asked her about the Underground Railroad, through which he hoped to channel slaves to join him at Harpers Ferry. He also asked her to recruit free blacks for the impending battle.

Clearly impressed with "General Tubman," as he called the militant black woman, Brown wrote a letter to his son about her. Curiously, he spoke of her as a man; perhaps he found it hard to believe that a woman could possess such strong qualities of leadership. "I came here direct with J. W. Loguen," said Brown's letter. "I am succeeding beyond my expectation. Harriet Tubman is the most of a man, naturally, that I ever met with. There is the most abundant material, and of the right quality, in this quarter, beyond all doubt."

During the following winter (1858–59), Tubman met with John Brown in Boston. There, the two conferred with Franklin Sanborn and other supporters of Brown's plan. Writing about that winter, Sanborn later noted that Brown "always spoke of [Tubman] with the greatest respect, and said that 'General Tubman,' as he styled her, was a better officer than most whom he had seen, and could command an army as successfully as she had led her small parties of fugitives."

Wendell Phillips, another great antislavery orator, met Tubman for the first time that winter. "The last time I ever saw John Brown," Phillips later recalled, "was under my own roof, as he brought Harriet Tubman to me, saying, 'Mr. Phillips, I bring you one of the best and bravest persons on this continent— General Tubman, as we call her.' "

Scheduled, delayed, and rescheduled several times, Brown's attack on Harpers Ferry would finally

Frederick Douglass shared John Brown's abolitionist goals, but he declined to join the old warrior's raid on Harpers Ferry, Virginia. "An attack on the federal government," Douglass warned Brown, "would array the whole country against us."

take place in October 1859. When the critical day arrived, however, Brown had neither of the black leaders he wanted at his side. Douglass, finally deciding that Brown's plan was doomed to failure, declined to join in the attack. Tubman, too, was absent.

Wholeheartedly admiring John Brown, Tubman had intended to join him for his historic battle. But in the summer of 1859, at the very moment she had planned to lend him her assistance, she fell ill. She had long suffered from the effects of the head wound she received as a young woman. Now almost 40, she found herself on the verge of exhaustion: The years of strenuous Underground Railroad journeys, combined with the heavy labor by which she supported herself and her parents, had caught up with her.

Tubman probably collapsed in Boston. In any case, friends took the sick woman to their home in New Bedford, Massachusetts, to recover. Meanwhile, Brown and his lieutenants had no idea where to find the "General," and she had no idea when the attack on Harpers Ferry would actually begin. In his biography of John Brown, the eminent black scholar W. E. B. Du Bois wrote, "Only sickness, brought on by her toil and exposure, prevented Harriet from being present at Harpers Ferry."

On the night of October 16, 1859, John Brown led his little band of abolitionist militants into the Virginia town and seized its federal arsenal. At his side were 5 blacks and 16 whites, 3 of them his sons. Almost immediately, Brown's fighters were attacked by citizens and local militia, who were soon joined by a company of United States Marines. With 10 of his men—including 2 of his sons—killed, Brown surrendered. Soon afterward, he was tried for treason, convicted, and hanged. Six of his remaining followers met the same fate.

When a horrified Tubman, still recovering from her illness, learned about the outcome of Brown's

raid, she must have recalled her dream of the previous winter; had those three stricken heads represented John Brown and his sons?

After Brown's trial, many abolitionists, including Tubman, kept as far away from the public eye as possible. They knew their names had been mentioned in the letters and papers that Brown had left scattered around the farmhouse from which he had staged his raid. Several prominent abolitionists, including Frederick Douglass, even left the country for a period. A Senate committee investigated the role played by the northern abolitionists, but in the end, none was accused of involvement in the Harpers Ferry raid. Tubman finally returned to her home in Auburn, still sick and now in mourning for the white man she had admired above all others of his race.

She must have been moved by Frederick Douglass's tribute to the slain visionary. "John Brown began the war that ended American slavery," said

Outnumbered and outgunned, John Brown's forces battle federal troops at the Harpers Ferry arsenal. Brown had hoped to enlist Tubman and Frederick Douglass in a mighty blow against slavery, but he went into action without either ally and with only 21 men behind him.

John Brown, a rope around his neck, heads for the gallows after his failed 1859 raid on Harpers Ferry. Devastated by the news of Brown's fate, Tubman said, "It was not John Brown that died. . . . It was Christ—it was the saviour of our people."

Douglass. "Until this blow was struck, the prospect for freedom was dim, shadowy, and uncertain. . . . When John Brown stretched forth his arm the sky was cleared—the armed hosts of freedom stood face to face over the chasm of a broken union, and the clash of arms was at hand."

By the following spring, Tubman was recovered and ready to renew her labors. In April, she staged her own raid, overwhelming scores of lawmen and rescuing fugitive slave Charles Nalle in Troy, New York. "Harriet Tubman's victory," commented biographer Earl Conrad, "was a high point of the fugitive slave history that racked the nation's breast for 10 years. If Brown's Virginia raid was a dress rehearsal for the Civil War, Harriet's action was a bugle call for the war to begin."

From Troy, Tubman went on to Boston. There, her friend and fellow Harpers Ferry conspirator, Frank Sanborn, escorted her from one gathering of social activists to another. She met many of the Bostonians passionately concerned with abolition, woman suffrage, economic theory, human rights, and civic reform. In a city preoccupied with the rights of women and blacks, Harriet Tubman became a highly sought-after speaker.

In drawing rooms all over Boston, men and women listened raptly as Tubman talked about her days as a slave, her travels on the Underground Railroad, and her association with the martyred John Brown. At one point, she said, "It was not John Brown that died at Charles Town [the Virginia town where he was hanged]. *It was Christ*—it was the saviour of our people."

Much of the talk in Boston revolved around the possibilities of ending slavery peacefully. Attired, as usual, in a well-worn gray cotton dress, its neck trimmed with lace and its full skirt reaching the floor, Tubman listened to such hopes silently but skeptically. At one point, Sanborn later recalled, she leaned toward him and whispered, "They may say, 'Peace, Peace!' as much as they like; I know there's going to be war!"

In Boston, Tubman spent most of her time with abolitionist groups, but she did make one speech at a women's rights convention, organized in 1860 by celebrated suffragists Susan B. Anthony and Elizabeth Cady Stanton. No record remains of Tubman's words, but a contemporary observer, author Robert W. Taylor, reported on their effects. "She made the weak strong, the strong determined, and the determined invincible," said Taylor. "After her words of untutored but fiery eloquence, her hearers stood like Martin Luther of old, body and soul and spirit devoted singly and untiringly to one end."

But for a woman of action, only so much time could be spent in drawing rooms and convention halls. As it happened, events in the fall of 1860 would plunge Tubman back into the tumultuous South. In November, Abraham Lincoln was elected president. Appalled by the victory of an abolitionist, South Carolina quickly seceded from the Union, virtually guaranteeing the flight of the rest of the cotton states. The specter of civil war loomed closer. Tubman, realizing that war would make it harder than ever to bring slaves out of the South, decided to make another foray into the Tidewater.

Supplied with traveling money by Boston abolitionists, Tubman headed for Maryland, where she picked up five slaves: Maria and Stephen Ennets and their three children, one of them a three-month-old baby. On her way north, Tubman collected two additional passengers, a man and a woman.

In December, Thomas Garrett of Wilmington sent a note to William Still of the Philadelphia Vigilance Committee. "I write to let thee know that Harriet Tubman is again in these parts. She arrived

By 1860, when he was elected president, Abraham Lincoln had made his position on slavery clear: "As I would not be a slave, so I would not be a master," he said in 1858. "This expresses my idea of democracy." Lincoln's election sparked South Carolina's secession from the Union and made civil war inevitable.

last evening from one of her trips of mercy to God's poor. . . . I gave Harriet ten dollars, to hire a man with a carriage to take them to [Philadelphia]. . . . I shall be very uneasy about them till I hear they are safe. There is now much more risk on the road . . . yet, as it is Harriet, who seems to have had a special angel to guard her on her journeys of mercy, I have hope."

The fugitives reached Philadelphia safely, and Still recorded their arrival in his book. Having learned from John Brown's mistakes, however, Still was now keeping less-detailed notes. The capture of Brown's letters and papers, he wrote, "with names and plans in full, admonished us that such papers and correspondence as had been preserved concerning the Underground Rail Road, might perchance be captured by a pro-slavery mob."

Tubman's 1860 Railroad trip was her last, although not by her own choice. As the North-South split widened, the South clamored ever more loudly for enforcement of the Fugitive Slave Act and for punishment of anyone who broke it. "Those anxious months, when darkness settled over our political prospects, were viewed by all classes with deep forebodings," Frank Sanborn recalled later. The times, said Sanborn, were especially dangerous "for those who, like Harriet, had rendered themselves obnoxious to the supporters of slavery by running off so many of their race from its dominions. Fear for her personal safety caused Harriet's friends to hurry her off to Canada, sorely against her will."

But Tubman was not to stay long in Canadian safety. In February 1861, the remaining six states of the Deep South (Alabama, Florida, Georgia, Louisiana, Mississippi, and Texas) withdrew from the Union to form the Confederate States of America. On April 12, Confederate troops opened fire on the federal garrison at Fort Sumter in Charleston, South

Confederate officers drive slaves away from approaching Union troops. Despite the rebels' efforts, thousands of blacks remained in South Carolina, flooding Union army bases in the Sea Islands and forcing overwhelmed commanders to call for civilian assistance. Heeding the call, Tubman headed south in 1862.

Carolina. The fort surrendered on April 13, and the nation went to war.

As Union troops advanced through Maryland in the spring and summer of 1861, large numbers of blacks left their plantations to join the northern soldiers. Officially called "contraband of war," these blacks were no longer slaves but were not yet legally free; Lincoln would not sign his Emancipation Proclamation, liberating the slaves of the South, until January 1, 1863.

In April 1861, when she learned that the federal armies needed help in caring for the "contrabands," Tubman headed south. Little is known of her activities during this period, but according to historian William Wells Brown, she remained on "the outskirts of the Union Army" until the fall, "doing good service for those of her people who sought protection in the Union lines."

Tubman was back in Auburn with her elderly parents when Union forces took Port Royal in South Carolina's Sea Islands. Plantation owners fled the islands for the mainland, leaving thousands of their slaves behind. These contrabands, many of them illiterate, malnourished and ill, flooded the Union army camps. Overwhelmed by this human tide, Union army commanders sent out a call for teachers

Newly released slaves line up out-side a contraband school. Adding to their other problems, the con-trabands around Beaufort spoke an African-flavored language that few outsiders—including Tub-man—could understand.

and nurses. Hundreds of northerners responded; among them, not surprisingly, was Harriet Tubman.

Arriving at Beaufort, South Carolina, in March 1862, Tubman discovered that she could barely communicate with the local black people. Still linked closely to Africa—the last (illegal) slave ship had delivered its cargo to the area in 1849—these former slaves spoke a dialect called Gullah, which contained many African words. "Why, their language down there in the far South," Tubman later told Sarah Bradford, "is just as different from ours in Maryland as you can think. They laughed when they heard me talk, and I could not understand them."

Adding to the language problem was suspicion. These blacks of the Deep South had little trust for whites or those who worked for them. Isolated on their offshore islands, they had never heard of Moses or the Underground Railroad. Tubman, assigned to the contraband hospital, had to win her patients' confidence step by step. She was entitled to army rations and supplies, but when she learned that the contrabands were jealous of her privileges, she gave them up. To supply her personal needs, she sold pies and root beer, which she made at night, after working in the hospital all day.

While she was in Beaufort, Tubman dictated a letter to her friend Frank Sanborn. In it, she described her patients as "very destitute, almost naked." She said, "I am trying to find places for those able to work, and provide for them as best I can, so as to lighten the burden of the Government as much as possible, while at the same time they learn to respect themselves by earning their own living."

Tubman nursed both the blacks who poured into Beaufort and white soldiers injured in the field. It was sometimes discouraging work. Years later, she described it to Sarah Bradford:

As a Civil War nurse in South Carolina, Tubman worked in this Beaufort manor house, converted into a hospital for contrabands. Eager to teach these impoverished and homeless people "to respect themselves," Tubman not only cared for the sick but helped find jobs for the healthy.

> I'd go to the hospital early every morning. I'd get a big chunk of ice and put it in a basin, and fill it with water; then I'd take a sponge and begin. First man I'd come to, I'd thrash away the flies, and they'd rise, like bees around a hive. Then I'd begin to bathe their wounds, and by the time I'd bathed off three or four [soldiers], the fire and heat would have melted the ice and made the water warm, and it would be as red as clear blood. Then I'd go and get more ice, and by the time I got to the next one, the flies would be around the first ones black and thick as ever.

Although she could not read them, Tubman kept many of the notes and orders she received at Beaufort. One note, addressed by a hospital surgeon to the base commissary, reveals the lack of supplies available to Tubman and other medical workers. "Will Captain Warfield," read the note, "please let 'Moses' have a little Bourbon whiskey for medicinal purposes."

Tubman worked at several southern locations, reporting when she was needed, then moving on. " 'Moses' was in her glory," wrote historian William Wells Brown, "and travelled from camp to camp, being always treated in the most respectful manner. The black men would have died for this woman."

From Beaufort, Tubman went to a military hospital in Fernandina, Florida. There, she later re-

When Tubman ran into her old friend Thomas Higginson in 1862, he was commanding the all-black 1st South Carolina Volunteers. Deeply impressed by his men's fighting abilities, Higginson told the War Department that "the successful prosecution of the war lies in the unlimited employment of black troops."

ported, soldiers were "dying off like sheep" from dysentery. When she discovered no medicine to treat them, Tubman searched the woods for certain roots; these she used to treat the men, achieving remarkable results in many cases. She also nursed soldiers and contrabands stricken with smallpox and "malignant fevers," or malaria. Despite her willing exposure to these highly contagious diseases, Tubman never contracted one herself. "The Lord would take care of me," she told Bradford, "until my time came."

Back in Beaufort in December 1862, Tubman heard a bit of interesting news. Her old friend Thomas Higginson was at nearby Camp Saxton, where he was organizing a regiment of black soldiers. In a letter to his wife, dated December 10, Higginson wrote: "Who should drive out to see me today but Harriet Tubman who is living at Beaufort as a sort of nurse & general care taker; she sends her regards to you. All sorts of unexpected people turn up here."

Tubman's days as a "general care taker," however, were drawing to a close. Among the needs of the Union army in South Carolina was information: Where were the enemy encampments? How many men did they have? How well were they armed? Aware of her work on the Underground Railroad, Union officers assigned Tubman to a new job: spy. In the spring of 1863, she organized a scouting service, leading a small band of black men deep into enemy territory and returning with information on Confederate movements. She reported to Colonel James Montgomery, an expert in guerrilla warfare who had fought at the side of John Brown in Kansas.

Perhaps the most celebrated of Tubman's military exploits took place in the summer of 1863. Deciding the time was ripe for a raid up South Carolina's Combahee River, General David Hunter, commander of the Union's southern forces, called on Harriet Tubman. Her mission: to take "several gunboats up the

Combahee River, the object of the expedition being to take up the torpedoes [mines] placed by the rebels on the river, to destroy railroads and bridges, and to cut off supplies and troops." Hunter also wanted Tubman to lead out the hundreds of blacks known to be in the Confederate-held area. Tubman accepted the assignment.

On the night of June 2, 1863, she and Colonel Montgomery started up the river with a force of 150 black soldiers in 3 steam-powered gunboats. The expedition, as the Boston *Commonwealth* later reported, "dashed into the enemy's country, struck a bold and effective blow, destroying millions of dollars worth of commissary stores, cotton, and lordly dwellings, and striking terror into the heart of rebeldom, brought off near 800 slaves and thousands of dollars worth of property, without losing a man or receiving a scratch."

Aware that the spectacular raid had been led by a black woman, humiliated Confederate commanders chose to blame their defeat on one of their own officers. "On this occasion," said the official Confederate report, "[the officer's] pickets were neither watchful nor brave; they allowed . . . a parcel of negro wretches, calling themselves soldiers, with a

Confederate soldiers and their dogs attack a black South Carolina regiment. Black fighting men faced double jeopardy: they could be killed on the field, or they could be taken prisoner and murdered by rebel soldiers, who refused to treat them as legitimate prisoners of war.

few degraded whites, to march unmolested, with the incendiary torch, to rob, destroy and burn a large section of the country."

Tubman knew that Colonel Montgomery, the white officer technically in command of the Combahee raid, would get most of the credit for its success. Ordinarily self-effacing, she allowed herself a touch of defensive pride on this occasion. In a letter she dictated to Frank Sanborn, she said:

> You have without a doubt seen a full account of the expedition. Don't you think we colored people are entitled to some of the credit for that exploit, under the lead of the brave Colonel Montgomery? We weakened the rebels somewhat on the Combahee River, by taking and bringing away *seven hundred and fifty-six* head of their most valuable live stock, known up in your region as "contrabands," and this, too, without the loss of a single life on our part, though we had good reason to believe a number of rebels bit the dust. Of those seven hundred and fifty-six contrabands, nearly or quite all the able-bodied men have joined the colored regiments here.

In the same letter, Tubman said, "I have now been absent two years, almost. . . . My father and

A trio of "contrabands"—southern blacks no longer slaves but not yet legally free—reports to a Union officer and his staff. At first regarded with suspicion by the northern military, contraband volunteers proved able and willing recruits.

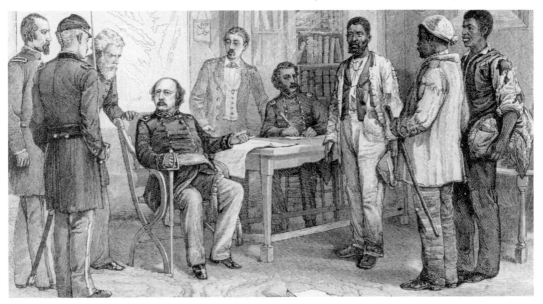

The 54th Massachusetts storms the parapet of Fort Wagner, in Charleston, South Carolina. Tubman probably saw the attack, which, observed the New York Tribune, "made Fort Wagner such a name to the colored race as Bunker Hill [Boston's revolutionary war battle site] had been for 90 years to the Yankees."

mother are old and in feeble health, and need my care and attention. I hope the good people [in Auburn] will not allow them to suffer, and I do not believe that they will. But I do not see how I am to leave at present the very important work to be done here."

Tubman would continue to perform that important work until the war ended, almost two years later. During that time, she would see some of the bloodiest battles of the Civil War. Among them was the celebrated Union assault on Fort Wagner, a Confederate bastion that guarded the harbor of Charleston, South Carolina. Leading the July 18, 1863, attack on Fort Wagner was the 54th Massachusetts, a black infantry regiment led by a 26-year-old white officer, Colonel Robert Gould Shaw. The battle marked the first important use of black troops, whose courage under fire was doubted by many whites, northerners as well as southerners.

Advancing through a murderous hail of shot and shell, the regiment captured Wagner's parapet, but

The men of Company E, 4th U.S. Colored Infantry Volunteers, prepare for inspection in 1865. President Lincoln vigorously supported the use of blacks in the army: "Abandon all the posts now possessed by black men," he said in 1864, "and we would be compelled to abandon the war in three weeks."

in the end, the entrenched Confederate position held. The 54th lost the battle, its young commander, and about half its men, but it demonstrated the extraordinary courage of its black soldiers. Their valor, however, failed to impress the South: When Colonel Shaw's father later asked for the return of his son's body, Confederate officers refused. "We have buried him," they said, "with his niggers."

But Fort Wagner transformed the North's view of the black fighting man. "Through the cannon smoke of that dark night," observed the *Atlantic Monthly*, "the manhood of the colored race shines before many eyes that would not see." After Fort Wagner, black soldiers fought on all fronts, with no one expressing doubts about their courage or ability.

Tubman probably witnessed the South Carolina battle. The night before, she served Shaw his dinner, and the next day, she helped bury the dead and nurse the wounded. Years later, she told historian Albert Bushnell Hart about a Civil War engagement that may have been Fort Wagner:

And then we saw the lightning, and that was the guns; and then we heard the thunder, and that was the big guns; and then we heard the rain falling, and that was the drops of blood falling; and when we came to get in the crops, it was dead men that we reaped.

For the next year, Tubman remained in the South. Taking part in numerous guerrilla operations, she earned respectful admiration from the military, foot soldiers and officers alike. As General Rufus Saxton, a Union officer responsible for organizing contraband regiments, later put it, "She made many a raid inside the enemy's lines, displaying remarkable courage, zeal, and fidelity."

8

"THIS HEROIC WOMAN"

Her face reflecting years of hardship and exhausting labor, Tubman sits for an Auburn photographer in the late 1860s. Despite her heroic war work as a nurse, spy, scout, and commando, Tubman never received a penny from the United States government.

IN MAY 1864, Harriet Tubman applied for leave from her duties at the Port Royal military hospital. Her boss, surgeon Henry Durrant, approved her request and gave her a note of reference. "I certify that I have been acquainted with Harriet Tubman for nearly two years," read the note, which Tubman saved. "My position as Medical Officer in charge of 'contrabands' in [Beaufort] has given me frequent and ample opportunities to observe her general deportment; particularly her kindness and attention to the sick and suffering of her own race. I take much pleasure in testifying to the esteem in which she is generally held." At the bottom of the note was a line signed by General Saxton: "I concur fully in the above."

Eager to see her aged parents, Tubman headed for Auburn, New York. Once there, her years of nonstop wartime service seemed to catch up with her; exhausted and ill, she suffered an intense bout of the sleeping seizures that had long plagued her. She spent almost a year in Auburn, resting and quietly visiting friends and neighbors. It was during this period that Tubman met and became friends with Sarah Bradford, the white woman from Geneva, New York, who was to become her first biographer.

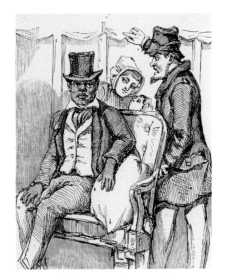

A northern conductor orders a black passenger out of a postwar whites-only railroad car. Although the North had fought to free the South's slaves, Tubman and other blacks soon discovered that northern whites could be as bigoted as their southern counterparts.

By the early spring of 1865, Tubman felt well enough to return to the war. She set out for South Carolina, but by the time she reached Washington, D.C., a string of Union victories indicated that the war would soon be over. Tubman decided to remain in the Washington area, where she worked as a nurse for the U.S. Sanitary Commission, that era's equivalent of the Medical Corps.

On April 9, Confederate general Robert E. Lee surrendered to U.S. general Ulysses S. Grant at Appomattox, Virginia. A few months later, a weary Harriet Tubman once again turned her eyes toward Auburn and home. The Civil War was over. But for Tubman and millions of other free black Americans, another war had just begun.

Carrying a half-fare military pass, Tubman boarded a northbound train in Washington. The white conductor who looked at the pass refused to honor it. Tubman later told Bradford the story. "Come, hustle out of here!" shouted the conductor. "Niggers," he said, were not entitled to travel at reduced rates. When she protested, he grabbed her arm and said, "I'll make you tired of trying to stay here." With three other men, the conductor then dragged her out of the passenger car. The train's white passengers watched in silence. No one came to Tubman's aid as her four burly assailants wrestled her along to the baggage car and literally threw her in.

Tubman rode north alone, cradling a severely sprained arm. She rarely complained about anything, but she must have noted the incident's bitter irony. Harriet Tubman, the woman who had led troops in battle for the Union, the daring rescuer who had escaped bullets, bloodhounds, and angry slave owners, had suffered her first war injury from a civilian in the "free" North.

Although Tubman had been entitled to military pay for her services as a scout and nurse, she had never demanded it—and never received it. In 1864, the Boston *Commonwealth* had called attention to this injustice. "This heroic woman," said the newspaper, "[and] her services to her people and to the army seem to have been inadequately recompensed by the military authorities, and such money as she has received, she has expended for others as her custom is."

Tubman had carefully saved her receipts and records from the war years. Using these documents, Tubman's friends concluded that the United States government owed her $1,800 for her military services. When her own requests for payment went unheeded, Tubman's old friend William H. Seward, now secretary of state, along with such influential allies as Colonel Thomas Higginson and General Rufus Saxton, petitioned Congress in her behalf. "I can bear witness to the value of her services in South Carolina and Florida," wrote Saxton. "She was employed in the hospitals and as a spy . . . and is as deserving of a pension from the government for her services as any other of its faithful servants."

Tubman desperately needed the money to support herself and her parents and to continue helping others. Astonishingly, nothing happened; Tubman's special case, it seemed, came under no official law. In one session after another, an indifferent postwar Congress refused to recognize the rights of this black woman who had worked and fought for her country. The debt was never paid.

When Tubman returned to Auburn, she was about 45 years old, penniless, and responsible for 2 aged parents. She was also in steady pain from the arm the trainmen had savagely wrenched. Nevertheless, she went about her affairs with her customary verve. She planted apple trees and broke ground for a large vegetable garden to feed her family and those who came to her door. With the help of well-to-do

Former slaves work at a county poorhouse. Determined to keep as many blacks as she could from such a disheartening life, Tubman resolved to open a home where the sick and elderly could find health care, companionship, and peace.

neighbors, she established a kind of refuge for the many impoverished blacks who passed through the area in search of work and homes. She fed them, nursed their sick, and helped deliver their babies. Apparently with strength to spare, Tubman also began a fund-raising campaign to support schools for newly freed blacks in the South.

Tubman's good-humored energy may have flagged in October 1867, when a friend sent her a clipping from the *Baltimore American*. Asking a neighbor to read it to her, Tubman learned that her former husband was dead. John Tubman, the satisfied free black man who had once threatened to betray his wife for running away, had been shot down in broad daylight by a white man. Although John Tubman had been unarmed, and although witnesses testified to the cold-blooded killing, an all-white postwar Maryland jury had found the white man not guilty. Harriet Tubman's reaction to the news can only be guessed; she never said a word about it.

Meanwhile, she was finding it increasingly hard to make ends meet. Sarah Bradford illustrated the black woman's plight with an anecdote about the winter of 1867–68. A blizzard had all but buried Tubman's little house on the outskirts of Auburn, preventing her from working or going out for food. "At length," wrote Bradford, "stern necessity compelled her to plunge through the drifts to the city." Calling on "one of her firm and fast friends," Tubman "began to walk up and down, as she always [did] when in trouble." Her eyes filled with tears, Tubman seemed unable to speak. Finally, "with a great effort, she said, 'Miss Annie, could you lend me a quarter till Monday? I never asked it before.' Kind friends immediately supplied all the wants of the family, but on Monday Harriet appeared with the quarter she had borrowed."

At about this time, Bradford began writing her biography. First printed in 1869 under the title *Scenes in the Life of Harriet Tubman*, the book carried a slightly apologetic preface by Bradford. "There are those who will sneer, there are those who have already done so, at this quixotic [impractical] attempt to make a heroine of a black woman, and a slave," she observed. Nevertheless, with financial aid from Wendell Phillips and other friends, Bradford published the book, then turned its proceeds—some $1,200—over to its subject. A considerable sum for the time, the money allowed Tubman to pay her expenses, continue to support southern schools for blacks, and feed the hungry strangers at her door.

Appearing at her door in 1869 was another kind of visitor: a tall, handsome man named Nelson Davis. Some years earlier, in 1864, Tubman had met him at a South Carolina army base. Davis, then about 20 years old, was a private in Company G of the 8th U.S. Colored Infantry Volunteers. Whether Davis came to Auburn in search of Tubman or by chance is unknown; what is known is that the former soldier asked the former spy to marry him. Despite their age difference—Davis was at least 24 years younger than Tubman—she accepted.

Surrounded by friends, both black and white, the couple married on March 18, 1869. The next day, the Auburn newspaper reported on the ceremony. "Before a large and very select audience Harriet Tubman . . . took unto herself a husband and made one [Nelson Davis] a happy man," noted the paper. "Both born slaves . . . they stood there, last evening, *free*, and were joined as man and wife."

By all accounts, the good-looking Davis seemed unusually robust, but his appearance belied the truth. He had contracted tuberculosis in the army, and his health was fragile. Some people believed that Tubman, ever the care giver, married him so she could nurse him. In any case, Davis apparently never worked during the 19 years of his marriage.

Among the guests at Tubman and Davis's wedding had been William H. Seward. He and Tubman had not agreed on every issue (Seward had, for example, never supported Harriet's idol, John Brown), but the two remained staunch friends for decades. Seward was to die only a few years later, in 1872; at his funeral, hundreds of people passed his casket and the mountains of elaborate floral displays surrounding it. When the service ended, mourners saw a small black woman walk to the casket and lay a wreath of wildflowers at its foot.

The years were carrying away Tubman's most cherished possessions, the people she loved. She lost her parents, both nearing 100 years of age, in the 1870s. Quaker Thomas Garrett of Wilmington died in 1869, Colonel James Montgomery (Tubman's col-

Tubman's shawl hangs from the bed where she slept in her later years. Her Auburn house was small and sparsely furnished, but it was palatial compared to the ditches and "potato holes" in which she had stayed during her Underground Railroad days.

league on the Combahee raid) in 1871, Wendell Phillips in 1884, Frederick Douglass in 1895. By the 1890s, of all the thundering abolitionist band, only Thomas Higginson, Frank Sanborn, and Harriet Tubman lived on.

Tubman never changed: Needy people could always count on a meal or a place to stay when they came to her door. She dreamed of building a home for the poor and helpless, but the closing decades of the century were lean times, even for this gritty, resourceful woman.

In severe need of money, Tubman fell prey to a pair of black swindlers who came to Auburn in 1873. The men told her they had found a chest in the South containing $5,000 in gold. They said they did not want to exchange the gold for greenbacks (U.S. dollars) because the government would seize the gold and leave them penniless. If Tubman could raise

$2,000 in cash, the men said, they would turn the chest over to her. Tubman, who had seen such treasures hidden away by slaveholders, believed the story and persuaded friends to back her with $2,000. She agreed to meet the swindlers in the woods on a dark night: There, they knocked her unconscious, took the cash, and vanished. The episode became something of a scandal, but Auburn's citizens, even those who had lost their money, soon forgave Tubman. They knew she had been as much a victim as themselves.

In these years, Tubman earned her living as a peddler, traveling from house to house and selling vegetables from her garden. Neighbors welcomed her, eager to hear stories about her days on the Underground Railroad and her wartime activities. One of these friends later recalled: "Harriet when I knew her in her matriarchal phase was a magnificent looking woman, true African, with a broad nose, very black, and of medium height. I used to often sit and listen to her stories when I could get her to tell them. We always gave her something to eat. She preferred butter in her tea to anything else. That was a luxury."

In 1890, 2 years after her husband, Nelson Davis, died at the age of 44, Tubman finally got enough money to buy a few such "luxuries" herself: Congress approved pensions for the widows of Civil War veterans. Ironically, the government allotted Tubman $8 per month (increased to $20 in 1899) as the survivor of a soldier, but it steadfastly refused to reward her for her own gallant service.

Although her own government never recognized her, Great Britain's ruler did. After reading Bradford's biography of Tubman in 1897, a clearly impressed Queen Victoria had sent the American woman a silver medal and a letter inviting her to come to England. She never went, but her friends later reported that Tubman looked at the letter so many times, it "was worn to a shadow." The former slave had never forgotten her 1856 trip to Canada, when she had ushered the despairing Joe Bailey into "Queen Victoria's dominions" and freedom.

Another woman long admired by Tubman was Susan B. Anthony. Tubman had heard the great suffragist speak on a number of occasions, and she wholeheartedly endorsed Anthony's goals. Anthony, who returned Tubman's respect, referred to her fellow activist as "this most wonderful woman." Late in her life, Tubman received a visit from Elizabeth Miller, leader of a local suffragist group. Miller later described the occasion. "I remember seeing you years ago at a suffragist convention in Rochester," she told Tubman. "Yes," responded Tubman, "I belonged to Miss Susan B. Anthony's organization." Miller said she would like to enroll Tubman as a life member in her group. "You certainly have assisted in bearing the burdens," Miller continued. "Do you really believe that women should vote?" Tubman paused. Then she said softly, "I suffered enough to believe it."

As Tubman grew older, she became increasingly determined to establish a home for sick and needy black people. She had long had her eye on a 25-acre lot across the road from her house; the site, she thought, would be perfect for the poor people's shelter. In 1896, the property came up for public auction, and Tubman saw her chance. She had almost no money, but she had her usual supply of optimism and determination. She later told an interviewer about the auction:

> They were all white folks there but me, and I was there like a blackberry in a pail of milk, but I hid down in a corner, and no one knew who was bidding. The man began down pretty low, and I kept going up by fifties. At last I got up to fourteen hundred and fifty, and then others stopped bidding, and the man said, "All done. Who is the buyer?"
>
> "Harriet Tubman," I shouted.

Tubman left the astonished auction crowd and headed for the local bank, where she got the money

Women's rights activist Susan B. Anthony (left) confers with colleague Elizabeth Cady Stanton in 1900. Although Tubman focused most of her energies on abolition, she was also a strong supporter of Anthony and her suffragist movement. "Tell the women," she said a month before she died, "to stand together."

Tubman worshiped regularly at Auburn's African Methodist Episcopal Zion Church, where her strong, clear voice rang out in such favorite songs as "Swing Low, Sweet Chariot" and "Go Down, Moses." According to local reports, many parishioners attended the church as much to hear Tubman sing as for religious motives.

for her new land by mortgaging it (using it as security for a loan). Still, she lacked the funds to build the home. Seven years later, in 1903, she deeded the acreage to the African Methodist Episcopal Zion Church, an all-black congregation at which she had worshiped for years. The church built the home of Tubman's dreams in 1908. She was delighted to see the first residents move in, but she objected strenuously when the home's managers decided to charge an admission fee.

"When I gave the Home over to Zion Church," she told a local reporter, "what do you suppose they did? Why, they made a rule that nobody should come in without a hundred dollars. Now I wanted to make a rule that nobody could come in unless they had no money. What's the good of a Home if a person who wants to get in has to have money?" Tubman and the church finally reached a compromise, and in 1911, she moved into the home herself.

MOSES OF HER RACE ENDING HER LIFE IN HOME SHE FOUNDED read the headline of an article in the June 25, 1911, issue of the New York *World*. "She was the friend of great men," said the story, "but now, almost a centenarian, she awaits the last call. Now with the weight of almost a hundred years on her shoulders, she seeks rest during the few remaining days."

Tubman enjoyed more than a "few remaining days." Clear of mind, her always hearty appetite undiminished, she spent almost two years at the home, receiving visitors, telling stories, and, in late 1912, making out a will. (She left her house and its garden to a niece, a grandniece, and Frances Smith, the black woman who managed the home.) In February 1913, she chatted with an old friend, Mary B. Talbert, president of the New York State Federation of Colored Women's Clubs. Tubman, recalled Frances Smith, told Talbert "of the sweet spirit in that home, and of the happiness she felt was there." As Talbert prepared to leave, Tubman reached for her hand.

Holding it tightly, she expressed her hopes for the suffrage movement. "Tell the women," said Tubman, "to stand together."

A few weeks later, on March 10, 1913, Harriet Tubman died of pneumonia at the age of 93. Friends who had gathered at her bedside joined hands and sang her favorite spiritual, "Swing Low, Sweet Chariot."

Most of Auburn attended Tubman's last rites, a military service led by local Civil War veterans. As

In this photograph, probably the last ever taken of Tubman, the old fighter looks at the world with her usual unflinching gaze. As William Still had said so many years earlier, "Her like it is probable was never known before or since."

Erected in 1932, an Auburn plaque boasts of one of the town's distinguished residents. Eighteen years earlier, almost everyone in Auburn had attended a memorial service for Tubman, who died at the age of 93. Blacks and whites, free citizens all, stood side by side as educator Booker T. Washington praised Tubman for bringing "the two races nearer together."

she was laid to rest, the old soldiers stood at crisp attention, mourners bowed their heads, a bugler played taps, and the flag of the United States snapped in the breeze. A year later, the town's citizens, black and white, took part in a memorial service for "the Moses of her race." The crowd listened intently as celebrated black educator Booker T. Washington spoke about the woman who had "brought the two races nearer together" and "made it possible for the white race to place a higher estimate upon the black race."

Harriet Tubman's dramatic work on the Underground Railroad has sometimes overshadowed her other accomplishments. She conducted hundreds of people to freedom; she was also a skilled military leader, a compassionate nurse, a tireless abolitionist, and a lifelong humanitarian. Carrying the scars of slavery through her long life, Tubman was willing to break the law when she believed it wrong. She stood by her people from start to finish.

Tubman never sought power, and she never had any. Uninterested in wealth, she remained poor all her life. Although she acquired scores of famous friends, she preferred to work quietly, shunning attention whenever she could. Of all the testimonials to this remarkable woman, perhaps the most incisive was delivered by Frederick Douglass in an 1868 letter to Tubman:

> The difference between us is very marked. Most that I have done and suffered in the service of our cause has been in public, and I have received much encouragement at every step of the way. You, on the other hand, have labored in a private way. I have wrought in the day—you in the night. I have had the applause of the crowd and the satisfaction that comes from being approved by the multitude, while the most that you have done has been witnessed by a few trembling, scarred, and foot-sore bondmen and women, whom you have led out of the house of bondage, and whose heartfelt "*God bless you*" has been your only reward. The midnight sky and the silent stars have been the witnesses of your devotion to freedom and of your heroism. Excepting John Brown—of sacred memory—I know of no one who has willingly encountered more perils and hardships to serve our enslaved people than you have.

CHRONOLOGY

———— ❧ ————

ca. 1820	Born Harriet Ross on the Brodas plantation in Dorchester County, Maryland
1827	Makes first attempt to escape from slavery
1835	Suffers a near-fatal blow to the head that leads to lifelong "sleeping fits"
1844	Marries John Tubman
1849	Escapes from slavery; befriends abolitionist leaders
1850	Makes first of 19 trips into the South as a conductor on the Underground Railroad
1852	Makes first trip to Canada
1857	Rescues parents from slavery; settles in Auburn, New York
1858	Meets abolitionist John Brown
1861	Travels to South Carolina to work with the Union army as a nurse
1863	Becomes a spy for the Union army; leads a raid on South Carolina's Combahee River; frees 750 slaves
1865	Works in Virginia hospital
1870	Marries Nelson Davis
1897	Receives a medal from Queen Victoria of England
1908	Builds a home for sick and elderly blacks
1911	Moves into home
1913	Dies of pneumonia

FURTHER READING

Aptheker, Herbert. *To Be Free: Studies in American Negro History*. New York: International Publishers, 1948.

Blockson, Charles L. *The Underground Railroad*. New York: Prentice-Hall, 1987.

Bradford, Sarah H. *Harriet Tubman: The Moses of Her People*. Secaucus, NJ: Citadel Press, 1974.

Campbell, Stanley W. *The Slave Catchers: Enforcement of the Fugitive Slave Law, 1850–1860*. Chapel Hill: University of North Carolina Press, 1968.

Conrad, Earl. *Harriet Tubman*. Washington, DC: Associated Publishers, 1942.

Duberman, Martin. *The Antislavery Vanguard: New Essays on the Abolitionists*. Princeton University Press, 1965.

Du Bois, W. E. B. *John Brown*. Philadelphia: Jacobs & Co., 1909.

Furnas, J. C. *Goodbye to Uncle Tom*. New York: William Sloane Associates, 1956.

Gara, Larry. *The Liberty Line: The Legend of the Underground Railroad*. Lexington: University of Kentucky Press, 1961.

McPherson, James M. *Battle Cry of Freedom*. New York: Oxford University Press, 1988.

Morris, Thomas D. *Free Men All: The Personal Liberty Laws of the North*. Baltimore: Johns Hopkins University Press, 1974.

Petry, Ann. *Harriet Tubman, Conductor on the Underground Railroad*. New York: Crowell, 1955.

Scott, John Anthony. *Hard Trials on My Way: Slavery and the Struggle Against It*. New York: Knopf, 1974.

INDEX

PICTURE CREDITS

———— ✲ ————

The Bettmann Archive: pp. 12, 20, 23, 27, 30, 31, 36, 38, 44, 45, 47, 53, 58, 63, 71, 76, 79, 80, 83, 87, 88, 90, 94, 96, 101; Cayuga County Historian: pp. 99, 102, 104; Library of Congress: pp. 10, 67; Louisiana Collection, Tulane University Library, New Orleans, Louisiana: p. 54; The Maryland Historical Society: p. 42; National Archives: pp. 43, 84, 85, 89; National Portrait Gallery, Smithsonian Institution, Washington, DC: p. 82; The Schomburg Center for Research in Black Culture, New York Public Library: pp. 2–3, 14–15, 16, 17, 18, 24, 25, 32, 33, 34, 35, 40, 46, 48, 50, 57, 60, 62, 65, 69, 72, 77, 86, 92, 103; Frederic Jean Thalinger, Library of Congress: pp. 3, 106; UPI/Bettmann Archive: pp. 28, 74

M. W. TAYLOR is the former editor of the *New York Times* and *Los Angeles Times* syndicates and also served as an editor at *Life* magazine. Currently a New York City–based book editor and writer, she is coauthor of *Facts on File Dictionary of New Words*.

NATHAN IRVIN HUGGINS is W.E.B. Du Bois Professor of History and Director of the W.E.B. Du Bois Institute for Afro-American Research at Harvard University. He previously taught at Columbia University. Professor Huggins is the author of numerous books, including *Black Odyssey: The Afro-American Ordeal in Slavery, The Harlem Renaissance,* and *Slave and Citizen: The Life of Frederick Douglass.*

Curiosities Series

MASSACHUSETTS
Curiosities

QUIRKY CHARACTERS,
ROADSIDE ODDITIES, & OTHER
OFFBEAT STUFF

*Bruce Gellerman
and Erik Sherman*

The
Globe
Pequot
Press

GUILFORD, CONNECTICUT

Text design by Bill Brown
Layout by Deborah Nicolais
Maps by XNR Productions © The Globe Pequot Press

Front cover photos: Hilltop Steakhouse and Cohasset light by Erik Sherman, and the Weathervane restaurant and the Skinny House by Bruce Gellerman.
Back cover photo: Hood Milk Bottle by Bruce Gellerman.

ISSN 1550-6932
ISBN 0-7627-3070-6

Manufactured in the United States of America
First Edition/First Printing

For Yulia, Andre, and Anna,
who make life infinitely curious.
—B.G.

To my parents, who taught me to question
the wisdom of convention.
—E.S.

Help Us Keep This Guide Up to Date

Every effort has been made by the authors and editors to make
this guide as accurate and useful as possible. However, many
things can change after a guide is published—establishments
close, phone numbers change, and facilities come under new
management.

We would love to hear from you concerning your experiences
with this guide and how you feel it could be improved and kept
up to date. While we may not be able to respond to all comments and suggestions, we'll take them to heart and we'll also
make certain to share them with the authors. Please send your
comments and suggestions to the following address:

The Globe Pequot Press
Reader Response/Editorial Department
P.O. Box 480
Guilford, CT 06437

Or you may e-mail us at:
editorial@GlobePequot.com

Thanks for your input, and happy travels!

NORTHEAST MASSACHUSETTS

THE TECHNOLOGY RING AROUND BOSTON

GREATER BOSTON

SOUTHEAST MASSACHUSETTS AND THE CAPE AND ISLANDS

CENTRAL MASSACHUSETTS

WEST MASSACHUSETTS, THE CONNECTICUT RIVER VALLEY, AND THE BERKSHIRES

CONTENTS

ACKNOWLEDGMENTS

As powerful as the Internet is in collecting the flotsam and jetsam of life, curious people are still the best sources for Massachusetts minutiae and we are indebted to many for sharing their knowledge and digging deep when we set them to task.

To Deborah Douglas, curator of science and technology at the MIT Museum, many thanks for introducing us to Kismet, the world's most emotive robot. Craig Le Moult and Siobhan Houton of Tufts University helped show us which way was up regarding the antigravity monument and the tale and tail of Jumbo, the elephant. Prof. Gordon Prichett from Babson College can actually tell you what an apple from Newton's tree tastes like, and we were blessed to make the acquaintance of Diane Shephard, archivist at the Lynn Museum, who introduced us to the God Machine.

Thanks, too, to Stephan Nonack, head of Reader Services at the Boston Athenaeum, who gave us the lowdown on the "skin book," and to Jennifer Spencer for opening up her skinny house. Roberta Zonghi, the keeper of rare books and manuscripts at the Boston Public Library, was a font of information about things curious about Boston, as was the entire staff at the Boston Historical Society. And the Worcester Historical Society is second to none when it comes to being friendly and helpful.

Heidi Wellman at Chandler's General Store in Colrain helped by providing information on Old Glory and getting us the inside scoop on the Arthur B. Smith covered bridge. Kate Wellspring, collections manager at Amherst College's Pratt Museum, offered a firm footing on dinosaur tracks, as did Kornell Nash.

Jarvis Rockwell was unfailingly generous with his time as we asked about his toy collection, and the staff of the Country

Charm Restaurant in Cheshire didn't blink an eye while seriously answering the question, "Just how tall is that rooster statue on the top of your building?" And a Global Positioning System enthusiast, with the handle Khao Mun Gai when he indulges in the sport of geocaching, led us to the Forty-Second Parallel marker.

David Olson and Susan Abele at the Newton History Museum at the Jackson Homestead always took our requests for information with a straight face, whether we were inquiring about Fig Newtons or worm farms. Chet Kennedy, founder of the Public Health Museum, is a man with a mission and a missionary zeal; and Rev. Steven Ayers, vicar of the Old North Church, was always ready with a quip and a quote about colonial Boston.

Ellen Berlin of the Boston Medical Center set us straight on the fate of Jack the Duck. Charles Ball, the president of World Smile Day, was a delight to work with. And we'll always remember Tom Smith from Woburn City Hall for remembering the *Maine* cowl and telling us about it.

If you want to know about the smallest church in the world, the Hudson Public Library and Vic Petkauskos are the place to go. Bert Cohen knows more about marbles than any person in the universe, and if you are really into bad art, the person to see is Louise Sacco, curator of the Museum of Bad Art. Deborah Henson-Conant has a taste for burnt food and curates her crispy critters and tofu dogs with aplomb. Dr. Stephen Gould is one of those rare people who actually stops and reads roadside monuments. Thanks to him for pointing out where "Jingle Bells" was written.

And many thanks to Marc Abrahams, editor and founder of the *Annals of Improbable Research,* for thinking we were curious enough, or just crazy enough, to write this book. We hope we've proven you correct on both counts.

INTRODUCTION

After working on a book like this for a while, you no
longer get embarrassed by asking such questions as,
"Excuse me, do you know where Mary's little lamb is?"
or "Are Jumbo the elephant's ashes kept in a jar of plain or
crunchy peanut butter?" or "Where can I find the world's
largest thermometer collection?" Yes, those around you still
look at you cross-eyed, but you no longer mind: It just goes
with the territory of being curious about Massachusetts, as
curious a place as ever there was. After all, it got its start by
Pilgrims who couldn't stand intolerance and European persecu-
tion, and who thus fled to a new land where they could have
the freedom to persecute and be intolerant of everyone else.
Upon reaching Cape Cod, one of the first acts of this largely
religious group was to steal corn that Indians had stored for
the winter. After finally coming to their last stop—which they
still thought was somewhere in Virginia—the Pilgrims set up
the first public utility, a grain mill. (You can thank them for
hundreds of years of misbillings and poor customer service.)
And you thought they survived that first winter on turkey?
We're lucky we're not munching on a giant loaf of corn bread
for Thanksgiving

You might think it easy to distill Massachusetts into a combination of Puritanism, rocky soil, and history—an image set
in native granite: predictable, solid, inflexible. We thought the
same when each of us moved here decades ago. And, like us,
you are in for a surprise. Massachusetts is a contradictory
land, full of unusual people, places, objects, ideas, and cranky
misfits. Talk about ornery: The settlers couldn't even form a
state, and instead chose to create a commonwealth.

Perhaps political unrest and opposing the usual order of
things was a healthy release for the residents, because all you

have to do is look at what happened when there wasn't some government to overthrow, action to protest, or election to contest. A colonial daredevil decided to challenge Puritanical Bostonians by flying from atop the Old North Church—more than 150 years before the Wright Brothers. The city leaders' reaction? You'd think that they'd be thrilled at the technical marvel. Nope. They got annoyed and banned flying. And what can you say of a place where people build giant seahorses and large granite towers, for the sole purpose of marketing? Or where a golf course includes an eighteenth-century grave or a monument to modern rocketry? Speaking of graves, you don't have to dig far to find some very curious final resting places. Massachusetts is the last stop for Jumbo, Mother Goose, and Mary Baker Eddy (founder of the Christian Science mother church). It's also the birthplace of Mary's little lamb, one of the Peter Rabbits (ah, the cotton tales of literary controversy), the Cat in the Hat, and the ubiquitous Kilroy. Here you will find what might be the country's oldest example of graffiti; an ancient bowling ball found in a privy; a place that always remembers the *Maine*; and museums dedicated to collections of dirt, shovels, and burnt food.

So, come meet the pirates and the healers, the artists and the ward heelers. See the house made of rolled-up newspapers, and the giant neon flag. Visit museums of plastic and of sanitary plumbing. Catch magic shows, ax murders, and lighthouse hauntings. Experience brightly painted gingerbread cottages on an island and entire towns smothered by a man-made lake. Just stifle your laughter, as the folks here can get touchy.

Massachusetts: You've got to love it. Or else.

North
Boston

Winthrop

East
Boston

(1A)

North
End

■ Boston
Common

Logan
International
Airport

(90)

(93)

South Boston

Boston Harbor

GREATER BOSTON

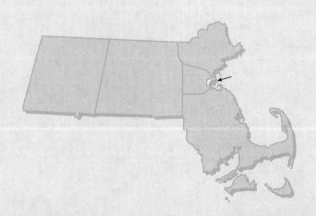

GREATER BOSTON

THE HUB OF THE UNIVERSE
Boston

Bostonians are a self-centered lot, and why not? After all, the city's immodest nickname is The Hub as in "the hub of the universe." The phrase is actually derived from something Oliver Wendell Holmes wrote in *The Autocrat of the Breakfast-Table* about the capitol building:

> Boston State-house is the hub of the solar system. You coud n't [sic] pry that out of a Boston man if you had the tire of all creation straightened out for a crow-bar.

Since Holmes wrote this whimsical essay in 1858, the so-called center of the universe has moved a bit. You'll now find it near Filene's Basement on a spot marked with a bronze plaque about 15 feet from the store's Washington Street entrance.

The hub of the universe is in the center of a fruit market on Washington Street.
Photo by Bruce Gellerman

Perhaps fitting for its top banana status, in order to see the center of the universe, you might have to move a bunch of bananas or two . . . and perhaps some onions and a crate of oranges. The plaque, marking the hub of the universe, is now in the center of a fruit market at 426 Washington Street.

F IGHTING J OE H OOKER
B o s t o n

A statue of Maj. Gen. Joseph "Fighting Joe" Hooker, on his mighty steed, stands in front of the entrance to the Massachusetts State House. One shudders to think what the statue might have looked like, considering what Hooker is best known for: lending his last name to the oldest profession.

Maj. Gen. Joseph Hooker lost his major battle at Chancellorsville even though he had twice as many troops as General Lee. We remember him for his activities off the battlefield.
Photo by Bruce Gellerman

Joe Hooker was a favorite son of Massachusetts. He commanded the Army of the Potomac during the Civil War, but Fighting Joe's men were a rowdy bunch and Hooker's headquarters was a den of iniquity. The encampment was said to be a combination barroom and brothel. Hooker allowed women who followed his troops to set up their tents nearby. Hence, the phrase "Hooker's Division" became the popular equivalent for prostitutes.

There is some evidence that the term "hooker" was used before the Civil War, but the story of Fighting Joe clearly was responsible for its common use today.

THE SACRED COD AND HOLY MACKEREL
Boston

Suspended over the entrance to the Massachusetts House of Representatives chamber is something you won't find hanging over any other deliberative body in the world: a cod fish. And it's not just any cod fish. It's the Sacred Cod Fish. Measuring 4 feet 11 inches, the pine carved fish is a constant reminder of the importance of the fishing industry to the state's early history. The Pilgrims and Indians feasted on cod along with turkey that first Thanksgiving, and it was the state's first export. We even named the Cape after the cod.

The fish that currently holds the place of honor above the legislative body's entry is actually the third-generation cod. The first was destroyed in a fire in 1747; the second, during the Revolutionary War. The current one has been hanging around since 1787, moved from the old statehouse to the new House chamber in 1895. It has hung there ever since, with one notable exception. In 1933 pranksters from the *Harvard Lampoon* "cod-napped" the state's seafood symbol by cutting the

The Sacred Cod.
Photo by Bruce Gellerman

The Holy Mackerel.
Photo by Bruce Gellerman

line holding it aloft, and they made off with their prize catch. Lawmakers were outraged. The state police were called in to investigate. The Charles River was dredged. Days later an anonymous tip led to the revered fish's recovery and it was hung 6 inches higher to prevent it from being stolen again.

Those who say something very fishy is going on in the Massachusetts statehouse have a basis for their claim. In 1974 the cod was elevated to the status of official state fish. Not to be outdone by the lower house, the Senate has in its chamber a wrought-iron chandelier with a fish in its design. It's called the Holy Mackerel.

Over in the House chamber, check out the second painting on the left behind the speaker's chair. It shows one of the judges from the Salem witch trials repenting for sentencing accused witches to death. The gesture is a bit late but still appreciated; after all, it's the thought that counts.

The Massachusetts State House is on Beacon Hill overlooking Boston Common on Beacon Street. Self-taught architect Charles Bullfinch designed the building, which was constructed between 1795 and 1797 on a pasture owned by John Hancock. Although it may look high now, the hill is 50 feet lower than its original height, as land from the hills was used to fill in Boston's Back Bay. The gilded dome, first made of wood shingles, is topped by a lantern and a pinecone (the latter is a symbol of the forests of Massachusetts.) The fish are indoors.

THE PARKER HOUSE HOTEL: REVOLUTIONARY ROLLS
Boston

Hotels make for strange bedfellows. John Wilkes Booth, Malcolm X, Ho Chi Minh, John Crawford, Ralph Waldo

Emerson, and John F. Kennedy have all spent time at Boston's Parker House.

The hotel, now known as the Omni Parker, is the oldest continuously operated hotel in the continental United States When it opened for business in 1855, it was the first hotel in Boston to have hot and cold running water and an elevator.

John Wilkes Booth stayed here the week before he shot Abraham Lincoln. Ralph Waldo Emerson, Nathaniel Hawthorne, and Henry Wadsworth Longfellow were members of the famous literary Saturday Club, which regularly met in the hotel's restaurant. Had the wordsmiths assembled some eight decades later, Malcolm X might have cleared their table; he worked as a busboy in the hotel restaurant in 1940.

The Parker House is famous for its rolls. Legend has it that this gastronomic delight is the happy result of an angry chef. The Parker House prided itself on meeting the needs of the pickiest patron, but in 1856, when one particularly demanding guest made one too many requests for a certain roll, it is said that a hotheaded German chef began throwing small balls of dough into an oven. Surprisingly, the rolls were delicious, and the talk of delighted guests gave rise to the famed Parker House Roll. The hotel kept the recipe a secret until Pres. Franklin Roosevelt requested it in 1933.

The Boston cream pie (which is actually a cake) was also concocted here. The origin of the pie/cake is not entirely certain. Some say it was created by a French chef named Sanzian. There is no truth to the story that the misnamed dessert was part of a Communist plot to confuse American diners, although revolutionary Ho Chi Minh did work as a baker at the Parker House from 1911 to 1913.

For a taste of Old World charm, and to imagine what it must have been like way back when chefs were tossing dough and bakers were plotting coups, check out or check into the hotel at 60 School Street, (617) 227–8600. You never know who you'll meet there.

WHAT A GRAPE CATCH

*I*n 1988 Paul Tavilla of Arlington, Massachusetts, earned a place in the Guinness Book of Records *by catching in his mouth a grape dropped from the top of the John Hancock building, sixty stories high.*
When it comes to grape catching, what goes down obviously also goes up. The longest distance a grape has been caught after being thrown into the air from ground level is 99.82 meters—precisely 327 feet and 6 inches. That great grape catch was accomplished on May 27, 1991, by, who else, Paul Tavilla.

BOSTON IS PLANET HOLLYWOOD
Boston

Boston University is home to the largest collection of Hollywood memorabilia on the planet. The University's Department of Special Collections includes the personal papers and effects of some 2,000 luminaries of the stage and silver screen. Included in the twentieth-century archive are materials from Mary Astor, Douglas Fairbanks Jr., Marilyn Monroe, Rex Harrison, Robert Redford, and Edward G. Robinson. The Oscar that Gene Kelly won for *An American in Paris* is on view, as are Fred Astaire's dancing shoes and Elizabeth Taylor's gloves.

Howard Gottlieb, curator of B.U.'s Department of Special Collections, began going through the attics and shoe boxes of the stars in 1963. His most prized catch is 119,000 pages of material from Bette Davis. Gottlieb called Davis twice a week for thirty years before she agreed to donate her scripts, scrapbooks, and 5,000-volume library specializing in theater history.

In all, the archives take up 7 miles of shelves in two underground vaults. The Department of Special Collections is at 771 Commonwealth Avenue, 5th Floor. Call ahead at (617) 353–3916 if you want to see something special.

OY, YOU SHOULD ONLY LIVE SO LONG AND PROSPER

*M*r. Spock from the TV series Star Trek comes from Vulcan via Boston. Leonard Nimoy, a.k.a. Spock, grew up in an Orthodox Jewish household in Boston. His religious background played a pivotal role in developing his Vulcan character.

According to Nimoy, the idea for the Vulcan salute, where four fingers of each hand are split, comes from a boyhood lesson he learned at temple. The gesture creates the Hebrew letter shin, representing the first letter of the Almighty and the word peace. Nimoy proposed the hand signal when the producers of the show were trying to come up with a salute for his character.

CAN YOU IMAGINE HOW BIG THE TEA BAG IS?
Boston

I t is only right and proper that the city where the most famous tea party in history took place would have the world's largest tea kettle. The giant pot was cast in 1873 and it hung over the Oriental Teashop until 1967, when it was moved

Tea for two . . . two thousand, that is. The giant teapot in Boston's City Hall Plaza has been spouting steam since 1873.
Photo by Bruce Gellerman

just a few doors down the street to its present site. The kettle holds precisely 227 gallons, 2 quarts, 1 pint, and 3 gills and blows steam through its spout.

Ironically, the kettle now hangs above a Starbucks store at 63 Court Street, near the Government Center metro station. Perhaps if the java chain had been around in 1773 we'd be calling it the "Boston Coffee Klatch" today.

JFK Ate Here
Boston

O bviously, John F. Kennedy ate at a lot of places in his hometown. One of his favorites was the Union Oyster House, where the Kennedy clan dined regularly on the restaurant's namesake mollusk. In the private upstairs dining room, you will find a plaque on Kennedy's favorite booth, number 18, dedicated to his memory in 1977.

Kennedy was just one of many Harvard students to frequent the restaurant. Supposedly, some were paid to eat there. Oyster House lore has it that an importer of toothpicks from South America hired Harvard students to dine at the restaurant and request the picks as a way to boost sales.

The Union Oyster House is located at 41 Union Street. To request a table or JFK's favorite booth, call (617) 227–2750.

LET THEM EAT
SANDWICHES!

*B*oston's first public playground was a sand-
box. The sand garden, as it was called in
those days, was built in 1886 by the philanthropic women of the North End Union. It was
created to serve the needs of immigrant Italian,
Irish, and Jewish children in the area.

At the time, Kate Gannet Wells of the philanthropic committee said, "Playing in the dirt is
the royalty of childhood."

The site at 20 Parmenter Street is across the
street from the North End branch of the Boston
Public Library, where you will find a diorama
of the Ducal Palace of Venice made by local
artist Louise Stimson in 1949.

GOT MILK?
Boston

The Hood Milk Bottle, near the Children's Museum at 300 Congress Street, is a pint-sized display—400,000 pints, that is, or 50,000 gallons, in case your math has gone sour. Either way, it would give you a giant milk mustache. The wooden bottle is 40 feet high and was built in 1938. During the summer it also serves as an ice cream stand and snack bar.

Milk with your tea? The giant Hood Milk Bottle
stands near the site of the Boston Tea Party.
Photo by Bruce Gellerman

THE BOSTON UNIVERSITY BRIDGE

*B*ostonians will tell you that the Boston University Bridge crossing the Charles River is the only bridge in the world where an airplane can fly over a person riding a bicycle, next to a car, going over a train, that's traveling over a boat. It's true—that is, if you don't count the Brooklyn Bridge, where the train (a subway in a tunnel) goes under the boat.

I'LL HAVE A VERY SHORT ONE: THE LITTLEST BAR
Boston

Without a doubt, Boston's most famous watering hole is the one from TV fame: the Cheers bar. Two establishments bearing this name cater to the tourist trade. One is at 84 Beacon Street and the other is in Faneuil Market. It's unlikely that anyone at either place will know your name, so if you want recognition and a little something to drink, take a short walk across Boston Public Garden to 47 Providence Street. The bar

For a wee bit of blarney, check out the tiny
basement pub the Littlest Bar.
Photo by Bruce Gellerman

there is so cozy that everyone will quickly learn your name. It's the smallest bar in Boston, appropriately named the Littlest Bar. Built in 1945, the Littlest is a wee small subterranean Irish pub just 16 feet wide and 22 feet long, seating just 38 patrons. Leprechauns would love it.

Don't forget to check out the minuscule bathroom. There you will find a plaque commemorating Irish Nobel Prize-winning novelist Seamus Heaney. It says, "SEAMUS HEANEY PEED HERE." Now there's something you won't see at Cheers. To find out if there's room for you, call (617) 523–9766.

A CLEAN GET-AWAY, EXCEPT FOR THE SMELL

*O*n January 17, 1950, robbers broke into the Brinks offices at 169 Prince Street in Boston's North End. They made off with $1,218,211.29 in cash and $1,557,183.83 in securities and checks. The Great Brinks Robbery was the biggest heist in U.S. history. It took six years and $29 million for the government to find and prosecute the crooks. Only $51,906 of the Brinks cash was ever recovered. A big breakthrough in the case came when one of the robbers tried to pass off money that he had hidden in the dirt. The buried loot became smelly and moldy and led to the case being cracked.

The building where thieves pulled off the Great Brinks Robbery still stands and is now known as the North Terminal Garage. It is on the National Register of Historic Places. The address is 600 Commercial Avenue.

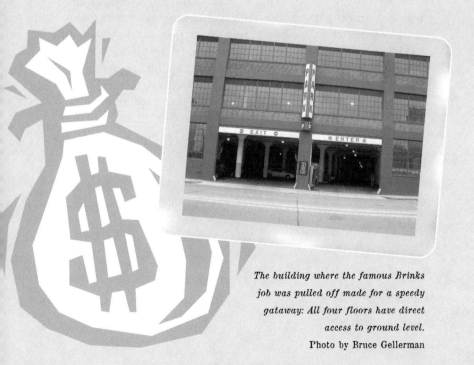

The building where the famous Brinks job was pulled off made for a speedy gataway: All four floors have direct access to ground level.
Photo by Bruce Gellerman

THE CHRISTMAS TREE IS THE PRESENT
Boston

If you want to see the most magnificent Christmas tree in the nation, forget about the ones at the White House and New York's Rockefeller Center. They dim in comparison to the one in Boston. For more than thirty years, Boston's official Christmas tree in Boston Common has run rings around any and all competitors. But don't take our word for it. The seasonal symbol comes from Nova Scotia, Canada, the self-proclaimed "Christmas Tree Capital of the World," as an annual gift selected after a six-month search. By tradition, the tree has to be at least fifty years old and 50 feet tall.

Why all the hubbub over the Hub's tree? It's a show of gratitude for the help Boston sent to Halifax during its time of greatest need. In early December 1917 a ship filled with munitions exploded in Halifax harbor. It was the largest artificially created explosion in history until the detonation of the atomic bomb. Halifax was flattened; thousands were killed and injured. Boston citizens braved a blizzard to deliver food, medical aid, and supplies to the city, and Halifax has never forgotten.

The traditional lighting of Boston's official Christmas tree takes place in early December in Boston Common.

WHAT'S UP, DUCK?
Boston

Robert McCloskey's *Make Way for Ducklings* is Massachusetts's official children's book. The children's classic features Mr. and Mrs. Mallard's darling little ducklings: Jack, Kack, Lack, Mack, Nack, Ouack, Quack, and Pack.

*After being "duck-napped," Jack the duckling is
back on his feet.*
Photo by Bruce Gellerman

A 38-foot-long bronze sculpture of the jaywalking duck-lings and their mom can be found in the northeast corner of Boston's Public Garden. The statue, sculpted by Nancy Schon, was installed in 1987 and quickly became a favorite of residents and visitors alike. Then in 1999 someone "duck-napped" Jack. Bostonians, usually unflappable about such matters, were incensed. Thankfully, a month later the statue was found under a desk at a Boston college. But the duck-napper had sawed Jack's legs off just above his webbed feet, so a new Jack had to be made. The one in Boston Garden is the new Jack. The old Jack, with his legs repaired, now has a new home at the rooftop playground outside Boston Medical Center's pediatric department at 84 Harrison Avenue.

A D EATH - D EFYING C OLONIAL D AREDEVIL
Boston

One if by land, two if by sea. Three if by air? Boston's Old North Church, perhaps best known as the place where Paul Revere got the signal that set him off on his midnight ride, also happens to be where colonial stuntman John Childs took the first flight in Boston history.

In 1757, eighteen years before Revere got his signal, John Childs used the church steeple as a launching pad. A plaque on a wall outside the Old North Church describes how Childs flew from the 190-foot steeple "to the satisfaction of a great number of spectators."

There are two versions of the event. One has Childs strapping on a leather umbrella-like contraption, putting a grooved wooden board on his chest, and sliding headfirst down a 700-foot-long guyline. The other version has him wearing canvas wings and gliding down. Either way, the colonial daredevil drew such a large crowd that he did it again the next day while shooting off pistols. The performance proved too much for Boston's Puritan prudes. They banned all future flights of fantasy, a prohibition on aviation that stands on the city's books to this day.

The plaque commemorating Childs's flight is the third from the left on the brick Washington Garden wall near the main entrance to the Old North Church, 193 Salem Street.

ONCE UPON A MIDNIGHT FROGPONDIUM

*A*lthough Edgar Allen Poe pondered weak and weary and died in Baltimore, the master of the macabre was born in Boston in 1809. Orphaned as a child, Poe lived in Boston only a short time, returning briefly in 1827 when he enlisted in the U.S. Army under the name Edgar A. Perry. While Poe was in Boston his first book of poems, Tamerlane and other Poems, was published, written anonymously "by a Bostonian." Poe had a love–hate relationship with Boston and may have been reluctant to have his name attached to the city of his birth; he often referred to Boston as "Frogpondium" after the frog pond on the Common.

Perhaps appropriately, Poe's exact birthplace is in dispute. Some put it at 33 Hollis Street; others say it was on Carver Street, which is now called Charles Street South. To avoid the dispute, the plaque honoring Poe is near 176 Boylston Street.

THE NUMBER 576

The colorful, charismatic, and corrupt James Michael Curley was the first mayor of Boston to have an automobile. His license plate, 576, represented the number of letters in his first, middle, and last names. The same sequence was used by every mayor of the city until 1993, when Thomas Menino decided to lease a car to save the city money. (How times have changed.)

Curley not only served as mayor of Boston, governor of the state, and congressman; he also served two terms in jail, for misuse of federal funds and for taking a civil service exam for a friend. Neither time was his prison number 576.

HEY NORTON, CHECK THIS OUT
Boston

You can never tell what you'll find when you spend $14.5 billion and dig through 16 million cubic yards of dirt.

Archaeologists working alongside excavators on Boston's Big Dig, the largest public works project in history, have unearthed the usual arrowheads, some clay tobacco pipes, and the oldest bowling ball in North America. If that doesn't bowl you over, perhaps this will: They found the ball under the floorboards in a "house of office," the seventeenth-century term for a privy.

The oak ball is flattened on two sides and is about the size of a grapefruit. It has a perforated middle to hold a lead weight to give the ball more play when rolled. Not that play was what the Puritans had in mind when they founded Boston: A statute forbidding bowling was passed in 1646 because it caused "much waste of wine and beer."

Perhaps a bowler taking a nip too much might explain why the ball was found in the toilet.

Today the oldest bowling ball in North America is on display at the Commonwealth Museum, 220 Morissey. Admission is free but you'll have to pay for shoes.

For more information, call (617) 727–9268 or visit www .state.ma.us/sec/mus.

AN AIRPORT NAMED FOR A VERY INFREQUENT FLIER

*B*oston's *Logan International Airport*, one of the busiest in the nation, is named in honor of Lt. Gen. Edward Lawrence Logan. Logan was born in Boston in 1875 and led a distinguished career as an elected official, judge, and war hero. He died in 1929.

The question is: Why did they name an airport after him? For all of his many accomplishments, Lieutenant General Logan never flew in an airplane.

THE RUNNING OF
THE BRIDES

*F*ilene's Basement's notorious bridal gown event has been likened to the running of the bulls at Pamplona. But according to the store's PR person, Pat Boudrot, some years it's more like a prize fight, as brides-to-be go head-to-head in an attempt to grab a designer wedding gown at a bargain-basement $249.

Some of the women arrive with retinues that include their moms and matrons of honor, ready to do battle. Boudrot says they come wearing boxing gloves and chomping on mouth guards. It's a knock-down, no-holds-or clothes-barred fight to the finish as the gals make a mad dash for the dresses, stripping themselves and the racks bare in just seconds. The record, witnessed by a CBS news camera team, is just 36 seconds. It's a scene that makes the floor of the New York Stock Exchange look like, well, a walk down the aisle.

Filene's Basement first emptied its warehouse of designer gowns for the one-day sale in 1947. Since then, on at least five occasions, starry eyed women, with their sights set on a "baaaahhhhgain" have broken down the doors to the store before they were opened.

The objects of their affections are dresses that come from manufacturers' overstocks, cancelled store orders, and, of course, cancelled weddings. The gowns may retail for up to $10,000 and sell for as low as $199 on this one lucky day. One memorable gown featured a peacock hand-painted in pastels; another had a map of the world laid out in Mercator projection on the skirt.

Marketing professors Ellen Foxman and Susan Dobscha have made a cottage industry of writing scholarly papers about the sale. Their latest, "Women and Wedding Gowns: Exploring a Discount Shopping Experience," is in the proceedings of the 1998 Conference on Gender, Marketing, and Consumer Behavior.

Filene's Basement has expanded the sale to many of its stores around the nation, but the one in the original store at Boston's Downtown Crossing is the first and still the most frenetic.

Brides strip the racks and themselves bare at
Filene's Basement Bridal Gown Sale.
Photo courtesy of Filene's Basement

THE SACCO AND VANZETTI
DEATH MASKS
Boston

There are many proud moments in Massachusetts's history, but August 23, 1927, is not one of them. That was the day when Italian immigrants Nicola Sacco, a shoemaker from Stoughton, and Bartolomeo Vanzetti, a fisherman from North Plymouth, were executed on the site that is now part of Bunker Hill Community College in Boston.

The men, followers of Italy's most radical anarchist, were found guilty of armed robbery and murder. Both men denied the charges up to their deaths. The evidence against the men was weak and circumstantial and their executions ignited protests around the world. The case became a landmark in the judicial history of the state and nation. Fifty years to the day of their execution, Massachusetts governor Michael Dukakis issued a proclamation apologizing to the men and their families.

Copies of Sacco's and Vanzetti's death certificates are housed in the rare books department of the Boston Public Library, along with a canister of their ashes, their death masks, a box of bullets, and other personal items. Boston Public Library is at Copley Square.

Visitors are asked to e-mail ahead of time so that the materials can be accessed. Write to rzonghi@bpl.org.

The Boston Public Library's special collections also contain more than over 700 anarchist newspapers and periodicals from around the world.

How sweet it isn't

*A*bout half past noon on January 15, 1919, a disaster like no other struck Boston's North End. A giant concrete-and-cast-iron tank, 52 feet high and 90 feet in diameter and holding 2.3 million gallons of molasses, exploded. The powerful blast propelled a gooey, 2-story tidal wave down Commercial Avenue at thirty-five miles an hour. Steel supports for a nearby elevated train line were severed and a fire station was crushed. Twenty-one people were killed, 150 were injured, and an untold number of horses drowned in the steaming, sweet lava. Left in its wake was a 2-foot layer of molasses that had spread for blocks. Cleanup crews and sightseers brought it on their shoes and clothes all over Boston and as far away as Worcester. While the sickly, sweet smell allegedly lingered for decades, there's not a trace of the molasses today. Not even a plaque marks the spot where the doomed tank once stood, but if you look down from Copp's Hill onto Commercial Avenue, you'll see a park next to an enclosed recreation center. That's the place.

TANKS VERMILION, HO HO HO CHI MINH
Boston

The world's largest copyrighted work of art is on permanent display just south of Boston in Dorcester on Route 93. It's the so-called Rainbow Tank, a 140-foot-tall liquid natural gas tank featuring five huge stripes of color: vermilion, orange, yellow, blue, and purple.

In 1971 Boston Gas commissioned artist Corita Kent to paint the tank. Kent, a former nun best known for designing the famous LOVE postage stamp, said the Rainbow Tank was an expression of peace. The war in Vietnam was raging, and Kent was a peace activist. Some say they can see evidence of Kent's anti-war sympathies hidden in the tank. Look at the middle stripe. See the profile of Ho Chi Minh? Who? Ho Chi Minh, the former leader of North Vietnam and a busboy at Boston's Parker House Hotel in the 1920s. Others say the roadside Rorschach test contains the image of the devil, Osama Bin Laden, or Fred Flintstone. And then there are those who say that sometimes a tank is just a tank.

Be careful: Don't use the access road leading to the tank. It's private property. There are remote cameras watching you and the property owners will call the police if you are on the road.

*The gas tank along Interstate 93 is a roadside
Rorschach test. Some people say they see Ho Chi
Minh's profile painted on the tank.*
Photo by Erik Sherman

You Definitely Save on Wall-to-Wall Carpet
Boston

Jennifer Simonic; her husband, Spence Welton; their daughter; and their dog and cat live at 44 Hull Street in Boston's North End. This 200-year-old, four-story town house has been beautifully restored, but it is easy to miss. The house is just 10 feet 5 inches wide. The home is so narrow that the front door is located on the side. The ceilings are 6 feet 4 inches high. (Spence Welton is 6 feet 1 inch tall.)

The Skinny House, as it is called, is the narrowest home in Boston—if not the entire commonwealth. Legend has it that the house was built out of spite to block the view of neighbors behind it. Admittedly, that's a pretty thin story. More likely, it is the last of a series of similar homes built in the area around 1800. At one time eleven people lived in the house. Ironically, the Skinny House has a spacious, 1,000-square-foot backyard, one of the largest in the densely populated North End.

The Skinny House is located directly opposite Copp's Hill Burying Ground. The house number is on the side.

The house at 44 Hull Street in Boston is the
skinniest house in the city, and perhaps in the
entire commonwealth.
Photo by Bruce Gellerman

ETHER OR EITHER
Boston

Boston printer Gilbert Allen never knew what hit him. After a few whiffs from an ether-soaked sponge, he was out. When he woke up, the human guinea pig learned he had made medical history. It was October 16, 1846, and Gilbert Allen was the first person to be successfully operated on while under anesthesia. Before then, undergoing an operation had meant enduring excruciating pain. Now, the ether-assisted surgery proceeded in silence as an astonished crowd of physicians looked on. Afterward, Dr. John Warren, the surgeon who performed the operation, told his incredulous colleagues, "Gentleman, this is no humbug."

Bah, humbug, indeed. The operation touched off a controversy of competing claims over who actually had invented the potent stuff, with two Boston dentists taking credit. When city authorities proposed a monument memorializing the inventor, they consulted Harvard physician and wordsmith Oliver Wendell Holmes. It was Holmes who coined the term *anesthesia* and, acting Solomon-like, suggested dedicating the statue to "Either or ether."

When Mark Twain learned that neither man would be named on the statue, he proclaimed that the ether monument "is made of hardy material, but the lie it tells will outlast it a million years." Well, either it will or ether it won't, but it has lasted since its unveiling in 1868 in Boston Common. It is the oldest monument in the country's oldest public park. The Ether Memorial can be found facing Arlington Street. Atop the red marble columns is a rendition of the Good Samaritan. Be sure to check out the weird reliefs behind the granite arches.

Patients breathed a lot easier after the invention of ether. This monument in Boston Garden pays homage to the pain-killing gas.
Photo by Erik Sherman

The surgical amphitheater in which the first anesthesia-assisted operation took place is called the Ether Dome. It was designed by the great architect Charles Bullfinch. Until 1873 it was used as an operating room. Then it served as a storage area, a dormitory, and a dining room for nurses. It is now a classroom. The Ether Dome is open to the public and is located at Massachusetts General Hospital, 55 Fruit Street.

THE GARDNER MUSEUM: WHAT YOU DON'T SEE IS WHAT YOU GET
Boston

T he magnificent Isabella Stewart Gardner Museum contains an eclectic collection of 2,500 paintings, sculptures, tapestries, pieces of furniture, manuscripts, and rare books. Mrs. Gardner, the grande dame of Boston's Brahmin high society, spent thirty years assembling the renowned collection and built a fifteenth-century Venetian palace with courtyard garden to house it.

But today what makes the collection a must-see for many tourists is what you do not see, as evidenced by the empty frames that hang on the walls. On St. Patrick's Day 1990, the Gardner Museum was the scene of the biggest art heist in U.S. history. Two men wearing fake mustaches and Boston Police uniforms stole thirteen priceless works of art. Among them were three Rembrandts (including the master's only seascape), five Degas sketches, a Manet, and Vermeer's *The Concert*. Despite a $5-million reward, none of the pieces has been recovered. The empty frames continue to hang on the walls because Mrs. Gardner stipulated in her will that everything in the house was forever to remain exactly as it was or all her possessions would pass to Harvard University.

The Isabella Stewart Gardner Museum is located at 280 The Fenway. For more information, call (617) 566–1401 or visit www.gardnermuseum.org. The Gardner is closed on most major holidays and usually on St. Patrick's Day.

GILLETTE EMPLOYEES GET WORKED UP INTO A LATHER
Boston

B ack in 1901 traveling salesman King Camp Gillette developed the world's first double-edged disposable blade, and the hirsute have never been the same. Today, from its World Shaving Headquarters in South Boston, where Gillette founded his international empire, the company turns out blades by the billions. To ensure that the company lives up to its claim that Gillette's razors are "the best a man can get" and that they get even better, Gillette employs 500 engineers and scientists in laboratories around the world who send their improvements back to Boston for evaluation.

More than 300 volunteers at the South Boston factory sign up for the shave-in-plant program to test-drive the latest experimental models. Each morning a select group of men take off their shirts, enter one of twenty booths, and lather up. Technicians in white lab coats register their reactions as the men shave the right side of their faces with one unmarked razor and the left side with another. The results are entered into a computer. After decades of studying shaving and blades under electron microscopes and in slow motion, Gillette has come to understand that making a blade shave smoother than a baby's bottom takes a lot more than science and technology. Because it sells blades from Armenia to Zanzibar, Gillette has to be sensitive to the different kinds of skin and hair types, and to cultural differences as well. Over the years, shaving scientists have learned that what constitutes a great shave is really a subjective experience; there's the sound of the blade slicing through whiskers, the feel of the razor in the hand. After all the testing and experimenting, it turns out that when it comes to shaving, beauty is in the eye of the beard holder.

YOU NEED THIS MUSEUM LIKE A HOLE IN THE HEAD
Boston

T he Warren Anatomical Museum is the kind of place to which Alfred Hitchcock might have brought a first date. The museum is fascinating in a macabre sort of way, and not without humor, with a vast collection of medical instruments, photos, anatomical models, machines, gadgets, specimens, body parts, and medical memorabilia. In all, more than 13,000 artifacts detail the evolution of modern medical science from the nineteenth to the twentieth century. You'll be astonished by how far medicine has come in such a short period of time . . . and perhaps be unnerved by just how primitive it was until not too long ago.

Dr. John Collin Warren started collecting unusual anatomical specimens in 1799, when he was just twelve years old. In 1848 he hung up his stethoscope (there are scores of models on display) and resigned his Harvard professorship, donating his world-class collection of weird artifacts to the medical school. His own skeleton is now part of the collection.

On display is the phrenological collection of Dr. Johann Gaspar Spurzheim, who studied skull bumps for clues about personality and brain function. In 1832 the famed German doctor died unexpectedly in Boston while on a lecture tour. His body is buried in Mount Auburn Cemetery in Cambridge, but his unusually large skull is on display at the Warren Museum.

The most popular exhibit is the skull of Phineas Gage. An on-the-job accident sent a thirteen-pound steel bar flying through Gage's cheek into his brain. Unexpectedly, Gage survived. His memory was intact but his personality took a turn for the worse. He became mean and lost his social constraints. Scientists studied Gage's skull for clues about personality. Seems they needed just such an accident, like a hole in the head, to discover the inner workings of the brain.

The Warren Anatomical Museum Exhibition Gallery is on the fifth floor of the Countway Library of Medicine, 10 Shattuck Street; (617) 432–6196.

Spurzheim Tomb is at the intersection of Fountain and Lawn Avenues, left sides, adjacent to the road in Mount Auburn Cemetery, Mount Auburn Street, Cambridge. Watch out for the bumps in the road.

A M E R I C A N S   " I N - V E S T "   I N   A N   I N S E C T
B o s t o n

S ince 1742, a 52-inch-tall, 38-pound copper grasshopper with glass doorknob eyes has looked down onto a good deal of American history. The 'hopper has watched from his weathervane perch 80 feet above the ground as the winds of change turned the colonies into a nation and the nation into a world superpower. From the grasshopper's vantage point atop Faneuil Hall, the insect has been an eyewitness to the Boston Massacre and the Boston Tea Party and watched as patriotic conspirators gathered at the Old Meeting House. Over time the grasshopper has survived wars, hurricanes, earthquakes, fires, and vandals.

But the statue is more than a priceless piece of Americana. The grasshopper is also a time capsule. Inside the insect's stomach vest area is a copper container. Each time the grasshopper has been handled and restored, people have placed objects into the vest and taken things out.

In 1761, following a devastating fire and an earthquake, a note inscribed "food for the Grasshopper" was inserted into the copper time capsule by the restorer. The note, detailing the gilded insect's trials and tribulations, is now in the Boston Public Library's archives.

In 1842 the weather vane was restored again. This time it was filled with papers and coins. It is believed that the first contents were removed and sold at auction in 1885. In 1889 some newspapers and coins from the period were deposited in the capsule, and in 1952 Boston's mayor inserted one of his business cards and a message in the copper vest.

In 1974 the grasshopper was reported missing and a massive insect hunt was started.

The 'hopper was discovered weeks later in the Faneuil Hall belfry underneath a pile of old flags. Seems painters had taken it down and forgot to put it back up. A tip from an ex-steeplejack who worked on the vane and was trying to beat a drug rap led to its recovery. Before the grasshopper was restored to its proper perch, Boston's mayor resealed all of the items in the vest, adding a letter of his own and two bicentennial coins.

The third floor of Faneuil Hall still houses the Ancient and Honorable Artillery Company. Founded in 1638, this is the oldest military company in the United States, and considered the third oldest in the world. Among its collection is one of the grasshopper's eye sockets. The Hall is adjacent to Quincy Market.

Now, Where Did I Put That Key?
Boston

T he giant Fortress padlock is a familiar, neck-bending icon for motorists on Interstate 93. When fully inflated, the 700-pound lock is 32 feet tall and 20 feet wide. To make sure the blow-up lock doesn't blow away, it's taken down for the winter and stored—where else?—in the super-secure, climate-controlled Fortress storage facility.

The giant padlock can be seen from
Interstate 93, just south of Boston.
Photo courtesy of the Fortress Corporation

The eight-story Fortress building at 99 Boston Street is also unique. Fortress, the largest provider of high-security storage in the United States, invented a giant carousel device that suspends the room-sized safety deposit vaults in midair and automatically delivers them to clients waiting in the lobby. The giant lock is in good company. Many museums use Fortress to store their works of art.

A Thin Tome from the Tomb
Boston

James Allen's autobiography is one book you can definitely judge by its cover. It is awful, inside and out. Allen admits he was a rotten scoundrel, and the book cover testifies to that. His autobiography is certainly him; the book is bound in his skin.

In 1833 Allen attempted to rob John Fenno Jr. near Powderhorn Hill in Chelsea. Fenno fought back and was shot, but he survived because Allen's bullet hit the buckle on Fenno's suspenders. Allen was arrested and sent to prison, where he wrote an autobiography of his troubled youth and his life as a highwayman.

Allen died on July 17, 1837, but before he did he asked to meet with Fenno, saying he wanted to shake the hand of a brave man. Then he made his fateful request. Figuring that once he was dead it would be no skin off his nose—or actually his back—Allen asked that a copy of his autobiography, bound in his skin, be given to Fenno and a second copy be given to Dr. Bigelow of Boston, the physician he requested attend his death.

Allen's skin was removed and bookbinder Peter Low tanned his hide and edged it in gold. The binding looks like pale gray deerskin and is inscribed in Latin: *Hic Liber Waltonis cute Compactus Est* ("This book by Walton bound in his own skin").

Binding his autobiography was no skin off James Allen's nose.
The cover came from his back. Photo by Bruce Gellerman

The full title of the book is: *Narrative of the life of James Allen, alias George Walton, alias Jonas Pierce, alias James H. York, alias Burley Grove, the highwayman. Being his death-bed confession, to the warden of the Massachusetts state prison.*

Allen's autobiography was donated to the Boston Athenaeum by one of John Fenno's descendants and you can still find it there today, but the copy given to the doctor has never been found. The Boston Athenaeum (617–227–0270) is located at an address Harry Potter would love: 10½ Beacon Street in Boston.

The Athenaeum's collection includes 600,000 volumes. James Allen's autobiography is the one most often requested. You can access the text of the thin tome on the Athenaeum's Web site at www.bostonathenaeum.org.

BRIDGES THAT "LIE" OVER WATERS

*A*s far as we're concerned it's all water under the bridge, but just to set the record straight, the Boston guidebooks have it wrong. Despite what they say, the iron bridge that crosses the swan lagoon in Boston's Public Garden is not the world's smallest suspension bridge. When it was built in 1866, the span, a quaint fifty-six paces long, was indeed a suspension bridge, but repairs in the early 1900s turned it into a plain old bridge.

Boston's newest bridge, the Leonard P. Zakim Bunker Hill Bridge, emerging from the underground Central Artery near Causeway Street, may also look like a suspension job, but it's not. It's a cable-stayed bridge. In fact, it's the widest cable-stayed bridge in the world. Both a suspension bridge and a cable-stayed bridge use two towers, but there is a difference in how the cables are attached to the towers. In a cable-stayed bridge, the cables run directly between the roadbed and the towers, and the towers bear the load. Suspension bridges have the cables slung over the towers, and they transfer the load to the anchorages on the other side.

While you are trying to figure out the difference, check out the new bridge's towers. They look just like the Bunker Hill Memorial to the east. The bridge is named after the famous battle and for Lenny Zakim, a Jewish activist who tried to bridge the difference of Boston's many racial, religious, and ethnic communities. For his work, Zakim was even named Knight of St. Gregory by Pope John Paul II in 1999.

The world's shortest suspension bridge, isn't.
Photo by Bruce Gellerman

THE PLYWOOD PALACE
Boston

Building the sixty-story John Hancock Tower, Boston's tallest skyscraper, was a real "pane in the glass." In 1973, soon after workmen began installing the first of 10,344 windows, the panes began to crack and many of the windows fell to the ground. Luckily, no one was killed or injured.

The entire exterior of the 790-foot building had been designed to be covered in special mirror-glass, but by April 1973 plywood had replaced more than an acre of the tower's high-tech windows. The building became known as the Plywood Palace.

Needless to say, lawyers had a field day—or, in this case, field years. There were lawsuits and countersuits and counter-countersuits. Scientists and engineers were perplexed. After much high-tech sleuthing, the problem was identified. However, the judge in the case imposed a gag order on the aggrieved parties that lasted seventeen years. It was not until 1990 that the public learned what was wrong. It seems that the bonding material that was supposed to hold the dual layers of insulated glass together, didn't.

All 10,344 windows were replaced with single sheets of tempered glass. Sensors were installed on each pane to provide an early warning if any pane began vibrating too much. Five thousand undamaged windows were sold to the public for $100 each. As for the plywood? It was used to board up abandoned buildings in the city.

The Hancock Tower is located on Clarendon Street and St. James Place near Copley Square. You can't miss it. It's the one with all the shiny windows.

The Hancock building was dubbed the Plywood
Palace after workers replaced fallen windows
with sheets of wood.
Photo courtesy of Peter Vanderwarker

"THE BRITISH ARE COMING. OPEN WIDE. THE BRITISH ARE COMING. BITE DOWN."

*T*rying to get sleepy colonists awake and aware that the British were coming must have been like pulling teeth for Paul Revere. It's a good thing, then, that our alarmist, patriotic midnight rider wasn't only a highly skilled silversmith but talented in the art of oral health and hygiene. On August 20, 1770, five years before his midnight ride, Revere took out this ad in the Boston Gazette and Country Journal:

> *Paul Revere Takes this Method of returning his most sincere Thanks to the Gentlemen and Ladies who have employed him in the care of their Teeth. He would now inform them and all others, who are so unfortunate as to lose their Teeth by accident or otherways, that he still continues the Business of a Dentist, and flatters himself that from the Experience he has had these Two Years (in which Time he has fixt some Hundreds of Teeth) that he can fix them as well as any Surgeon-Dentist who ever came from London. He fixes them in such a Manner that they are not only an Ornament, but of real Use in Speaking and Eating. He cleanses the Teeth and will wait on any Gentleman or Lady at their Lodgings. He may be spoke with at his Shop opposite Dr. Clark's at the North End.*

CURIOSITY OF THE MONTH
Boston

When Jeremy Belknap founded the Massachusetts Historical Society in 1791, he asked the public to submit unusual contributions to the organization's collection. Since then, the Society's "curiosity collection" has grown to hold some very unusual artifacts including a five-dollar bill featuring Santa Claus, issued in 1850 by the Howard Banking Company (it was legal tender back then); a letter from Boston native Benjamin Franklin describing his attempt to electrocute a turkey; and a World Series medal from the 1912 Boston Red Sox. Little is known about the medal, but it is obviously very rare. The last time the Red Sox won the series was in 1918, the year they traded Babe Ruth to the New York Yankees and so began "the curse of the Bambino."

The Massachusetts Historical Society is at 1154 Boylston Street, (617) 536–1608. The Society maintains an "object of the month" online showcase of some of its more unusual artifacts at www.masshist.org/welcome.

FINDING BERT COHEN'S MARBLES
Boston

Bertram Cohen readily admits he's crazy about his hobby, but obviously he hasn't lost his marbles. In fact, he had 300,000 at last count. In his Victorian town house in Boston's Back Bay,

Bert Cohen has all his marbles . . . and then some.
Photo by Bruce Gellerman

Cohen has amassed what just might be the largest collection of marbles in the world. They fill his basement, hallways, and a study; they're in bags and bins, buckets and barrels. He's got onion skins, Joseph's coats, sulfides, immies, aggies, and, of course, cat's eyes. The marbles are everywhere, along with a huge collection of books about the history and playing of the game and assorted historic photos and marble memorabilia.

Bert has been a marble consultant and historian for more than forty years, collecting, swapping, and selling marbles large and small, old and new. His largest marble is a custom-made job that rolls in at thirty-three pounds; the smallest is just one-sixteenth of an inch in diameter. One of his most unusual and valuable marbles is 4,000 years old, which is kid stuff when you consider that the game goes back 10,000 years.

Bert doesn't play anymore himself; but he does give out mass-produced marbles by the shovelful to worthy causes, such as the Boy Scouts. He gets them from a factory in Mexico that churns out fifteen million a day. Collectors who share Bert's mania for marbles gather at an annual event he has organized for the past quarter-century in Marlborough.

Now, having the world's largest collection of marbles might be enough for some people, but not for Bert Cohen. He's an admitted pack rat and also has an extensive collection of glass-ware and what certainly must be the largest, if not only, collection of toys made by the long-gone Irving Corporation, maker of some of the first plastic toys.

Visits to Bertram Cohen's marble museum and toy emporium are by special invitation only, but you can learn more about his marbles at his Web site at www.marblebert.com/publications.htm.

SIGNS OF THE TIMES
Boston

Soaring 200 feet high over Kenmore Square, seemingly float-ing in midair, is one of Boston's more obvious and beloved landmarks: the Citgo sign. Built by City Services Oil Company in 1965, the giant ad—60 by 60 feet—glows orange, red, and white from 5,878 neon tubes.

The Citgo sign sits atop 660 Beacon Street in Kenmore Square. The building, originally known as the Peerless Motor Car Building, now houses a bookstore.
Photo by Bruce Gellerman

Appropriately enough, the brightly lit sign is located on Beacon Street and is used by Bostonians to orient themselves around the city. However, in 1973 residents wandered around confused and directionless when the lights were turned off for a year as a symbol of conservation during the energy crisis. Then from 1979 to 1982 there were again lost souls in the streets when the sign was turned off once more to save electricity.

Just how important the Citgo sign had become to residents became clear in November 1982, when workers arrived to dismantle the sign. Before they could remove a single bulb, the Boston Landmark Commission intervened, saying the sign was a "prime example of roadside culture." There was talk of designating the sign an official city landmark, but Citgo would have had to pay to move it. Instead, the company paid $450,000 to refurbish the sign and return it to its original glow. On August 10, 1983, as the song "You Light Up My Life" filled the air in Kenmore Square, 750 people attended the relighting ceremony. Today the beloved Citgo sign is as much a part of Boston as the Old Meeting House or Faneuil Hall, and they don't have a single neon tube.

L A D Y   M A D O N N A
E a s t   B o s t o n

Not far from Suffolk Downs Racetrack and overlooking Logan Airport is the Madonna, Queen of the Universe National Shrine. The 35-foot bronze-and-copper statue was created by Italian–Jewish sculptor Arrigo Minerbi and set on the site in 1954.

Driving up the winding road to the shrine, you will see a 50-foot cross atop a hill. The hill is where the second battle of the American Revolution was fought. The views of Boston and the airport from the top of the hill are terrific. A gift shop near the shrine offers unusual religious object for sale.

The Madonna, Queen of the Universe National Shrine (617–569–2100) is at 111 Orient Avenue, East Boston. Follow the signs on Route 1A.

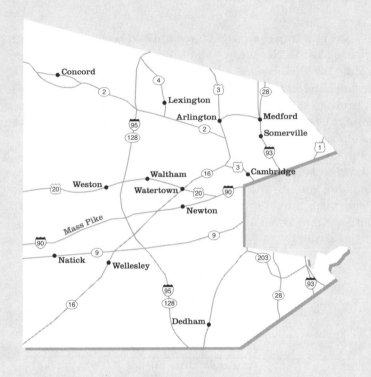

THE TECHNOLOGY RING AROUND BOSTON

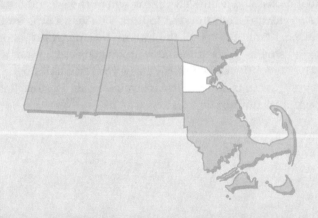

THE TECHNOLOGY RING AROUND BOSTON

A WELL-DONE MUSEUM
Arlington

Where there's smoke, there's Deborah Henson-Conant. Put a harp in her hands and boy, can she cook! With her long beaded hair and leather halter top, she plays the heaven-sent instrument with the fire of a bat out of . . . well, you-know-where.

Doc Severinson calls Henson-Conant a wild woman of the harp, serving up blues, jazz, Celtic, and folk music with a generous serving of humor. But put her in the kitchen of her Arlington, Massachusetts, home and the menu changes dramatically.

Henson-Conant is the founder of (and curator, and primary contributor to) the Museum of Burnt Food, an ever-expanding collection that celebrates the art of culinary disaster. Sometime in 1989, while heating a pot of apple cider on her stove, she was distracted from her task by a lengthy telephone call. By the time she returned, the cider had turned to cinder (exhibit A). She proudly mounted and displayed the piece and, voila, the Museum of Burnt Food was born. The Museum's motto: "To cook the museum way—always leave the flame on low . . . and then take a long nap."

For a meal Smokey Bear might love, check out
the Museum of Burnt Food.
Photo courtesy of Deborah Henson-Conant

There's nothing half-baked about this eccentric collection of fire-fossilized food. Over the years Henson-Conant has cooked up, entirely by accident, the Forever Shrimp Kebab; Well, Well Done Soy Pups; and Trice-Baked Potatoes.

The entire collection is on limited public display in Henson-Conant's home by invitation only, but it can be viewed by the masses at http://burntfoodmuseum.com.

HEY, CITGO SIGN, CLAM UP!
Cambridge

Literally and figuratively sitting in the shadow of Boston's famous Citgo sign is one owned by competitor Shell Oil, just across the Charles River. Built in 1933 and in operation continuously ever since, the giant scallop-shell neon is one of two that were constructed for Shell's regional headquarters on Commonwealth Avenue in Boston. In 1944, possibly in response to wartime restrictions, the company removed the signs. One was dismantled; the surviving spectacular neon sign was relocated to the existing Shell gas station on Memorial Drive. The Cambridge Historical Commission deemed the sign an artifact of early commercial development in the city. The Commission designated the Shell sign a historic and protected landmark, and in 1994 the sign was put on the National Register of Historic Places.

The Shell sign is at the intersection of Magazine Street and Memorial Drive, Cambridge.

Memorial Drive in Cambridge is home to the giant Shell Oil sign.
Photo by Bruce Gellerman

IT'S MIT BY A SMOOT
Cambridge

The techies who attend Massachusetts Institute of Technology (MIT) deal with precise standard units of measure: the angstrom, the meter, the light year, and the smoot. The latter, while perhaps unfamiliar to lay persons, is an exacting measure: precisely 5 feet 7 inches.

There are just two things in the known universe measured in smoots: the Harvard Bridge connecting the MIT campus in Cambridge to Boston's Back Bay (364.4 smoots plus one ear) and Oliver R. Smoot Jr., MIT class of '62 (one smoot).

In October 1958, when O. R. Smoot Jr. was an MIT freshman pledge to the Lambda Chi Alpha fraternity, a fraternity brother decided it would be useful if students walking back to campus from Boston during the fog and snow knew how much further they had to walk. Smoot, the smallest of the pledges, was measured with a string, and the unit known as the smoot was born. The fraternity members marked off the smoots in paint on the bridge. When a police van appeared at about the 300-smoot mark, the measurers took off, returning later to finish the job.

Today the pledge class of Lambda Chi Alpha repaints the smoots with a new color twice a year, and the police are no longer a problem. In fact, officers use the markers to indicate locations on the bridge when writing up accident reports. To make matters easier, the Continental Construction Company of Cambridge now makes concrete sidewalk slabs 5 feet 7 inches long to coincide with the smoots, instead of the usual 6-foot increments.

Can it be too much longer before the Boston Marathon is measured in smoots, not miles?

The Harvard Bridge is measured in smoots . . .
plus one ear.
Photo by Bruce Gellerman

You can count the smoots yourself by walking over the Harvard Bridge from Massachusetts Avenue in Cambridge to Boston. (By the way, MIT named the span Harvard Bridge, even though it is located next to the MIT campus. The school considered it an example of inferior engineering and gave the dubious honor to its arch-rival down Massachusetts Avenue.)

GEORGE WASHINGTON'S PHEASANTS UNDER GLASS
Cambridge

Harvard's Museum of Natural History is an eclectic and eccentric collection of stuffed stuff, embalmed animals, and mounted fossils. It includes a dodo, giant tape worms, a thirty-five-million-year-old bee, the world's largest frog, and the only known kronosaurus, a 42-foot-long prehistoric marine reptile. The museum is also home to the Ware Collection of Blaschka Glass Models of Plants. The unique collection of lifelike plants made out of glass was the life's work and passion of Leopold Blaschka and his son Rudolph. There are over 3,000 plants representing more than 800 species.

A pair of George Washington's pheasants reside in a glass corner case, a gift to the founding father from the Marquis de Lafayette. When the pheasants died, a taxidermist had them stuffed and mounted. The birds must have overheard a foul (or is it fowl?) mouthed visitor, because they were recently put on indefinite loan to a museum in Philadelphia.

The museum building itself, at 26 Oxford Street in Cambridge, belongs in a museum. It's a nineteenth-century throwback to the days when museums had rich wood paneling on the walls, high ceilings, and white frosted globe lights. Set aside a couple of hours to see all of the exhibits, and be sure to stop by what may be the most curious oddity in the entire museum: the antique wooden telephone booth on the second-floor staircase. It may be the last of its kind in Cambridge, if not in all of Massachusetts, and it still works.

IT MAKES WAR AND PEACE
LOOK LIKE A SKIRMISH
Cambridge

If you wanted to snuggle up for a little bedtime reading with the book *Bhutan: A Visual Odyssey Across the Last Himalayan Kingdom,* you'd better have a very big bed. Actually, the book is so big it could *be* your bed. According to the *Guinness Book of Records,* the 114-page tome is the largest commercial book ever published. It is 5 feet high, opens to

Michael Hawley, publisher and author of Bhutan—A Visual Odyssey
Across the Last Himalayan Kingdom, *standing next to the world's
largest published book at Acme Bookbinding where the books are made.*
Photo by Paul Parisi/Courtesy of Michael Hawley

nearly 7 feet wide, and weighs more than 130 pounds. Two gallons of ink are needed to print each volume, which costs $10,000. Most of the proceeds go to charity to send students from Bhutan abroad to study.

The hefty read is the creation of Michael Hawley, director of special projects at the Massachusetts Institute of Technology. Hawley was inspired by numerous trips to the remote Shangri-La kingdom. He also wanted to demonstrate state-of-the art publishing technology.

Bhutan's leaders have charted a unique course for their country. The government's stated economic plan is to achieve the highest level of "gross national happiness." Television was not even allowed into the country until 1999, no doubt because the Bhutanese are very big readers.

The Acme Bookbinding Company in Charlestown, Massachusetts, is the exclusive builder of *Bhutan: A Visual Odyssey Across the Last Himalayan Kingdom.* Acme calls itself not only "the world's oldest book bindery," but also the world's "largest book" bindery. Acme has more information about the big book on its Web site, www.acmebook.com/index/2003/12/15.

WHO SAID GRIME DOESN'T PAY?
Cambridge

Since 1977, Elizabeth Magliozzi's sons have been driving radio listeners nuts and sending them reaching for their dials. Her boys, Tom and Ray, better known as Click and Clack of the weekly show *Car Talk* are a public-radio phenomenon. These days they have 2 million listeners a week, from Sweden to Sheboygan. The gregarious grease monkeys are a mega-industry perpetually trying to unload their books, records, T-shirts, and whatever else they can get away with on their

Car Talk Plaza, appropriately located above the Curious George shop in Harvard Square, is the intergalactic headquarters of public radio grease monkeys Click and Clack.
Photo by Bruce Gellerman

shameless e-commerce Web site. The entire shenanigans come out of *Car Talk*'s dumpy offices high above Harvard Square in Cambridge, a.k.a. "our fair city," and can be found above the Curious George store at the intersection of Massachusetts Avenue and JFK Street.

Whatever you do, don't drive like these brothers.

THE THAIS THAT BIND
Cambridge

In Cambridge, at an intersection at the edge of Brattle Square (which is actually just an intersection on the edge of Harvard Square), you will find yet another square with a curious name. King Bhumibol Adulyadei Square commemorates the reign of the only monarch born on American soil. His Majesty, King Bhumibol of Thailand, was born at Mount Auburn Hospital in Cambridge in 1927 while his parents studied medicine at Harvard.

King Bhumibol ascended to the Thai throne in 1946, and in 2000 he became the longest-reigning ruler in the world. King Bhumibol is also the only reigning monarch ever to win a gold medal—or any medal, for that matter—at an international sporting event. He won a medal for sailing in the Southeast Asian Peninsular Games. The King was also the first member of a royal family ever to receive a patent. In 2003 he received his fourth patent, for inventing an artificial rainmaking technique.

A photograph of the King can be found next to the elevators on the maternity floor at Mount Auburn hospital.

If you want to learn more about the Cambridge–Thailand connection, ask for Joe at the Union Oyster House in Boston. In addition to being the owner of the restaurant, Joe Milano is Honorary Counsul of Thailand.

HARVARD UNIVERSITY'S FAMOUS
OVER-ACHIEVING NON-GRADS
Cambridge

Some of the most distinguished people in the world have earned diplomas from Harvard University, including seven U.S. Presidents, poet T. S. Eliot, authors Norman Mailer and John Updike, educator W. E. B. DuBois, jurist Oliver Wendell Holmes, Sen. Elizabeth Dole, and many more household names.

And then there is the list of equally distinguished Harvard students who walked the same hallowed halls but never graduated. Among those who dropped out of Harvard or were otherwise "excused" are actor Matt Damon; poets Robert Lowell, Robert Frost, and Ogden Nash; and Edwin Land, inventor of the Polaroid camera and holder of more than 500 patents. R. Buckminster Fuller dropped out twice—once during midterms so he could take a dancer and her entire chorus to dinner. William Randolph Hearst got the boot after sending personally inscribed chamber pots to his professors while they were considering his academic probation, and bazillionaire Bill Gates left Harvard in his junior year to devote his energies to his fledgling start-up, Microsoft.

Pop singer Bonnie Raitt never made it through. Neither did folk singer Pete Seeger, although he was honored years later with the Harvard Arts Medal, telling the crowd that he "was tempted to accept (it) on behalf of all Harvard dropouts."

THE ARCHIVE OF USELESS RESEARCH
Cambridge

At last count, there were fifty-six current or former members of the MIT community who had won a Nobel Prize. The Institute is a center for superb scholarship, intellectual excellence, innovative entrepreneurship, and some of the craziest, crackpot pseudoscientific research you will ever find in one place. In room 14N–118 of the Hayden Library's Special Collections, collection number MC 187 consists of six large boxes known as MIT's Archive of Useless Research. It's a reminder that sometimes scientific exploration respects no boundaries, even when it should.

The archive began at MIT's Engineering Library as "the American Institute of Useless Research," a collection of crank files sent to the school's researchers over the years. In 1940 Albert Ingalls, an editor for *Scientific American,* began adding useless but invaluable research that had come his way, and the Institute morphed into today's current archive. Although the archive stopped adding to the collection in 1965, it certainly was not for lack of ongoing kooky research.

The collection is a celebration of screwball science, unpublished articles, self-published books, and rejected theories sent to MIT researchers over the years and deemed deserving of preservation for posterity. Included are such breakthrough studies as "Darwin as a Pirate" and "The Riddle of the Universe *Solved.*"

The archive can be seen at the Hayden Library, 160 Memorial Drive, Cambridge. The archivist suggests you call ahead at (617) 253–5690 so they can retrieve this fascinating collection in advance of your visit.

Bring your aluminum foil helmet.

IT'S KISMET, THE ROBO SAPIEN
Cambridge

Kismet is a moody infant. One minute sad; the next happy; a few seconds later, angry; then calm, bored, or surprised. If Kismet were a baby with colic, you could understand, but Kismet isn't a baby. Kismet is a robot—more accurately, a seven-pound robot head. Still, that is enough to land Kismet in the *Guinness Book of Records* for being the most emotionally responsive robot ever built.

Kismet is the world's most expressive robot, but MIT robo-scientists did not quit while they were ahead. They have built a robot with a body, too.
Photo by Bruce Gellerman

Created by Dr. Cynthia Breazeal at the Massachusetts Institute of Technology, Kismet has movable facial features that can express basic human emotions, and electronic eyes and ears to interact with its environment and people. If you stop playing with Kismet, it acts bored; shake a doll in front of the dismembered head and it looks agitated. Kismet's gremlinlike features are powered by twenty-one motors and fifteen huge computers.

It is a good thing that Kismet has been retired to the MIT Museum, or it would have the look of envy that comes with sibling rivalry. Back in the lab, Kismet has a big brother, COG, a 7-foot-tall artificial humanoid with arms, hands, a sense of touch, and the ability to talk. To make COG even more humanlike, researchers are working on a biochemical system to run it. Ultimately, it is hoped that COG will have the intelligence equivalence of a two-year-old child.

It's the stuff of science fiction, complete with profound philosophical implications. Of course, there are also practical concerns. Perhaps robo-researchers will know they have gone too far when the machines they create in their own image start asking for the car keys.

You can see Kismet and videos of it interacting with its creator at the MIT Museum, 265 Massachusetts Avenue. For more information, check out the museum's Web site, http://web.mit .edu/museum/ or call (617) 253–4444.

MIT Eager Beavers
Reach for the Brass Rat
Cambridge

G raduates of the Massachusetts Institute of Technology receive a special badge of honor and symbol of intellectual distinction and achievement for studying day and night, sweat-

By tradition, the Brass Rat contains secret
codes and symbols. In this design, hidden in the waves of the Charles
River along the MIT campus, are the letters "A=B=C=P" representing the fact that
the class of 2005 was the last to have pass/no record in their entire freshman year.
Notice the hand of the student drowning in the river. The "ZZZ" to the right of the
beaver's tail is for the constant attention to the student's lack of sleep. See if you
can find the letters IHTFP. Photo courtesy of MIT

ing through brain-bending tests, and ruining their social lives. It's a brass rat. That's the name affectionately bestowed on MIT's class ring, which, since 1930, has featured the MIT mascot, the beaver. After all, like MIT students, beavers are nocturnal, industrious, and master builders, but on the ring, the beaver, which is an aquatic rodent, looks like a rat. Hence, the nickname.

The design changes each year, created by a committee from each class that spends the better part of a year meeting in secret. By tradition the design contains the letters *IHTFP*, an acronym with a number of interpretations underscoring the love-hate relationship MIT students have with their school. Some say it means, "I Have Truly Found Perfection." Others say it stands for "I Hate This !$@#% Place." Both camps proudly wear the brass rat; nearly 95 percent of the student body buys one.

Another tradition is the way the students wear their rings, which they purchase in their sophomore year. As undergraduates, the bottom of the beaver faces in toward the student; at the graduation ceremony, the class *en masse* removes the rings and turns them the other way. The saying is that while they are students, the beaver excretes on them, but after they graduate, it excretes on the world.

TRUTH BE TOLD, HARVARD'S STATUE IS A LIAR
Cambridge

For a university whose motto is "Veritas," you would expect the truth, the whole truth, and nothing but the truth. But check out the statue of the venerable school's namesake, John Harvard, standing right in front of University Hall. It's a pack of lies. In fact, it is informally called the Statue of Three Lies.

The inscription beneath the statue reads JOHN HARVARD, FOUNDER, 1638. Not a word of it is true.

John Harvard was not the founder of Harvard University. The college (it was a college back then) was founded in 1636 by the Massachusetts Bay Colony in what was then the village of Newtowne and later became Cambridge. John Harvard was an

The Statue of Three Lies sits in Harvard Yard.
Photo by Bruce Gellerman

early benefactor of the college and it was named for him in 1639 after he donated his library to the school. Nor is the statue a likeness of John Harvard. There were no pictures or images of him, so the sculptor, Daniel Chester French, randomly chose a student as his model and dressed him in seventeenth-century garb.

And, truth be told, the statue actually contains *four,* not three, lies. The statue is *not* of John Harvard, who was *not* the founder of Harvard University, which was *not* founded in 1638, and does *not* stand in Harvard Yard in front of University Hall. It sits.

WHAT YOU GET WHEN YOU CROSS EINSTEIN WITH THE THREE STOOGES
Cambridge

You have to hand it to those techno-nerds at MIT: They sure know how to hack. Since the technical institute first opened in 1861, the brainy students have been pulling creative practical jokes that are both technically challenging and devilishly clever. Over the years the ever-more-ambitious hacks, as they are called, have become an institution.

Some pranks have been elegantly simple, like the stoplight altered to read "don't walk–chew," instead of "walk." Others were more scientifically challenging. In 1976, for example, hackers consulted an arachnologist and used an electron microscope to study spider webs before weaving a wicked-big one out of 1,250 feet of wire and rope and installing it in a campus building. The real trick, as with all hacks, was not to get snared by the police.

In 1982, during the Harvard–Yale football game, hackers hid a weather balloon inscribed with "MIT" under the turf of Harvard's 40-yard line. The pranksters inflated the balloon by remote control. The crowd and teams looked aghast as the balloon grew to 6 feet in diameter and exploded in a burst of white smoke. MIT one, Harvard–Yale zero.

MIT's famed domes have long been favorite places for hackers to pull their pranks. One Halloween, hackers dressed the Great Dome in a 20-foot-tall witch's hat. Another year the huge dome was transformed into the Star Wars robot R2D2. The dome has been topped with a working telephone booth that rang when officials tried to remove it. Hackers also turned the pinnacle into a parking space for a full-size replica of a campus police car, complete with working lights, with a box of doughnuts on the front seat.

The 1982 weather balloon inflator that disrupted
the Harvard–Yale football game.
Photo by Bruce Gellerman

Hacks have to be harmless as well as humorous. Self-deprecating humor works well. In 1996 MIT student hackers transformed the Great Dome into a giant, working propeller beanie. Who says nerds have no sense of humor?

A PLACE TO BE CAUGHT DEAD IN
Cambridge

There are almost as many people buried in Mount Auburn Cemetery in Cambridge (93,000 and counting) as there are living in the city (101,000). The historic cemetery is a popular place for very permanent residents and visitors alike. More than 200,000 people a year visit the burial grounds, making it one of Cambridge's most popular tourist destinations.

Founded in 1831 by the Massachusetts Horticultural Society, Mount Auburn was the first landscaped cemetery in America. Its creation marked a dramatic change in the prevailing attitudes about death and burial, as it was designed not only to be a decent place of interment but also to serve as a cultural institution. Mount Auburn, unlike other early city cemeteries, utilized landscape architecture in its planning. This influenced the creation of no less than fifteen other park–cemeteries in the United States. Besides its obvious function, Mount Auburn also serves as a museum, a sculpture garden, an arboretum, and a wildlife sanctuary.

Among the notables making the 175-acre garden their final residence are Oliver Wendell Holmes, Winslow Homer, Fanny Farmer, B. F. Skinner, and Buckminster Fuller.

The gravesite of Mary Baker Eddy, founder of the Church of Christ, Scientist, is one of the more spectacular. And contrary to long-standing rumors, she did not have a telephone installed in her crypt. During the construction of her monument, Eddy's body was kept in the cemetery's receiving vault. A guard was hired to stay with the body until it was interred and the tomb was sealed. A telephone was installed at the receiving vault for the guard's use during that period. There was never a phone at Eddy's monument.

Mount Auburn Cemetery is open every day of the year from 8:00 A.M. to 5:00 P.M. During daylight saving time hours are extended to 7:00 P.M. Drive-by and walking audio tours are available on tape for rent or purchase at the entrance gate or the office. The cemetery is located at 580 Mount Auburn Street, Cambridge. For additional information, call (617) 547–7105.

HEARD ON THE GRAPEVINE: SOMETIMES YOU DON'T REAP WHAT YOU SOW
Concord

Ephraim Wales Bull is buried in Concord's Sleepy Hollow Cemetery alongside some very distinguished company. Here, along Authors Ridge, you will find the gravesites of Henry Thoreau (1862), Nathaniel Hawthorne (1864), Ralph Waldo Emerson (1882), and Louisa May Alcott (1888) and her father, Bronson Alcott (1888). Okay; admittedly, Ephraim Wales Bull's name is not as familiar as these literary greats, but his contribution to the nation looms just as large. You see, Ephraim Wales Bull is the "father of the Concord grape." Today U.S. grape farmers harvest more Concord grapes than all other varieties combined.

Now, by all rights you should not even be able to grow grapes in Massachusetts. The grape killing frost comes early in fall and lasts until late spring. Nevertheless, Bull was, well, bullheaded. He persevered for ten years to develop his plump, purple berry, testing thousand of seedlings on his Concord farm before he came across his hardy, all-American variety.

Bull sold cuttings from his divine vine for $1,000 each, yet despite the horticultural breakthrough he died a poor man. His gravestone is inscribed, "He sowed—others reaped."

Among those who reaped was Vineland, New Jersey, dentist Thomas Welch, who began squeezing Bull's grapes with vigor in 1869. His company, Welch's, began producing unfermented sacramental wine. In 1913 Secretary of the State William Jennings Bryan served Welch's Grape Juice instead of wine at a state dinner for the outgoing British ambassador. The uproar in the press resulted in months of free publicity.

Ephraim Wales Bull's farmhouse, Grapevine Cottage, still stands on Lexington Road. The original vine from which all of the world's Concord grapes are descendants can still be seen.

An interesting note: A Massachusetts law regulates the taking of photographs and movies in a public cemetery for commercial purposes. To receive permission to do so, contact the cemetery department at (978) 318–3233.

Sleepy Hollow Cemetery is on Bedford Street just off the rotary in the center of Concord.

A R T   T O O   B A D   T O   B E   I G N O R E D
D e d h a m

T he Museum of Bad Art (MOBA) is testimony to the wisdom of writer Marshall McLuhan, who said, "Art is anything you can get away with." The museum is dedicated to "the collection, preservation, exhibition, and celebration of bad art in all its forms and all its glory." In short, it's a permanent repository for art too bad to be ignored.

What started out in 1995 in a suburban basement as a humble assemblage of spectacularly awful artwork has evolved into a full-fledged museum, complete with the requisite gift shop. The MOBA holds a special place near and dear to connoisseurs

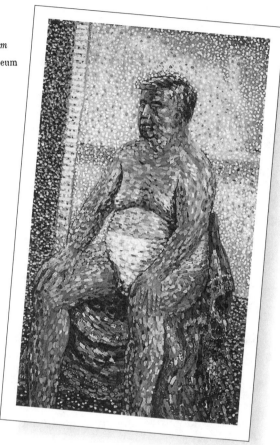

Sunday on the Pot with George *sits in the Museum of Bad Art.* Photo © Museum of Bad Art, Dedham, Massachusetts

of misunderstood masterpieces. It's also located within earshot of the men's room at the Dedham Community Theater.

To qualify for an esteemed place in the museum's collection, an artist's ambition has to vastly exceed his or her ability. One classic museum piece, for example, portrays a naked woman in stiletto heels and red leg warmers sitting on a stool milking a unicorn. The unicorn looks startled but not displeased by the experience. It's truly a head-snapping, jaw-dropping sight.

MOBA curators are constantly searching Salvation Army stores and landfills in search of the highest caliber bad art. The majority of the collection came from bequests of the public refuse system. Submissions are always welcome. The curators have imposed a $6.50 limit on acquiring new works but once offered twice that amount as a reward for a piece that was stolen. (Alas, even at that price the painting was never recovered.)

MOBA's permanent gallery is at the Dedham Community Theater, 580 High Street in Dedham Center. For more information visit www.glyphs.com/moba.

THE MAN WHO INVENTED MONEY
Lexington

Charles Ponzi was a small man with a taste for the finer things in life. He loved luxurious houses and large automobiles, and he dressed in the finest top hats, walking sticks, and suits. Too bad he couldn't afford them. No matter; the former dishwasher, convicted smuggler, and scam artist was "the man who invented money." At the peak of his pyramid scheme in 1919, Ponzi was raking in a million dollars a week. He created 40,000 "millionaires" and at one point sauntered into the Hanover Trust Company, opened a suitcase with $3 million in cash, and bought a controlling interest in the bank.

The pyramid scam is probably as old as, well, the pyramids. But it took Charles Ponzi, an Italian immigrant living in Boston, to raise it to new heights in the world of modern finance. The scam is simple: Borrow from Peter to pay back money you borrowed from Paul. Repeat over and over again and, voila: You have a Ponzi scheme. A bit like Social Security, the system works as long as you bring in enough new investors at the bottom to support those at the top of the pyramid.

Ponzi employed a new twist on the old scam. He promised investors a 50 percent return on their money in ninety days if they purchased international postal reply coupons, which were coupons he bought overseas for a penny and exchanged in the United States for six cents. (Unfortunately, it wound up costing more money to ship and exchange the coupons than they were worth here, but that was a minor detail to Ponzi.)

Ponzi's house of reply coupons finally collapsed when a Boston newspaper questioned the con. Ultimately, five banks went belly-up in the scam. Ponzi wound up spending seven years in a Boston jail and died penniless in Rio de Janeiro. He left behind an unfinished manuscript for a book, appropriately titled *The Fall of Mr. Ponzi.*

As Ponzi's wife, Sophie, watched, investigators searched their twenty-room mansion in Lexington, Massachusetts, for securities and evidence of fraud. All they found were one hundred gallons of homemade Italian wine.

The stucco house in Lexington still stands. It's the third on the right on Slocumb Street, off Massachusetts Avenue.

BLACK DAHLIA MONUMENT
Medford

One of the stranger monuments in Massachusetts was designed and paid for by documentary filmmaker Kyle J. Wood, whose film *Medford Girl* chronicles the life and death of Elizabeth Short, "the Black Dahlia." Short was born in Hyde Park, Massachusetts, in 1924 and grew up in Medford. She quit school at age sixteen, seeking fame and fortune in Hollywood. Her mutilated body, severed in half at the waist, was found in a vacant lot in Hollywood in 1947—one of the most celebrated unsolved mysteries of its time.

The Black Dahlia monument is located at 115 Salem Street in Medford.

JUMBO IN A JAR
Medford

Although students at Tufts University are called Jumbos, it's not that they are especially big. They hold that nickname because the school's original mascot was P. T. Barnum's famous elephant, Jumbo. Born in Africa in 1859, Jumbo grew to 12 feet high at the shoulder and weighed more than six tons. Barnum, ever the showman, billed the huge pachyderm as the largest land animal ever in captivity. Big as he was, today all that remains of Jumbo are some ashes stored in a fourteen-ounce Peter Pan peanut butter jar locked in the safe of the school's athletic director.

The story of how Jumbo went from circus center ring to a crunchy peanut butter jar at college begins in 1882, when Barnum bought Jumbo from the London Zoo for $10,000. Jumbo traveled the circus circuit in a specially built railroad car until 1885, when he was hit by a train and died. The pachyderm underwent taxidermy and the stuffed hide was taken on a four-year world tour. Jumbo then came to his final resting place at the Barnum Museum at Tufts University, where the ringmaster was a school trustee. He stood there for eighty-six years, while generations of students stuffed his trunk with pennies and pulled his tail for good luck on tests. In 1942 Jumbo underwent an overhaul and his original over-tugged tail was archived at the school's library.

All was well until 1975, when a fire destroyed the Barnum building, rendering everything, including the elephant, into a pile of ashes. Mindful of the mascot's importance to Tufts, a member of the school's athletic department scooped up what he assumed were Jumbo's ashes and put them into the container

A jar of crunchy Peter Pan Peanut Butter is the
final resting place of Jumbo the Elephant.
Photo by Bruce Gellerman

he had on hand—an empty peanut butter jar—which is now
kept in a safe in the athletic director's office. To this day Tufts
Jumbos rub the jar for luck just before a big game.

The tail on Jumbo's tush is in Tufts' Tisch Library Digital
Collections and Archives. Say that three times fast and win a
Kewpie doll.

ELEPHANT MAN HAS A HERD INSTINCT
Medford

It's probably a good thing that John Baronian did not attend the University of California–Santa Cruz or Cal State–Long Beach. Otherwise, you might be reading about the world's largest collection of banana slugs or dirtbags. Baronian, you see, collected miniature models of his alma mater's mascot. As luck would have it, he went to Tufts University, home of Jumbo, the elephant, and so for fifty years Baronian collected elephant figurines.

Baronian began gathering his mini-menagerie of mini *objets d'pachyderm* soon after graduation. Today he has more than 3,000 figurines in his collection—probably the largest assemblage of pachyderm art on the planet. (If you've heard of a bigger herd, let him know.) He has elephants made out of wood, glass, bronze, porcelain, and yes, ivory. He even has an elephant crafted out of camel hide. There are elephant ashtrays, mugs, jewelry, and bookends and a pachyderm jigsaw puzzle.

Baronian is not just any Jumbo alum, he's *the* jumbo Jumbo supporter. On campus he is known as "Mr. Tufts" for his long volunteer service and generosity to the University. A man with a big heart and a herd to match, he ran out of space for the collection in his home, so he donated it to the school. It now resides in the Remis Sculpture Court at the Aidekman Arts Center, 40R Talbot Avenue on Tufts' Medford campus. Call ahead for hours at (617) 627–3518.

*"Mr. Tufts," John Baronian, with members of his
mini-elephant menagerie.*
Photo by Bruce Gellerman

THE CHRISTMAS
LIGHTS FANTASTIC

*R*esidents living on Greystone Court in
Medford (locals pronounce it "Meffuhd") go
to extreme measures to make sure all their
Christmases are bright. When the owners of the
thirteen houses on this cul-de-sac throw the
switches on their illuminated santas, reindeers,
and other lighted lawn tchotchkes, you need to
stand back. It is truly something to behold. Tens
of thousands of lights erupt in a dazzling display of December decorating. What makes the
display so remarkable is that the tradition is
unorganized. Surprisingly, there are no meetings, leaders, or plans for the show. It's an
unspoken tradition going back to the early 1990s
that neighbors here will try to out-illuminate
each other during the holiday season.

Word has spread and thousands of spectators in cars and by the busloads cruise the
street each night—a far cry from 1659, when
Massachusetts fined people for celebrating on
December 25. (It seems the Pilgrims had a dis-
trust of Christmas. Thankfully for folks in
Medford, the law was repealed in 1681.) The
electricity bills are enough of a fine for anyone.

This Sign Will Sleigh You
Medford

We hate dashing your Christmas spirit, but one of the most popular songs sung around the holiday has nothing to do with Christmas. "Jingle Bells" was written by Medford resident James Pierpont in 1850, inspired by the annual one-horse open-sleigh races on Salem and Pleasant Streets between Medford Square and Malden Square. Pierpont penned the racy little ditty in Simpson's Tavern, a boardinghouse that had the only piano in town. The lyrics tell the story of picking up girls while hot-rodding through the snow.

The song was originally titled "One-Horse Open Sleigh," and initially it was a flop. But after a Boston publishing house released it as "Jingle Bells" in 1859, the rest was history, albeit controversial history. It seems that Savannah, Georgia, thinks it's the "Jingle Bells capital of the world" because Pierpont was living there when the song was released and is also buried there. However, a plaque at 21 High Street near the corner of Forest Street in Medford sets things right. As residents in Medford are quick to point out, Pierpont wrote the tune while in Massachusetts . . . and racing a sleigh in snowless Savannah doesn't make much sense, anyway. (In fairness to Savannah, it too has a plaque commemorating the composer of "Jingle Bells.")

Medford is also where the lyrics for another famous festive song were written. Town resident Lydia Maria Child's poem "Boy's Thanksgiving" became the song "Over the River and Through the Woods." Child lived in the Greek Revival house at 114 Ashland Street on the corner of Salem Street, not far from where Pierpont sleighed them with "Jingle Bells." Behind Child's house are the woods she went through and the Mystic River over which she traveled to get to Grandfather's house. We're told the horse knows the way.

THE COCKROACHES THAT
ALMOST ATE NATICK
Natick

On the battlefield of the future, it may be the suit that makes the soldier. The uniforms warriors will wear decades from now are being designed at the U.S. Army Soldier Systems Center in Natick, about 20 miles due west of Boston.

The Center is a high-tech laboratory that designs and develops everything a soldier wears, carries, or consumes. Established in 1954, the lab created the technology that led to freeze-dried food. During the Vietnam War it created a boot sole in the shape of a bare-footed VietCong soldier to confuse the enemy, and it designed a camouflage Jewish prayer shawl.

The Natick lab is best known for developing the field combat rations called *MREs*, or Meals Ready to Eat. The MRE menus provide high-calorie, relatively palatable foods with a shelf life that rivals enriched uranium.

In 1974 Army scientists were experimenting with a new way to control pests by zapping them with ultraviolet rays. Unfortunately, the experiment went out of control. The zapped bugs were put in plastic bags with a chemical, then disposed of at a local dump. The chemical ate through the bags and the bugs' eggs hatched and escaped into Natick. The insects, 4-inch flying Madagascar cockroaches, drove residents buggy. The cockroaches were resistant to most pesticides and the Army had to call in the "big guns" and use DDT.

Researchers at the Natick facility are now working on projects designed to protect our men and women in uniform with fabrics that change color depending on their surrounding environment, and spray-on clothing.

Due to budget cuts and the cost of fighting current wars, the Soldier Systems Center is not conducting tours for the public. However, its Web site, www.natick.army.mil, provides a good overview of the ongoing research. The bugs won't get out as easy that way, either.

NEWTON'S CONTRIBUTION TO COOKIEDOM
Newton

In 1891 James Henry Mitchell invented a contraption that could squish figs into jam and smear the substance between two layers of soft, crumbly cookie dough. The cookies were a smash hit, and soon the Kennedy Biscuit Works in Cambridge was turning them out by the truck load.

The Big Fig, as usual, is right in the middle of things.
Photo courtesy of Newton History Museum at the Jackson
Homestead, Newton, Massachusetts

The famous cookie got its name from the plant manager at the bakery, who liked to name his cookies and crackers after surrounding Massachusetts towns. Thankfully he didn't decide to dub his latest concoction after Cow Yard, Massachusetts, or Marblehead, and instead settled on the suburban city of Newton.

An apartment building now stands at 129 Franklin Street on the site near MIT where the original factory baked Fig Newtons by the billions. Several of the original biscuit ovens have been preserved there, and above the front door is a giant rendition of the cookie itself.

Nabisco Brands eventually bought the Kennedy Biscuit Works, and to commemorate the one-hundredth anniversary of the Fig Newton, it threw a bash for the cookies' namesake community. The Big Fig acted like the fruit he is and, of course, was right in the center of things.

BEAUTIFUL BLABBERMOUTH BRIDGE
Newton

Echo Bridge is one of the highest stone arches in the world—its crown is 51 feet above the Charles River—but what makes it truly remarkable is that, as the name implies, the bridge talks back to you, and back to you, and back to you.

Built in 1876 to carry water to Boston, the 500-foot-long aqueduct consists of seven arches. The largest segment, spanning the Charles, is 130 feet long, and it is this arch that produces the remarkable reverberation. It's said that on a still day the granite walls can bounce a human voice back and forth as many as eighteen times. (Be forewarned: You might not always like the responses you get. Try yelling the word *July* under the archway.)

For a spectacular view of the Charles River, stand atop the bridge's pedestrian promenade. The span is located at the end of Chestnut Street, north of Route 9 in the Upper Charles River Reservation. It is open from dawn to dusk year-round.

MARATHON MAN
Newton

ohn Kelley likes to run and run and run. Between 1928 and 1992, John "the Elder" Kelley, a Massachusetts native, ran the Boston Marathon sixty-one times, finishing all but three races. He came in first in two races (1935 and 1945), took second place a record seven times, and finished in the top ten eighteen times.

At the foot of Heart Break Hill is the monument
to Boston Marathon man John Kelley.
Photo by Bruce Gellerman

Kelley ran his last marathon when he was eighty-five and became the first road runner elected to the National Track and Field Hall of Fame. Officials waived the retirement rule because they figured he might never retire.

A statue dedicated to the amazing marathoner as a young man and as an older participant is located at Heart Break Hill, on the corner of Walnut Street and Commonwealth Avenue in Newton, across from City Hall.

In the 1996 centennial running of the Boston Marathon, 39,708 official entrants participated in the race. According to the *Guinness Book of Records,* this is the largest number of runners in a single race in history.

MAYBE IT WAS SO THE WORMS DIDN'T HAVE TO USE THE STAIRS?
Newton

It's called simply the Old Stone Barn, but don't let the plain name deceive you. This is one strange structure. Built in 1839, the huge stone building (100 feet by 50 feet) has an architectural feature you don't see every day: All four stories have access to ground level. The architectural feat was accomplished by building the barn into dirt embankments. The sub-basement faces the east; the basement, the south; the first floor, the west; and the second floor, the north, off Cliff Road.

Historians are not sure why the barn was built this way, or even if it was originally intended to be a barn. The owner, Otis Pette Sr., never told anyone why he had it constructed. After it was built it lay empty for years until it was used as a stable. Some speculate that Pette meant for the barn to house a silk-

The Old Stone Barn has access to ground level from all four stories.
Photo courtesy of Newton History Museum at the Jackson Homestead,
Newton, Massachusetts

worm hatchery and constructed it out of stone because his textile factory had burned to the ground earlier that year. However, the silkworm industry quickly unraveled in colonial New England. (The cold killed the mulberry bushes.)

The Old Stone Barn, or whatever it was, still stands and is used as a warehouse. It can be seen at 38–44 Oak Street, off Cliff Road in Newton Upper Falls.

THE ORIGINAL AIRHEAD AND HIS
IGNOBLE IG NOBEL PRIZES
Somerville

M arc Abrahams is an airhead and proud of it. In fact, as
publisher of the *Annals of Improbable Research,* or *AIR,*
Abrahams is head airhead. *AIR* is what would happen if the
editors of *Mad* magazine and the *National Lampoon* conspired
to publish *Scientific American.* And lest you think being an airhead is somehow an ignoble distinction, the magazine has
eight Nobel Prize laureates on its editorial board.

Since 1990 *AIR* has injected spoofs, parodies, and satires
into the otherwise straightlaced world of science and scientists.
Example of typical articles include: "Why the Chicken Must
Come First," "Mass Strandings of Horseshoe Crabs," and an
inquiry titled "What Does Crime Taste Like?" A regular feature
queries Nobel Prize winners with the most pressing questions
of our time, such as, "Do you shave with a blade razor or electric?" and "Do you often give people nicknames?"

The highlight of the year for Abrahams and *AIR* is the
annual Ig Nobel Prize ceremony, honoring people whose
achievements "cannot or should not be reproduced." This take-
off on the Stockholm proceedings includes some of the pomp
along with a heavy dose of Swedish slapstick. Abrahams sports
a tuxedo and top hat to announce the winners, including a biol-
ogist who studied how various flavors of chewing gum affect
brain waves. Karl Kruszelnicki of the University of Sydney
received his Ig Nobel Prize for his comprehensive survey of
human belly button lint: who gets it, when, what color, and
how much. Chris McManus of University College, London was
honored for his excruciatingly balanced report, "Scrotal Asym-
metry in Man and in Ancient Sculpture." Anders Barheim and

Hogne Sandvik received their Ig Nobel Biology Prize in 1996 for their monumental discovery that sour cream stimulates the appetite of leeches. Jerald Bain and Kerry Siminoski won the Ig in Statistics in 1998 for their landmark study, "The Relationship among Height, Penile Length, and Foot Size."

The Ig ceremony, featuring opera, interpretive dance by Nobel laureates, and drama takes place in Sanders Theater at Harvard University the first week of October, and is broadcast on National Public Radio's *Science Friday,* the day after Thanksgiving. Check your local listings and be prepared to fall out of your seat.

ANY SEAT IN A STORM

New England Nor'easter snowstorms are legendary for their ferocity. So are folks from Somerville, Massachusetts. After residents shovel out their parking spaces along the city's narrow streets, they jealously guard their clearings by putting lawn chairs, chaise longues, even sofas in the street to hold "their" spots. It's not unusual to see bundled-up Somervillians sitting on their furniture, waiting for the family car to return.

Saving shoveled-out spots in the snow is a time-honored winter tradition in Somerville, and heaven help those who violate the unwritten rules of the road. If you do, make sure you have towing insurance and are prepared to buy four new tires.

ONE ARTIST YOU DEFINITELY DON'T
WANT TO PAINT YOUR PORTRAIT
Watertown

P art of the permanent collection at the Armenian Library and
Museum of America in Watertown, Massachusetts, are pictures painted by Dr. Jack Kevorkian. Known to many as "Doctor
Death," Kevorkian is a controversial physician who promotes
assisted suicide and has been jailed for practicing what he
preaches. Kevorkian is also an oil painter of some note, and
being an ethnic Armenian, he has donated a number of his
works to the Armenian Library and Museum. Two of his oils,
Very Still Life and *Genocide,* are hanging in the museum at 65
Main Street, Watertown. For more information, call (617)
926–2562.

Dr. Jack Kevorkian's
Very Still Life *hangs*
in the Armenian
Library and
Museum in
Watertown.
Photo by Bruce
Gellerman

AS THE WORLD DOESN'T TURN
Wellesley

One of the largest worlds in the world can be found on the campus of Babson College in Wellesley. The giant Babson Globe was built in 1955. It weighs 21.5 tons and is 38 feet in diameter. It is literally meant to provide an out-of-this-world experience, to give you an idea of what Mother Earth would look like if you stood 5,000 miles away in space. Each inch on

The 21.5-ton globe at Babson College stopped
revolving in 1993.
Photo by Bruce Gellerman

the steel ball represents 24 miles. The globe rotated on its base and spun on its axis until sometime in 1993, when the mechanical turning-and-spinning device broke. The earth has stood still ever since.

Truth be told, there are larger globes. The Unisphere, from the 1964 New York World's Fair in Queens, is 120 feet in diameter. The world's current world record holder, Eartha, installed at the DeLorme Map company in Yarmouth, Maine, is about 41 feet in diameter.

To get up close and personal with the Babson Globe, the one-time largest world in the world, go to Babson College in Wellesley sometime during daylight hours. It's that giant round thing fixed in space outside the Coleman Map Building. There is no admission charge. Who says nothing in the world is free?

UNDERSTANDING THE GRAVITY
OF THE SITUATION
Wellesley

It was Roger Babson's dream that what went up would not necessarily have to come down. To accomplish this gravity-defying feat, Babson created the Gravity Research Foundation in 1948. Its goal was to investigate ways to block and harness the force of gravity.

The idea of violating a basic law of physics may sound far out, but Babson was a man who had his feet firmly on the ground. A self-made millionaire who earned his money revolutionizing the financial services industry, Babson also founded two universities, ran for president of the United States against FDR (he came in third out of eight candidates), and authored forty-seven books.

In one of his books, *Gravity—Our Enemy No. 1* Babson explained his quest to tame the pull of the earth. It was a personal battle, as he blamed gravity for his son's death in an airplane crash and for his sister's drowning, writing of the latter, "She was unable to fight gravity, which came up and seized her like a dragon and brought her to the bottom."

The Gravity Research Foundation, which recently relocated to Babson College in Wellesley, holds an annual convention and essay contest. Although the contest does attract its share of crackpots, it also receives submissions from some of the best minds of our time. Famed cosmologist Stephen Hawking has won the foundation's cash prize five times.

The foundation has also installed a number of granite monuments on college campuses where distinguished anti-gravity research was being done. One monument was installed in 1961 on the Tufts University campus in Somerville, Massachusetts, where it soon became a source of myth and mirth. The inscription reads: THIS MONUMENT HAS BEEN ERECTED BY THE GRAVITY RESEARCH FOUNDATION. IT IS TO REMIND STUDENTS OF THE BLESSINGS FORTHCOMING WHEN A SEMI-INSULATOR IS DISCOVERED IN ORDER TO HARNESS GRAVITY AS A FREE POWER AND REDUCE AIRPLANE ACCIDENTS.

A year after the monument's installation, a group of students dug a hole around the stone to test whether it would defy gravity. (It didn't.) Another group dug it up again and moved it to a different location. Thus began a cycle of burying and digging up that lasted several years. In 1968 Tufts groundskeepers dug up the stone to make way for a sidewalk and buried it in a secret locale. It remained hidden until 1971, when members of the Mountain Club unearthed it by sheer accident. In 1975 it was moved again. Then in 1977 the administration confiscated the stone and moved it to an undisclosed location after students had used it to block the doors of (P. T.) Barnum Hall. In the 1980s the stone was finally set to rest in its present location between Eaton Hall and Goddard Chapel.

THE MASSACHUSETTS VIKINGS

*T*hree public monuments in eastern Massachusetts lay claim that it was Viking Leif Erikson in 1000, not Christopher Columbus in 1492, who was the first European to step foot on North America. The monuments were built by Eben Norton Horsford, a Harvard professor of chemistry turned amateur archaeologist who was convinced that "Leif the Lucky" was the first European in the New World.

Professor Horsford made a fortune in the mid-nineteenth century selling "Horsford's Cream of Tartar Substitute," a new-formula baking powder, and used the money to fund excavations in Cambridge, Weston, and Watertown. According to Horsford, Erikson landed on Cape Cod, sailed up the Charles River, and built a house in what is now Cambridge. Horsford said he found some buried Norse artifacts near the intersection of Memorial Drive, Mount Auburn Street, and Gerry's Landing Road. He built a small monument there marking the spot.

Further upstream stands Norumbega Tower. Horsford built the structure in 1889 to commemorate the site on which he believed the Vikings had constructed the legendary Norse settlement of the same name. A summary of Horsford's theory is engraved on a plaque on the tower. To see it, take Route 128 to Route 30 West to River Road North.

The third monument to Horsford's fanciful theory is located at Charlesgate East on Commonwealth Avenue, near Kenmore Square in Boston. It was unveiled in 1887 and depicts Leif the Lucky on a pedestal scanning the distant horizon. The back of the memorial is inscribed: LEIF THE DISCOVERER SON OF ERIK WHO SAILED FROM ICELAND AND LANDED ON THIS CONTINENT AD 1000.

Leif Erikson in
Kenmore Square.
Photo by Bruce
Gellerman

Horsford's theories were later debunked as just bunk, and he's considered a crackpot today. But recent scientific analysis of a controversial parchment drawing, the so-called Vinland Map, and an accompanying manuscript called "The Tartar Relation" seem to suggest that maybe the chemist was onto something archaeological after all.

A CHIP OFF THE OLD BLOCK
Wellesley

T he story about how Sir Isaac Newton got clunked on the noggin and discovered gravity isn't as far-fetched as it may sound. On the campus of Babson College stands a fifth-generation apple tree grown from a cutting of a tree from young Isaac's home in Woolsthorpe Manor, Lincolnshire, England. You'll find the area around the fenced-in tree littered with apples, proving Sir Isaac correct.

Babson College founder Charles Babson was fascinated with gravity and Newton. In addition to the Newton apple tree now growing in the center of campus, Babson also purchased the fore-parlor from the great mathematician's last London residence. He had the room disassembled and rebuilt in the Babson College library.

A chip off Newton's block grows on the campus of Babson College.
Photo by Bruce Gellerman

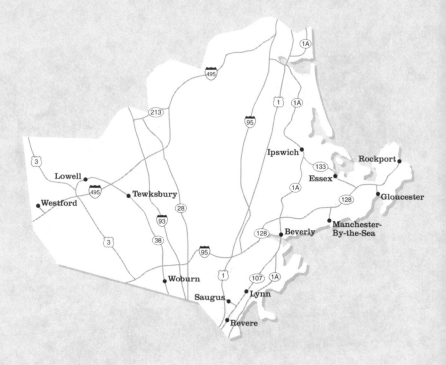

NORTHEAST MASSACHUSETTS

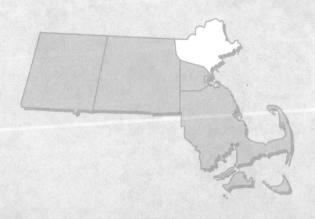

NORTHEAST MASSACHUSETTS

THERE'S DEFINITELY SOMETHING UP HIS SLEEVE
Beverly

It seems the only thing magician Cesareo Palaez can't make disappear is his magic show. In 1972 Palaez conjured up "Le Grand David and his Own Spectacular Magic Show" out of thin air, little money, and a bunch of volunteers. Today the act is the longest-running stage magic show in the world.

The magic is not limited to the stage. It begins as soon as you enter the theater. Palaez and his troupe perform Le Grand David in two vaudeville theaters that they have meticulously restored to their former gilded glory. In the lobby, members of the troupe, many who have been with Palaez since the very beginning (and, in some cases, their children and even grand-children) entertain patrons before the stage performance starts. It's multigenerational, multitasking magic. The sets are magnificent, the costumes opulent. Members of the cast make both.

Taking center stage, of course, is Palaez, who says it's his passion for "wonder, mystery, and enchantment" that brings so many people under his spell. A professor emeritus of psychology, Palaez is also a past president of the Society of American Magicians and was voted Magician of the Year several times. He came to the United States from Cuba, hoping to re-create the magic shows he had watched as a boy. He left his home just after Castro took power, in what he calls his greatest escape.

Palaez, starring as Marco the Magi, performs on select Thursdays at 7:30 P.M. at the Larcom Theater, 13 Wallis Street, and Sundays at 3:00 P.M. at the Cabot Street Theater, 286 Cabot Street. For more information, call (978) 927–3677. Every performance is another record-breaker.

AW, SHUCKS, I DO
Essex

The fried clam is the claim to fame at the restaurant Woodman's of Essex. It was here on Main Street, along a marshy road, that Lawrence and Bessie Woodman say they invented the world's first munchy mollusk. Although others make the crunchy clam claim, they don't have the evidence the Woodmans have. Right on the back of their marriage certificate, it says they dunked the first mollusk into a deep-fryer on July 3, 1916. They said "I do," and they did. If anyone claims otherwise, let them come forward or just clam up.

The idea certainly wasn't half-baked. Come during the summer and expect a line out the door. Woodman's of Essex is on Route 133, Main Street. For more information, phone (978) 768–6057 or (800) 649–1773 or visit www.woodmans.com. (Or is it "dot-clam?")

A deep fryer and clams are a marriage made in heaven at Woodman's.
Photo by Bruce Gellerman

HUNTING FOR BABSON'S BIG BOULDERS
Gloucester

By 1830, Dogtown, Massachusetts, had literally gone to the dogs. First the men left, then the women, leaving behind their canine companions. The abandoned, unincorporated town was purchased by philanthropist Charles Babson, founder of

Words to the wise can be found in Dogtown.
Photo courtesy of Don Noll © 2004 (www.don.noll.com)

Babson College. Babson hired Swedish stone carvers to chisel words to the wise into huge glacial boulders that littered the property. And today Dogtown is best known for the big boulders bearing their messages. The messages include: "Never Try, Never Win," "Be on Time," "Help Mother," and our favorite, "Get a Job."

Dogtown is now part of Gloucester and has become a favorite haunt for trail-riding bicyclists. You may have to hunt a bit to find the place. (Don't forget to take insect repellant with you.) Take Route 127 just outside of Gloucester to Reynard Street. At the end of Reynard, turn left onto Cherry Street. You'll see a small sign for Dogtown Commons. Hey, never try, never win.

A GREASY POLE AND A TOUGH ITALIAN
Gloucester

Since 1931, Gloucester's Italian-American fishing community has paid homage to the patron saint of fishing by holding its annual Saint Peter's Fiesta. Here, commercial fishing is a way of life and, too often, death. Gloucester was the hailing port of the *Andrea Gail,* which encountered the Perfect Storm.

Each year contestants squirm along this greased
pole to capture a red flag.
Photo by Bruce Gellerman

According to Alphonse Millefoglie, vice president of the Fiesta Committee, the celebration's most unusual event is the Greasy Pole Contest. A heavily greased, 45-foot telephone pole is extended over the water, 200 feet off Pavillion Beach. Contestants must wiggle and squirm their way along the pole and capture a red flag nailed to the end. The winner then swims back to the beach. All the other contestants lift the victorious pole walker onto their shoulders and parade around the town.

The first round is traditionally a trial run without capturing the flag. In 1979 one contestant broke the courtesy rule and was quickly confronted by a contest enforcer, Anthony "Matza" Giambanco. Matza presented the offender with a knuckle sandwich, the flag was once again nailed to the pole, and the competition commenced.

The Fiesta is a five-day event held on the June weekend closest to the Feast of Saint Peter. It's a time for prayers, food, a parade, food, sporting events, and food . . . sometimes a knuckle sandwich. For more information, visit www.stpeters fiesta.org.

The greasy pole is a permanent fixture and can be seen year-round. It's off shore, in the harbor right behind the Cape Ann Chamber of Commerce on Commercial Street.

THE INVENTIVE GENIUS WITH AN ITCH FOR DISCOVERY
Gloucester

Couch potatoes everywhere owe a debt of gratitude to their patron saint, John Hays Hammond Jr. This inventive genius was one of the early pioneers of radio electronics and is considered "the Father of the Remote Control." Dr. Hammond patented more than 430 inventions, second in number only to

A knight in shining armor and a pipe organ reside at the
eclectic castle built by inventor John Jay Hammond Jr.
Photo by Bruce Gellerman

Thomas Edison. Hammond's inventions reflect his wide interests, whimsical sense of humor, and taste for the flamboyant.
In 1914 the good doctor spooked sailors and spectators when
he guided a crewless "ghost ship" by remote control on a 130-
mile round-trip cruise from his home in Gloucester Harbor to
Boston. Among his other inventions was a hypodermic meat
baster, a stove that cooks food without using a pan, and a mag-
netic bottle cap remover. Alas, his cure for baldness failed, succeeding only in turning his scalp green.

Most of Hammond's creations had military applications. During World War II he offered the United States and Great Britain his patent to a fire bomb. Although the Allies turned him down, Hammond was arrested for treason when Germany subsequently used it on England. He was freed only after one of his staff members admitted to selling the weapon to the enemy.

Hammond did much of his inventing in a medieval-style castle he constructed in Gloucester from 1926 to 1929. In the Great Hall Hammond designed and built the largest pipe organ in a private residence in the world. It has more than 10,000 pipes. (No he's not *that* Hammond.)

When Dr. Hammond died in 1965, he was buried with his mummified cats, who tour guides claim were placed in mayonnaise jars, in a crypt not far from the castle. According to his instructions, the spot was covered in poison ivy. However, despite the fortification, someone broke in to the burial chamber, smashed one of the mayo jars with a cat mummy, and stole Hammond's head. A ransom was paid and the skull was eventually returned.

The castle, complete with pipe organ, drawbridge, and a dungeon, is open to the public at 80 Hesperus Avenue in Gloucester. Directions and hours of operation are available at www.hammondcastle.org or by calling (978) 283–7673.

DANCES WITH WOLVES. NOT.
Ipswich

If Little Red Riding Hood had traveled to Wolf Hollow, she would have learned a lot more than Grandma without having to take a single step into the forest. Wolf Hollow was founded in Ipswich in 1988 to allow people to experience wolves in the animals' natural habitat and to dispel the many myths surrounding the much-maligned creatures.

Wild wolves once populated all forty-eight continental U.S. states. Today they're endangered in forty-seven of those states. Humans are the wolves' only predators. The North American Wolf Foundation, which runs Wolf Hollow, contends that the wolf can harmoniously co-exist with humans and other mammals; it is a matter of understanding wolf behavior and the pack's social order. According to the Foundation, there is not a single documented case of a healthy wild wolf attacking a human. But just in case, the pack at Wolf Hollow is enclosed in a large meadow protected by a 12-foot-high chain fence. Visitors are cautioned not to stare a wolf in the eye or to show their teeth. The founders of Wolf Hollow, the late Paul Soffron and his wife, Joni, learned firsthand the laws of the pack. They even slept with young pups to create a lifetime bond.

Wolf Hollow is open year-round and there are one-hour structured presentations, weather permitting. Check ahead. There are also special seminars and events such as one observance that poet Allen Ginsberg might have enjoyed, "Howl Night." Grandma never had it so good.

Wolf Hollow is about 3 miles east of Ipswich on Route 133. For more information call (978) 356–0216 or visit www.wolf hollowipswich.com.

HEY, IF THE SHOE FITS...
Lowell

Lowell is perhaps best known as the home of beat-generation author Jack Kerouac. But if you are on the road looking for something lowbrow but upbeat and find yourself in the historic mill town, drop by the Lowell Historical Society. There you will find two curious items that have almost nothing to do with Lowell history.

The first is a helmet made out of a coconut and a sea urchin. It was worn by a Lowell soldier who served in the Philippine Insurrection of 1899–1901. The second item is a mummified ankle and foot. No one seems to know how the preserved appendage got to the museum, where it came from, or what it really is. Until a few years ago, it was thought to be a mummified child's foot from ancient Egypt, but recently an expert identified it as being from South America and perhaps belonging to a woman.

Both items are in storage but are taken out on special occasions. The Historical Society is located at the Boote Cotton Mills Museum, 400 Foot of John Street in Lowell. (No, we're not kidding, and no, it's not John's foot. That's just the address.)

DUNGEON ROCK
Lynn

Legend has it that in 1658 pirate Thomas Veal sailed up the Saugus River and anchored at Pirate's Glen. Although three of his buccaneers were captured and hung by British soldiers, Veal escaped into the woods and hid in a cave all alone with a stash of ill-gotten gains. Suddenly a violent earthquake shook Lynn, entombing Veal and sealing his treasure trove in what has come to be called Dungeon Rock.

Over the centuries there have been numerous attempts by psychics and the certifiably insane to recover the loot. The most famous attempt began in 1852, when Hiram Marble, a spiritualist from Charlton, Massachusetts, his wife, and his son Edwin, purchased five acres of land in the area and, "guided by the spirit of revelation," started digging for the hidden treasure.

Dungeon Rock is the site of two graves and pirate's treasure.
Photo courtesy of Dan Small

To help raise money for their project, the Marbles gave tours of the site and sold bonds for a dollar each, promising investors a share of the loot. The Marbles also sought guidance from the spirit of Pirate Veal, who perhaps advised the abrupt changes in direction apparent in the tunnel today. It is more likely that the spirits assured the Marbles that, like Moses wandering the desert for forty years, it was necessary for them to toil before reaching their reward.

Hiram Marble died in 1868. His son continued digging until his own death, in 1880. By that time the duo had dug 145 feet through solid rock, a rate of about a foot a month. Edwin's last wish, to be buried at Dungeon Rock, was granted. You will find a large pink rock at the top of a set of stairs next to an old cellar hole marking his grave.

While the gravel debris from the Marbles' blasting and remnants from many structures they built in the area can still be seen, the pirate treasure, if there ever was any, remains to be found.

Curiously, the Marbles were not seeking the treasure for themselves. Their first goal was to prove that the dead could communicate from the afterlife. They didn't have much luck there. Hiram Marble also hoped to use the pirate's treasure to purchase land in the area for the people of Lynn to enjoy forever. He largely succeeded. Soon after Edwin's death the city of Lynn purchased the family's land for their new park, the Lynn Woods.

The entrance to Dungeon Tunnel is sealed with an iron gate but open to the public from May through October and by request. Bring a flashlight; it's really dark and scary.

In late October the Friends of Lynn Woods hold a Dungeon Rock Day celebration, where people dress as pirates and tell stories.

The shortest walk to Dungeon Rock is from the Rose Garden entrance to Lynn Woods. Maps are available at the entrance. For more information, check out the Lynn Woods Reservation Guide at www.flw.org or call the rangers at (781) 477–7123.

THE GOD MACHINE
Lynn

The era of the 1850s was a high-water mark for spiritualists in the United States, and High Rock, with its commanding view of Boston to the south, was something of a magnet for séances and spiritualists. Molly Pitcher, said to be clairvoyant, lived at the base of High Rock until her death in 1813. She was legendary among sailors whose fortunes she foretold before they set sail. In 1846 a man named Jesse Hutchinson bought High Rock and erected Stone Cottage on the side of the hill. It became home to Hutchinson and his eleven brothers and sisters, who formed the world-famous group the Hutchinson Family Singers. Jesse Hutchinson was a social activist and spiritualist who organized a meeting of spirit-minded people on High Rock. Reportedly, in 1852 spirits from twenty-four countries gathered on the mound. A year later nineteenth-century spiritualist John Murray Spear made the High Rock scene.

Although many say High Rock is as close to heaven as a Lynn poet can get, it obviously wasn't close enough for Spear.

In 1853 Spear and a group of philanthropic spirits he called the "Band of Electricizers" gathered atop the 170-foot-tall granite hill to build "Heaven's last, best gift to man." They set about constructing the New Messiah.

The Electricizers, led by the spirit of Benjamin Franklin, provided Spear and his followers with step-by-step instructions to build the New Messiah. It was later dubbed the God Machine.

Slowly the God Machine took shape on a dining room table. It was a mass of metal spheres, magnets, and coils of zinc and copper. There was a flywheel in the center of the contraption, with wire connections. When it was complete Spear encased himself in a shroud of metal plates and gemstones and for about an hour came in contact with the machine. Not much happened, although later a follower of Spear's went into labor while touching the God Machine, even though she claimed she wasn't pregnant. Spear insisted that at the moment of the baby's birth the machine became animate for an instant.

The contraption was later dismantled and moved to upstate New York, where an angry mob of nonbelievers reportedly mauled and mangled the God Machine. No trace of it has ever been found.

Today High Rock is still a place for those looking toward the heavens. Atop the tower built on the summit in 1906 are an observatory and a new computerized telescope. The observatory is open to the public on Tuesday nights or by appointment for large groups. For more information visit www.ci.lynn.ma.us/ public_documents/lynnma_resources/highrock27.

To get to High Rock, take Essex Street and make a left on Rockaway Street. Turn up High Rock Street to Circuit Avenue and park at the end of Circuit.

CARRYING A TUNE IN A BUCKET
Manchester-By-the-Sea

D inah Shore it's not, but Singing Beach really does sing . . . sort of. Shuffle your feet over the sand or pull your hands through it quickly and you'll hear a squeaking sound, not unlike a high-pitched violin (or Dinah on a bad day.) To get the full experience, try the sand closest to the bathhouse. It seems to be the most mellifluous.

Naturalist and writer Henry David Thoreau wrote about the sonorous sands of Manchester-By-the-Sea in the mid-nineteenth century, but scientists are still not sure of the exact mechanism of its tonal quality. It's thought that the uniform size and round shape of the grains is responsible for the phenomenon. Whatever the cause, even if you could never carry a tune in a bucket, now you can.

Singing Beach is at the end of Masconomo Street off Route 127 in Manchester-By-the-Sea. Parking is limited to town residents with special stickers, so you will have to park your car in town about a half-mile away and walk to the concert that awaits you.

BILLINGS OF SWEET NOTHINGS
Revere

B ack in the 1920s there were at least thirty-two candy manufacturers in the Boston area churning out sweet stuff by
the megaton. One is still going strong. The New England Con-
fectionery Company, or NECCO, recently celebrated its 150th
anniversary, making it the oldest continuously operating
candy company in the United States.

Until 2003 NECCO was located in a huge building next to
the MIT campus in Cambridge. It was the largest factory in the
world whose entire space was devoted to candy production. The
company has since moved to Revere, north of Boston.

NECCO is literally a sweetheart of a company. Besides its
signature Necco Wafers, it produces eight billion Sweethearts
Conversation Hearts a year. They're the chalky-tasting, heart-
shaped candies bearing saccharine sayings such as "Kiss Me,"
"Be True," and "Be Mine."

The Valentine's Day amore mottos have been updated in
recent years to include "Girl Power," "Swing Time," and "Got
Love." For a minimum order of $7,600, you can even have a
custom-made cupid-saying printed on the hearts. You will have
a whole lot of loving to go around. That's about 1.6 million
candy hearts.

EXTRA! EXTRA! READ ALL ABOUT IT!
Rockport

At 52 Pigeon Hill Street in Rockport is an unusual home you not only can read about; you can actually read the home itself.

The house and most of the furnishings are built out of old newspapers. Elis F. Stenman constructed the house as a hobby. Perhaps his talent for paper construction had something to do with being a mechanical engineer who built machines to make paper clips. Certainly he had a passion for newspapers. He read three a day.

In 1922 Stenman started experimenting with newspapers as insulation for the cottage he was constructing. The material proved so strong that he decided to varnish it. The outer walls are 215 pages thick, and the roof is lined with newspapers but has a wood outer shell. It took Stenman two years to build the house and eighteen years to construct the clock, chairs, tables, and piano that furnish it. Although the fireplace is made of bricks, the mantelpiece is built from the magazine sections of Sunday newspapers.

The Paper House is located at 52 Pigeon Hill Street in Pigeon Cove in Rockport. Take Route 127 to Pigeon Cove; after the Yankee Clipper Inn, take the second left onto Curtis Street and then turn left onto Pigeon Hill Street. On Curtis Street you will see handwritten signs on telephone poles directing you to the house. Of course, they're written on paper.

Visitors are on the honor system to make a contribution. To read an interview with Elis Stenman, go to www.rockportusa .com/paperhouse/.

The Paper House is black and white and read all over.

Photo by Bruce Gellerman

ROUTE 1:
THE (R)ODE TO INDIVIDUALITY
Saugus

Ten miles north of Boston you will find a major dose of road-side America circa 1960. The strip of Route 1 stretching from Saugus to Peabody is a six-lane tabernacle to garish taste and unbridled individuality. It is a road that tells it like it was; a time when your mother wore a bouffant, your dad motored happily with a tiger in his gas tank, and the family saw the U.S.A. in a Chevrolet. You'll want to yell, "Hi dad, hi mom, hi Beaver" as you pass the Bel-Aire diner and the Fern Motel, a place Norman Bates would feel right at home. And if you want to whack a few balls, stop at Route 1 Miniature Golf, where an orange Tyrannosaurus Rex, a national landmark, guards the links.

In its heyday, Route 1 had more restaurants per mile, serving more people, than anywhere else in the nation. The eateries were an exuberant celebration of tacky taste and entrepreneurial chutzpah, and the road was a mecca for marketing meals run amok. Different was better. Biggest was best.

Atop a hill overlooking Route 1 in Saugus, you can still see the huge pagoda-shaped Weylus, once said to be the largest Chinese restaurant on the planet. It featured cuisine from every Chinese canton in a style you might call "Saugus Early-Elvis Dynasty." They could serve up egg foo yung for 1,400 with no sweat. Alas, the last egg roll left the Weylus kitchen in the late 1990s. But fear not; you won't go hungry along the Route 1 kitschway today. If you have a hankering for a slab of beef the size of Plymouth Rock, you can still head to the Hilltop Steakhouse, the place with the 68-foot neon cactus right next to the giant plastic grazing cows. Feel like Italian? A bit

The 30-foot-tall Hilltop Steak House cactus.

Photo by Bruce Gellerman

The two-masted Weathervane restaurant.

Photo by Bruce Gellerman

farther north is Prince Restaurant. It's the one with the three-story LEANING TOWER OF PIZZA sign, just across the road from Kowloon, a humongous grass-hut Polynesian restaurant with giant Tiki statues out front and a bubbling volcano inside. Diners looking for a nautical motif can chart a course a bit farther north to the life-sized, two-masted Weathervane restaurant. The "ship" is anchored between a Yankee Candle Shop and a Christmas Tree Shop. Guiding the way is a faux lighthouse in the parking lot. You can't miss it.

Yet despite the best efforts of kitsch preservationists, this roadway—architecturally littered with a kind of joyful abandon you just don't find much anymore—is slowly but surely giving way to staid chain stores and look-alike fast-food franchises. Nonetheless, there is enough of the old Route 1 still standing to make a trip down memory lane at forty miles an hour worth it. Just hop in your Chevy, put the top down, turn up Dean Martin on the AM radio, and cruise the road. It's *amore*.

HEY, BARTENDER, I'LL HAVE ANOTHER ONE OF THOSE MEDICINES
Tewksbury

In the old administration building of what is now known as Tewksbury Hospital is the only public health museum in the United States.

The hospital was established in 1852 as an almshouse for the poor. Its most famous patient during the nineteenth century was Anne Sullivan, later the tutor and companion of Helen Keller. In 1994 the bottom floor was converted into the unique public health museum by Chet Kennedy, former art director for the Massachusetts Department of Public Health, "to show to the world what a great heritage we have in this part of

*The Public Health Museum's collection of patent
medicines might not be good for what ails you.*
Photo by Bruce Gellerman

the country" and to sing the praises of public health pioneers.
Colonial Massachusetts passed the first laws to register births
and deaths; it was the first state to require lead testing in children; and it was the first with a tuberculosis hospital. It's hard
to remember now that in 1900 TB was a major cause of death
in the United States.

The Queen-Anne-style museum building itself is an exhibit, listed on the National Register of Historic Places. The eight rooms in the museum include a nurses' classroom and a hospital room from the 1920s. The Mural Room features a four-wall mural from the Works Progress Administration in the 1930s. The steep staircase up one wall leads to a little room used to store records of venereal disease.

Massachusetts was also the epicenter for the patent medicine industry, as evidenced by the museum's extensive collection of bottles and advertisements. Included are bottles of Turtle's Elixir, Atwood's Jaundice Bitters, and Bee's Laxative Cough Syrup. Prominently displayed are patent medicines produced by Lydia Pinkham. In 1876 Pinkham began manufacturing her nostrum, Lydia E. Pinkham's Vegetable Compound, in nearby Lynn promising to cure "the worst form of 'Female Complaints'—everything from 'General Debility' to cancer." The elixir was based on a formula Pinkham's husband won in a card game. Lydia Pinkham became known as "a lady's best friend" during Prohibition, and no wonder: The elixir was 90 percent alcohol.

Pinkham's cure-all was a phenomenon and her salesmanship made her one of the most successful women in U.S. history. Indeed, although she died in 1883, customers were still encouraged to write to Mrs. Pinkham for medical advice. In 1905, twenty-two years after her death and countless letters later, the *Ladies' Home Journal* exposed the scam in an article that included a photograph of Mrs. P's tombstone, located at the Pine Grove Cemetery in Lynn within sight of the maintenance garage, 145 Boston Street.

The Public Health Museum in Massachusetts is located off Interstate 93 at exit 42 West. More information is available at the museum Web site, www.publichealthmuseum.org.

What's a Knight Like You Doing in a Place Like This?
Westford

H istorian Frederick J. Pohls says "fuggetabout" Columbus sailing the ocean blue in 1492. In his book, *Atlantic Crossings Before Columbus,* Pohls makes the case that it was a seafaring Scot in 1398 who first "discovered" America. According to Pohls' research, Henry Sinclair (Earl of Rosslyn, Prince of Orkney and Lord of Shetland, Duke of Oldenburg and Premier Earl of Norway) set out to explore newly discovered Newfoundland but wound up getting chased away by natives. It seems he then got caught in a New England Nor'easter, sending Sinclair's armada to the coast just north of Boston, where he had better luck with the local inhabitants. Maybe it was all his titles, or maybe it was his kilt. In any case, Sinclair and his crew of one hundred were allowed to spend the winter on shore. In the spring they trooped inland and climbed what is now called Prospect Hill in Westford, perhaps seeking a place to hide the Holy Grail some say they carried with them. Historian Pohls writes that one of Prince Henry's men died there and the Scots memorialized him by carving a marker into a flat, 8-foot-square hunk of granite. Although the weatherworn carving is faint, you might be able to make out a roughly life-sized portrayal of a fourteenth-century knight with a sword, shield, and crest, wearing a helmet.

"Holy Grail, shmoly grail," say nonbelievers who contend that the Westford Knight is nothing but a weather-beaten rock. Decide for yourself. From the Westford Common, make a right on Lincoln Street onto Main Street and a left onto Depot Street. Park near the Abbot School and walk 50 yards up Depot. A commemorative marble marker marks the spot where Prince Henry may have left evidence of his discovery of the New World, or maybe not.

THE SCOOP ON THE BATTLESHIP MAINE
Woburn

Do you remember the *Maine*? The USS *Maine* was the battle-ship that mysteriously blew up in Havana Harbor in 1898, setting off the Spanish–American War. To remember more, go to Main Street in Woburn, where you'll find remains of the *Maine,* specifically one of the ship's ventilator cowls (an air scoop that looks like a crushed tuba and is enshrined in a glass case).

When residents of Woburn had requested a piece of the *Maine* in 1911, Congress rejected them, stating that only non-profit, patriotic organizations could apply. The citizens got Local Post 161 of the Grand Army of the Republic to submit an application, and it was approved by Congress. The 315-pound, barnacle-encrusted cowl was put on display in the front window of Whitcher's Drug Store (now a sushi restaurant) on Main Street. A year later it was encased on the Common and dedicated on July 4, 1913.

As they say, "from sea to shining sea."

Visitors can remember the Maine *on Main Street in Woburn.*

Photo by Bruce Gellerman

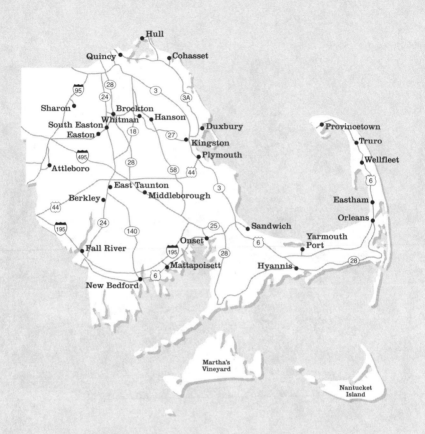

Hull

Quincy

Cohasset

28

24 3 3A

Sharon

Brockton

Whitman Hanson

South Easton
Easton 18

Duxbury

27 Kingston
Plymouth

495

Attleboro 28

58 44

East Taunton
Berkley Middleborough 3

44

24 140

195

Fall River

Onset 25

195 6

Mattapoisett 28

New Bedford 6

Provincetown

Truro

Wellfleet

6

Eastham

Orleans

Sandwich

Yarmouth
Port

6

Hyannis 28

Martha's
Vineyard

Nantucket
Island

SOUTHEAST MASSACHUSETTS
AND THE CAPE AND ISLANDS

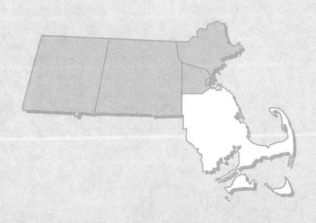

SOUTHEAST MASSACHUSETTS AND THE CAPE AND ISLANDS

I'M DREAMING OF A LIGHT CHRISTMAS
Attleboro

I f you are of a certain age and cultural background, you spent many youthful hours among cloaked figures—silent, swift, certain. We're talking nuns here, those powerful and virtually omniscient harbingers of order, guilt, and swift retribution. Also of humor, teaching, an understanding ear, and a mean swing on the softball field. It all depends—hardly surprising—on the individual. But uniforms can be deceiving and even leveling. Part of the raiment, at least in the Northeast in the 1960s, was strands of rosary beads, which are a physical system for tracking a series of prayers, like a spiritual abacus. In those days, when you were six, those beads seemed large, far bigger than marbles. In Attleboro at the La Salette Shrine, however, you will find a rosary that dwarfs those once sported by the nuns, with beads as big as bowling balls. The site, originally intended to be a sanatorium, was purchased in 1919 by the Methodist Church. It was called Attleboro Springs, named for the springs on the property. The Methodists used it as a

At Christmas, visitors enjoy the lighter part of the shrine.
Photo by Erik Sherman

retreat for a time, finally closing the facility in 1938. In 1942
representatives from a French Catholic order called the Mis-
sionaries of Our Lady of La Salette bought the property and,
ten years later, began building a shrine commemorating a supposed appearance of Mary to two children in France. The Giant
Rosary, which stretches over a walkway arch, is part of the
scene, as are other religious statues and peaceful gardens.

    A particularly bright and uplifting time to visit is during
the annual Christmas Festival of Lights. Tens of thousands of
miniature lights illuminate the trees and grounds and draw
hundreds of thousands of visitors. The lights go on at 5:00 P.M.
from Thanksgiving through the first few days of January. To
see the beads and lights, follow the blue-and-white signs on
Route 152 in Attleboro or from Exit 5 on Route 95. For more
information, visit http://lasalette.shrine.tripod.com.

AMERICAN GRAFFITI
Berkley

K ids who "tag"—draw large and elaborate versions of graffiti on anything that doesn't move (and on some things that do, if you look at subways in New York)—might think they are on the cutting edge of generational revolt. Oh, if only they realized that the graffiti in this land even makes their parents look young. Dighton Rock is a noted bit of sediment: an 11-foot boulder covered in petroglyphs (fancy talk for lines carved into a rock) that was originally on the Taunton River at Berkley. Think that urban tagging can be hard to read? These ancient inscriptions were left by unknown people with a meaning that is more obscure than a political party's press release. Back in 1712, when Cotton Mather wasn't looking for witches, he was trying to figure out what the markings meant. He even made a copy of the figures and sent them to the Royal Society in London for a translation, but the experts there were undecided.

Was this the literary equivalent of crop circles and mysterious Mayan hieroglyphs? It could be that what you can see is actually the musings of an international group of ancient punks. Over the years many have argued that the petroglyphs aren't a single language, but several. Some scholars think that they have deciphered bits and pieces. One of those pieces is the name *Thorfinn Karlsefni* and the phrase, "Miguel Cortereal by will of God, here Chief of the Indians," along with the date 1511 and a Portuguese coat-of-arms. (Not all students of language and history agree with even these fragmentary—or is it figmentary?—translations.) What is clear, however, is that Dighton Rock became a veritable billboard for graffiti enthusiasts over many years. To avoid having the rock face damaged by tides and weather and the modern tagging practitioner, it now sits in a museum in Dighton Rock State Park.

We have our own theories on what was meant by the writing. Either this is an old variation of *Kilroy was here,* or an early comic dramatic masterpiece, *Dighton Beach Memoirs.* If you visit, be sure to bring a picnic lunch for the eighty-five acres of grassy areas and shade trees. There is also boating, fishing, and hiking. Dighton Rock State Park is on Bay View Avenue; for more information, call (508) 822–7537 or visit www.state.ma.us/dem/parks/digr.htm.

A LASTING IMPRESSION
Brockton

Imelda Marcos has nothing on the city of Brockton when it comes to shoes. She only had hundreds of pairs at hand (or would that be "at foot?") But the Brockton Shoe Museum lifts shoe obsession to an art. Those who are interested in fashion—whether leather or lace—can see how boots and sneakers can be a veritable foundation for a look. Not only does this shoe showplace examine the footwear-making craft from the sixteenth century on, but it also has entire theme collections, like military shoes from the Civil War to Desert Storm. If your mother wore combat boots, they may be here.

Then there are the celebrity shoes, including those worn by Ted Williams, Arthur Fiedler, and Rocky Marciano. (Marciano was a Brockton native.) There is even a pair, size twenty-four, used by an Italian boxer of the 1930s. And don't forget those of the political persuasion: Mamie Eisenhower, President Gerald Ford, and President Bill Clinton, whose sneakers are fast enough to get out of almost any scrape. If you get tired of Shoes, the Exhibit, then you can move on to Shoes, the Movie—actually, a video of shoes. We won't be heels and give the end-

The Brockton Shoe Museum features the size 24 shoes worn by
1930s world champion Italian boxer Primo Carnera.
Photo by Erik Sherman

ing away. But we do have a bone to pick with the people who
have designed the attraction's marketing message. The Shoe
Museum bills itself as "the only authentic shoe museum in
America." We beg to differ and offer as evidence the closets of
virtually all the women we have ever known. You can judge for
yourself at the Brockton Heritage Center, 216 North Pearl
Street. For more information, or to find out if they have your
size, visit www.brocktonma.com/bhs/shoe.html or call (508)
583–1039.

HEAVY LIGHTHOUSE
Cohasset

Whoever said that watching over a lighthouse was easy work, let alone even safe? Sure, turn the switch on and turn it off—and make out your last will and testament. Just off the coast of Cohasset is Minot's Ledge Light. Erected in the mid-nineteenth century, it is the most wave-swept lighthouse of the United States Lighthouse System (USLHS). This is the Hawaii of the lighthouse set, where the biggest and baddest waves break—and, sometimes, so do the light keepers. After the lighthouse's initial construction, the first keeper complained about how dangerous the waves were and immediately quit. The next keeper also complained. The year after the lighthouse went up, it came down in an April storm, killing the two assistants who were on duty. The USLHS wanted a light there, since this was a dangerous stretch of water, so it rebuilt on the site. Some people can't take no for an answer. Replacing the building was quite the trick, using 1,079 blocks of granite from Quincy—more than 3,500 tons in all—cut to fit together like a well-made joint on a dresser drawer. It took the USLHS five years to put all the blocks in place. Impressive, but the engineering wonder still left keepers wondering why, in the name of all that was holy, they should sit out there. People quit, right and left—that is, when they didn't become violent or literally lose their minds. Reports of hauntings include the mysterious polishing of lenses, odd noises, and a figure screaming in Portuguese for help while hanging off a ladder. Talk about your hostile working environments.

Amusingly, the Minot's Ledge Light is also known as the "I love you" light, because it flashes in a 1–4–3 pattern, mirroring the number of letters in each word. (Imagine what conditions would have been like if it hated you.)

The memorial of the Minot's Ledge Light honors the two men who died when the lighthouse collapsed.

Photo by Erik Sherman

These days the lighthouse itself is automated, working off solar power, and is closed to the public. The lighthouse keeper's abode has become a private club and a pleasant venue for functions. But you can read about the storm and the men who died (although not the ones who went off the deep end, so to speak) by going to the memorial at Cohasset Harbor. The memorial includes a replica of the top portion of the lighthouse on granite blocks from the original structure. The light keepers' residence also makes an interesting place for a social gathering. Set sail for a driveway that runs off Border Street, next to the small bridge.

LADY OF THE LIGHTHOUSE

Working in a lighthouse was always a lonely job, perhaps making the appearance of ghosts not all that unwelcome. Maybe previous occupants didn't want the new ones to feel isolated. One such place is Plymouth Light, formerly known as Gurnet Light, established in 1768 on the property of John and Hannah Thomas at the tip of Duxbury Beach. It was one of a dozen colonial stations and John was the lighthouse keeper until he was killed during the Revolutionary War. That left Hannah as the first official female lighthouse keeper on the continent. According to accounts at the time, Hannah was good at what she did. She was also very loyal, refusing to leave the lighthouse during her life. She worked until her death, at which point her son took over. The original lighthouse is long gone, having been replaced in 1803, rebuilt in 1843, and then rebuilt again in 1924.

In 1994 Bob and Sandra Shanklin, world-famous lighthouse photographers, enthusiasts, and authors, came to photograph the building and stayed at the keeper's house. In the middle of the night, Bob woke and saw the apparition of a woman's face, dark clothing, and shoulder-length hair. Could Hannah be the lighthouse keeper emeritus?

Although Plymouth is technically the closest city to the lighthouse, the only way to approach is by four-wheel-drive or by foot from Duxbury Beach. The lighthouse is generally closed to the public, though it is open on such special occasions as the annual Opening of the Bay each May in Duxbury.

GOOD WORKS AND GOOD EATS
Eastham

*S*aving souls is serious work, but that doesn't mean that you can't have some fun while you do it. The Methodists have long understood that part of spiritual development was being in the proper atmosphere, and they have been drawn to beautiful seaside areas in the hot days of summer. In Eastham is Millennium Grove, an oak grove in which as many as 5,000 of the faithful would camp and pray with some 150 ministers. Henry David Thoreau witnessed this on one of his walking trips of the Cape and later wrote about it. While it's easy to build an image of what this must have been like, it's easy for that image to be wrong. Life at the camp was not one of deprivation; the worshipers were apparently open to sustaining the flesh as well as the spirit. Thoreau wrote of his visit: "I saw the heaps of clamshells left under the tables, where they had feasted in previous summers, and supposed, of course, that that was the work of the unconverted, or the backsliders and scoffers. It looked as if a camp-meeting must be a singular combination of a prayer-meeting and a picnic." We can only imagine the difficulties the faithful must have faced: mounds of shellfish and not a drop of melted butter in sight. To get a feel for the old surroundings, let the spirit move you to Campground Road and look for the old lobster bibs.

D*IGGING* C*ULTURE*
Easton

I f you liked watching *Home Improvement,* or if going to
Home Depot is your idea of a night out on the town, then
the Arnold B. Tofias Industrial Archives at Stonehill College
will give you fun by the spadeful. This special collection of
the school's Stonehill Industrial History Center, located in the
Cushing-Martin Building on the campus, is nicknamed the
Shovel Museum. There's a good reason for the moniker, as this
could well be the largest historic retrospective of that most
essential icon of earth movement. It's not to everyone's taste;
according to a researcher, in 1995 only 200 people visited the
collection. What do most people think it must be, a hole in the
ground? Absolutely not: There are papers—diaries, sales
ledgers, and catalogs—of the O. Ames Company, which happened to make shovels. And you will also find more than 800
shovels and shovel components, as well as trowels, trenchers,
and other related tools.

The business had its start in the Revolutionary War, when
Capt. John Ames, a blacksmith by trade, made shovels and
muskets in West Bridgewater. His son moved the business to
an abandoned nail factory in Easton in 1803. Because merchandise from England was relatively cheap, Ames concentrated on
making expensive, high-quality shovels. The company thrived
in Easton until it merged with another in the 1950s and moved
out of town. In the process of the move, the new owners managed to leave an attic full of shovels in the old building. Thus
was born the collection. Family members are still in the area,
and one donated the paperwork a few years ago. A gallery is
open where you can view the shovels through glass, but if you

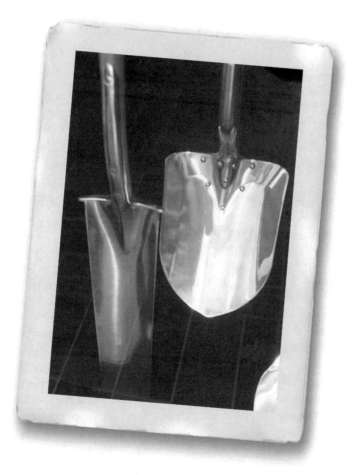

More than 800 shovels and shovel components are
displayed at Stonehill College.
Photo by Erik Sherman

want to dig into the subject more, call the curator at (508) 565–1403 to arrange for a walk through the *objets d'dirt,* or visit www.stonehill.edu/archives/sihc. The historical big dig is at the Cushing-Martin Building, Stonehill College, 320 Washington Street.

POP-TOP ART
East Taunton

College students who spend their hours hardly studying and partying heartily might seem to be wasting important intellectually formative years. Yet we'd like to think that an entire genre of beer art has been the result. Unlike much cultural philanthropy, this is not a category that owes much to wealthy patrons or even government underwriting. Beer art is something that the average person on the street supports, sip by sip. There are the nameless people who have done their small share, and then there are the heroic figures who, each like a modern Hercules, move and direct the rivers of frothy liquid. It is the latter category that features the East Taunton Beer Can and Breweriana Museum. Kevin "Kevbo" Logan, the owner and curator, was introduced to this collection pastime by his cousin in Galveston, Texas. Since then Kevin has collected more than 1,000 cans, along with roughly the same number of coasters, half a dozen beer trays, and assorted glasses and bottles from around the world. His best find was in 1980, cleaning out a woman's basement; she told him to keep anything he found. In an old running refrigerator were two rare Schaeffer 1964 World's Fair Special Steel Flattops, one of which now sits in the museum. (The other went to cousin Patrick, a belated but much welcomed, we assume, thank-you.) On his Web site, Kevin answers what might seem obvious: Why would someone collect beer cans? "Beer cans are pretty fascinating, really." We are sure that the display-preparation phase, which includes draining the contents (from the bottom) doesn't hurt. In fact, it's probably good for what ales you. The collection is large, but the number of visitors is only about forty a year. To arrange a visit or just to take a virtual tour, go to http://kevslog.tripod.com/beercanmuseum—it's the yeast you could do.

S HELL G AME
Fall River

T he USS *Massachusetts* never lost a sailor in combat but the government nearly lost the *Massachusetts*. In the early 1960s the Navy was going to sell the battleship—home to 2,300 sailors during World War II—for scrap. The ship, built in 1941 in the city of Quincy, Massachusetts, had joined the War in November 1942. In a battle with the ship *Jean Bart* during the

Battleship Cove is home to the world's largest collection of historic naval ships, including the USS Massachusetts.
Photo by Erik Sherman

drive into North Africa, the *Massachusetts* let loose the war's first American 16-inch shell. (This piece of artillery was nothing to trifle with—it was nearly a foot and a half in diameter.) On August 9, 1945, less than a month before the end of the war in Asia, the *Massachusetts* shelled the Kamaishi, Honshu, ironworks with, as it turns out, what were probably the War's last American 16-inch shells.

Luckily, before the Navy could sell the *Massachusetts*, a group of citizens organized a battle plan and turned the valiant ship into a museum worthy of the name. They rescued not only the *Massachusetts*, but an entire fleet, adding a destroyer, a submarine, two PT boats, a mechanized landing craft, and even some foreign craft, such as a Russian warship and a Japanese suicide-attack boat. Now the *Massachusetts* hosts camping adventures where youth groups can see what a sailor's life was like. That includes meals served on board, berthing in crew's quarters, movies about Navy ships and Navy life, and Morse code classes for those who want to join the signal corps and pursue radio licenses. There are even facilities for functions and meetings for those above the recruitment age. Stop by headquarters at Battleship Cove; the Web site www.battleshipcove .com gives directions, hours of operation, and other details.

A HATCHET JOB
Fall River

F orget television movie re-creations of sensational crimes or even reality shows. If you have an ax to grind with second-hand titillation, you might find a trip to the Lizzie Borden Bed and Breakfast Museum intriguing. This was the site of the double-hatchet murder of Andrew J. and Abby Borden and the trial of their spinster daughter, Lizzie. Legal authorities not

The old Borden house is now a bed-and-breakfast.

Photo by Erik Sherman

only charged Lizzie with the murder of each parent, but they also accused her of an additional charge of killing both of them—sort of a double double-homicide.

Lizzie was tried and eventually acquitted—whether fair or not we couldn't say, as that would be splitting hairs. But much of the defense's success seemed to lie in excluding testimony Borden gave during the inquest that contradicted what she said at the trial, as well as having certain other testimony labeled inadmissible. Oh, and there was that mysterious man who had been hanging around the Borden home. No matter about the verdict, though, as the town didn't forgive her. That rhyme about "giving her mother forty whacks and when she was done giving her father forty-one" had to hurt, and it was untrue—mom got nineteen and dad, only eleven.

Now, thanks to the time-honored commercial tool of exploiting the macabre, you can experience the Borden house up close and personal by spending the night in the very dwelling that was the site of the deeds. You can even have a suite that includes Lizzie's room. The meal portion is actually similar, so we read, to the ones the Borden parents had the morning of that . . . uh . . . unfortunate incident: bananas and jonny-cakes, washed down with coffee and sugar cookies.

There are tours of the house on weekends in May and June, and daily in July and August, but the hours vary. For more information, go to www.lizzie-borden.com or call (508) 675-7333. To reach that (hopefully not) final resting place, go to 92 Second Street.

OLD TECH

*I*s he a curator, or simply a pack rat? We're not sure, but Mark Vess of Hanson certainly has come up with the best excuse for keeping an overwhelmingly large collection of old stuff. Calling his obsession with antiquated technology a "museum" seems unfair. After all, it's not a public institution and you can't drop by to see it. But the founder and curator does give a few tours each year to school groups and collectors.

Vess started saving old radios and phones when he was a child, and if his own mother couldn't stop him, who can? Now, decades later, he keeps the bulk of the collection in the hayloft of his barn, though it does spill out into other parts of the house, and some things—a tractor, a number of antique autos, and a player one-man band (piano with other instruments)—require a bit more space planning.

A number of the items, such as the Edison wind-up phonograph and the manual typewriters, are obvious in their function . . . or they would be, for those old enough to remember records and carbon paper. Then there are things that could use descriptive panels, like the electrical coils that doctors of the late-nineteenth century used to (unsuccessfully) treat stomach aches and bad pregnancies. But not everything is hand-powered: Vess also has a selection of handheld transistor radios. Those lucky enough to tour past the wooden display tables will also see cameras, flashlights, telegraph keys, light bulbs, sewing machines, and even antique shaving blades. The world may be waiting for a better mouse trap, but when society moves on, you can bet that Mark Vess will have the old model.

READY OAR NOT
Hull

Most museums are happy with just telling about the past. The Hull Lifesaving Museum does that and goes a bit further, though with a twist. The U.S. Life Saving Service, established in the 1870s to assist mariners in distress, had stations up and down the East Coast, and the branch in Hull was certainly busy. But the present-day museum actually has a program for putting people into the water, not taking them out. It sponsors various open-water rowing races, and you have to wonder about the conditions when you hear some of the names: the Snow Row and the Icebreaker. (Undoubtedly the museum staff doesn't have to worry about people falling out of the pilot boats, dories, wherries, and whale boats, as they would probably just bounce off the frozen surface.)

If you don't catch one of the races, there is still a lot to see—and to think about. This part of the state has had a long relationship with the sea, and the loss of life in its waters has been real and historic. Sometimes the rescuers from the local station would take boats out to pull mariners from the rough waters off the shore. When the weather was too rough, a canon would shoot a ball and line out to sea so those in trouble could pull themselves back to land (if they were lucky).

The Hull Lifesaving Museum is open year-round and has both artifacts and hands-on exhibits. Be sure to go up into the children's space and climb into the cupola, which, on a clear day, offers a view of the harbor and the neighboring lighthouse that can't be beat. Row, row, row your way to 1117 Nantasket Avenue. Just don't forget your life preserver. For information, call (781) 925-5433, or go to www.bostonharborheritage.org/main.htm.

D *IZZY* D *ISPLAYS*
Hull

E ver feel like you're going around in circles? It's an unpleasant hazard of modern life. Instead of giving up, try a little
sublimation: Head to the end of the small boardwalk-like strip
in Hull, and check out of the rat race and into childhood at the
Paragon Carousel. Before the turn of the twentieth century,
this area was a major New England resort, complete with an
amusement park. In 1928 its owners installed this carousel,
number eighty-five of the eighty-nine built by the Philadelphia
Toboggan Company, known for its realistic hand-carved figures. Back in those days Hull was a resort town, and people
would flock to the shore to enjoy a vacation in the cool breezes.
Times changed, and the seaside community became a bit run-
down. It transformed into a blue-collar residential area as plane
travel became more prevalent and could take the wealthy to
real tropical destinations. The Paragon Amusement Park, long
a fixture, finally came down in the mid-1980s, the victim of a
condominium development. Most of the history is just a paper
memory, but thanks to the efforts of community activists and
sentimental supporters, three investors purchased the carousel
and set it up on land provided by the state. Fate does have a
way of going in circles, and the owners decided that they
wanted "off" the merry-go-round when their interests changed.
They put the carousel on the market again, and it appeared
that it was going to be dismantled and sold piecemeal to
antiques buyers. Rather than let the beloved amusement be
taken for a ride, its fans from neighboring towns raised more
than a million dollars to purchase the carousel and save it for
posterity. Today the carousel's mighty Wurlitzer band organ
plays on. The sixty-six wooden horses and two Roman chariots

The carousel in Hull is a mechanized taste of
summer, whether you ride or watch.
Photo by Erik Sherman

have been taking turns undergoing restoration, and today they await to take you away from care. Just hop on and enjoy the satisfyingly long ride. Next to the carousel is a great local ice cream store, and the beach across the street has its own appeal, as long as you aren't horsing around. The carousel is at 205 Nantasket Avenue; call (781) 925–0472 or visit www.enjoy-hull.com for information.

G RAVE E NTERTAINMENT
Hyannis

M ost people think you need a campfire, dirt, and mosquitoes for a good ghost story. But why not add some comfort to your scare? At the Ghost Theater you sit among haunted furniture and household items. Your hostess, Madame Theresa Coffin (M. T. Coffin—get it?), spins tales based on her research and experiences. Is it real? Fancy? Does it matter? Neither the Madame nor her husband, who helps run things, has a theatrical background. Nevertheless, Madame Theresa has long been intrigued by funeral homes and stories of the hereafter and she has received high marks from local reviewers. Her tales entangle audiences and leave them at times in considerable fright, if the candid pictures on her Web site are any evidence. To help keep idle hands busy, the couple also builds realistic Victorian morning clothing and other costumes, which they sell to theater groups and museums. A newly renovated performance space keeps the cutting tables out front, so visitors can appreciate all aspects of the business. There are two regularly scheduled performances: a recitation of the Madame's encounter with the spirit of the victim of a suicide (called a "psychological thriller") and a series of scary stories, all told with the lights so low that you might as well close your eyes, but don't—you never can tell when you'll have to make a sudden break for the door inches ahead of some avenging spirit. Reservations are not required for public shows, for which the box office opens fifteen minutes before the terror starts. But check ahead (508–833–1807 or www.mtcoffin.com) for the current schedule and fees, or if you want to bring a group. You don't want to be disappointed. After all, you might be dying to see it. Coffin's Ghost Theater is at 523 Main Street.

PARALLEL PARKING
Kingston

We like straight lines—they're so orderly. And what better order do they provide than when arranged as longitude and latitude, giving direction and guidance to us all? Okay, okay, so the latitude bands that run parallel to the equator and the longitude lines passing through the poles are actually big circles, and not straight at all. The point is that without them, we'd be totally lost. Those who appreciate the niceties of navigation can enjoy the pure mathematics of the way the numbers look. And one of the coolest things for the aficionados is finding a spot where either latitude or longitude is a complete whole number, with no fractions. Think of it as directional geek chic. You can enjoy a small sample of it by driving down Loring Street in Kingston, between Parks and River Streets. On the east side of the road, look for a granite slab celebrating the 42nd parallel. On that spot, you are at exactly 42 degrees latitude. Isn't it good to know where you are?

HOG WILD
Martha's Vineyard

Some motorcycle lovers says that Harley Davidsons make a deep-throated rumble that is music to their ears. It seems that the people at Panhead Mike's Offshore Cycle have taken that idea to an extreme. Sure, they tune Hogs—and totally rebuild and restore vintage bikes as well as giving attention to the more ordinary examples. But how many cycle shops expand into more cultural aspects of life? Panhead Mike's is also the rehearsal space for a local band that ended up taking its name—the Offshore Cycle Band—from its digs. And Panhead Mike's is also the official mechanic and enabler of the Flying Horses, the nation's oldest operating platform carousel. The merry-go-round was brought from New York's Coney Island to Oak Bluffs on the Vineyard in 1884. If you were born to be wild, thanks to the shop, you can still take a spin from Easter Sunday through Columbus Day and grab for the brass ring that gives a free ride. You'll be on a hand-carved horse, but if you'd rather try a Hog, head to the shop at 348 State Road, Vineyard Haven or call them at (508) 693–7447. For the carousel, go to the end of Oak Bluffs Avenue near the beach in Oak Bluffs . . . and don't forget the leather jacket.

WHAT RELIGION HATH WROUGHT
Martha's Vineyard

We'd love to tell you when you can enjoy Illumination Night in Oak Bluffs—really, we would. It's a warmly glittering affair celebrating the end of summer. After a sing-along concert, the oldest member of the community lights a Japanese lantern. Then hundreds of similar lamps are lit as they hang on the Tabernacle, a wrought-iron open-air auditorium seating more than 3,000. (The Tabernacle was built for religious services by the Methodists, who knew a good location for a religious revival when they saw one.) And there are even more lanterns on the nearby gingerbread cottages. These brightly painted wooden structures once housed those attending the camp and are now private homes. Footpaths lead all around the courtyards, so you can take a stroll and appreciate the colorful dwellings in the glow.

So why don't we cough up the details of when you can see all this? It's because we don't know. The event takes place sometime in late August, but the exact date is kept a secret until about a week before it happens. You can try to pry the secret out of someone, or at least get the schedule for concerts and other activities at the Tabernacle, by calling (508) 693-0525. And if you do miss the celebration, you can still have some fun near the Tabernacle. See the cottages in the daylight or learn about the life of the early fervent inhabitants at the Cottage Museum, One Trinity Park in Oak Bluffs.

"*SEA*" *THE BIG HORSE*
Mattapoisett

If you are traveling along the main drag in Mattapoisett, an aqua-equestrian sight might leave you crying, "Whoa, Seabiscuit!" More than fifty years ago, a gift shop owner wanted something to attract attention and customers, so he asked sign maker Theodore Tetreault to build an 8-foot-tall sea horse to place on the road. And build it he did. But in the grand scheme of things, how impressive is that? The finished product was hardly taller than some professional basketball players. Once it was finished, the original owner thought that the landscape swallowed it up. So Tetreault, with the help of his two sons, went back to the stable (or was it the fishing hole?) and built a 38-foot plywood sea horse. When done, it looked almost the way it does today. (Tetreault returned later with some boat builders to add a fiberglass layer, the better to protect the steed from its native element in liquid or frozen form.) Long after the original business owner was gone, the icon stayed. After all, where does an almost 40-foot sea horse sit? Anywhere it wants.

Salty the giant sea horse has gone from kitsch to landmark.
Photo by Erik Sherman

A few years ago the sea horse came down for some rest, recreation, and rehabilitation. The decades of exposure to the elements had been hard, and eight months of work were a wonderful restorative: a new tubular frame, the removal of rotted material, fresh sherbet-colored paint, another coat of fiberglass, and a new name: Salty. Tetreault died in 2001, but his monument lives on. The land around it is now a park. How fitting: After years of working to bring in the customers, the sea horse is happily put out to literal pasture. To see it, take a drive down Route 6 by North Street.

IT'S A SMALL WORLD
Middleborough

The lesser things in life are usually those that qualify for small talk, and these days, the public is interested in bigger and better. However, today's small was the mid-nineteenth century's big. Mercy Lavinia Warren Bump, born in Middleborough, was more—or is it less?—than diminutive. At 32 inches tall, she was one of the two most famous midgets in the country. (The other was her husband, Charles Sherwood Stratton, otherwise known as "General" Tom Thumb.) Lavinia had a sister who was also only 32 inches tall. Her other sister was normal sized, and all four of her brothers grew to over six feet. Yet she gained a level of fame that towered over that of her siblings. She spent a few years working on a relative's steam boat show on the Mississippi, then was hired by P. T. Barnum when she was 21 and dubbed "the Little Queen of Beauty." Although we're sure she was attractive, to be fair, there probably weren't a lot of contenders to the crown. Her future husband already worked for the master showman, and it would seem destiny that the two should marry, or at least form a conglomerate of their interests. Barnum turned the engagement announcement into a money-maker, putting the future bride on display for tens of thousands of people. The wedding, in 1863, was a major event in New York City, with more than 2,000 guests. The honeymooners spent time touring the world. As the years passed, both grew to 40 inches tall. After her husband's death, Lavinia lived in retirement until her marriage to Count Primo Magri, an Italian dwarf. She lived until the age of sixty-four and is buried in South Amenia, New York. But some of the personal effects of both Lavinia and Charles are on display in the Middleborough Historical Museum, which has the world's largest collection of Tom Thumb memorabilia, including his 12-inch walking stick. The collection is behind the town police station, on Jackson Street. Call ahead (508–947–1969) for the hours, though the management has been known to set up appointments at other times.

THERMOMETER MAN
Onset

What's the difference between a personal collection and a museum? Maybe just a degree of interest. Some people get all hot and bothered about a subject, but Richard Porter could be called positively mercurial—literally. He has assembled thousands of items in what he claims is the world's largest—actually, he claims that it's the world's only—thermometer museum, which sits in the basement of his home. It's also, at last check, the only museum in Onset on Cape Cod. Here are big thermometers, little thermometers, thermometers shaped like animals. There are two pill-sized thermometers that John Glenn had to swallow on his last mission on the space shuttle, which match the backup model that traveled to the moon on *Apollo 9*.

There is a thermometer that came as a prize in a Cracker Jack box, and another used in deep-sea studies. A model from Alaska reads to –100 degrees F. Some float; some are scientific instruments. Many came from flea markets and others are from Porter's travels in the United States, Europe, South America, and Africa. Porter, a retired science teacher, started his collection decades ago after a friend told him, "If you don't collect something in retirement, you may just collect dust." His teaching activities have not been left out in the cold. He regularly gives presentations at schools, museums, and conferences. You can see the collection yourself by traveling to Onset, where the museum's motto is "Always open and always free with over 3,000 to see." Call (508) 295–5504 to arrange a visit.

CABLE ENTERTAINMENT
Orleans

Sociologists and economists would argue that the telecommunications industry leaves a mark on society. We have learned that this is literally true. Just check the French Cable Station Museum, which celebrates what was a straightforward business investment of the day. Despite the reputation Yankees have of being taciturn and uncommunicative, Massachusetts became a hub of firsts in communication. Granted, this was largely because the innovators were from Europe. Alexander Graham Bell, a Scot, invented the telephone in Boston, and although the weather was against him, Italian Guglielmo Marconi looked to Cape Cod to provide a base for the first transatlantic radio broadcast—probably a good excuse to write off a vacation. But what the French Cable Museum commemorates is the time when the French, in 1869, laid their first transatlantic telegraph cable. It ran from the western tip of France to New-

The French Cable Station Museum in Orleans
celebrates the French connection.
Photo by Erik Sherman

foundland, to Orleans, and finally over to Duxbury. Given the
difficulties of ocean travel, this was an impressive engineering
feat. It was also a slow one, as the Atlantic Telegraph Company
had managed to make a transatlantic hop a few years before.
Yet being in second place didn't hinder the cable's usefulness. It
was the mechanism by which the United States learned of
Charles Lindbergh's successful landing in Paris. News from the
French end was cut off in the spring of 1940 with the message
"Les Boches sont ici—The Germans are here." The sister station
in Brest finally resumed transmission—in 1952. (We figure
that one of those famous French labor strikes might have
slowed things down after the end of the war.)

The museum is not the only legacy of the cable. To this day, you will find many Norgeots, Deschamps, and Ozons in local phone directories. These are the descendants of men who came from a French-owned set of islands near Newfoundland to work at the station. To check out the museum, go to 41 South Orleans Road, which is near the intersection of Cove Road and Route 28. It's open various hours, though not at all times of the year, so call (508) 240–1735 ahead of time to be sure.

WERE THE PILGRIMS REALLY STIFFS?
Plymouth

The Pilgrims have a reputation for being unbending—religious, industrious, and no fun at all. Yet there is stiff, and there is . . . stiff. At the Pilgrim National Wax Museum, you can find representations of the sect that are entirely unmovable. Interest in our national forerunners is hardly unusual, and wax museums are common enough. But how many wax museums are completely devoted to the people who landed at Plymouth Rock? This one is located on Cole's Hill, where the Mayflower immigrants secretly buried their dead after their first winter on this continent so that the Wampanoag Indians would not know how their number had dwindled (amusing, as the group would have disappeared had the natives not helped them). Here, though, the dead still live. A series of dioramas show scenes of the Pilgrim's past: being jailed in England, signing the Mayflower pact, the first Thanksgiving, the blossoming love of John Alden and Priscilla Mullins. There are twenty-six scenes in all and a total of 180 figures. That's a lot of wax. If you get tired of the educational tour, then step outside, cross the street, and take in the salt air of the harbor. Just remember that this is a unique experience. In fact, you might say that no other attraction holds a candle to it. The museum is at 15 Carver Street. You can get more information at (508) 746–6468.

PILGRIM'S GRIND
Plymouth

et's thank the Pilgrims for all they have done: opening a new land to colonization, kicking out anyone who didn't agree with their religious views, and introducing the concept of the public utility. That's right: The next time you get angry at the electric company, remember that you have people from the seventeenth century to thank. When the Pilgrims almost starved and froze to death their first year here—obviously not having read the visitors' information—the Wampanoags taught them to grow and store corn. But the settlers had increasing numbers of residents to consider, and the process of grinding corn with a mortar and pestle was either too inefficient or had become an entirely too overwhelming drag. Enter John Jenney, who knew that he could make use of the settlers' laziness. In 1636 he received permission to build a grinding mill, starting a tradition of disputed charges and poor customer service that has lasted to this day. At least reliability was there—although the original burned down in 1847, a 1970 reconstruction brought it back to working order; it still grinds corn, and you can buy bags of meal. Next to it is a fish ladder, so the herring can go upstream to spawn.

If you want to see where it all started and take a tour, head to the corner of Leyden and Water Streets. Walk through the park area, called Brewster Gardens; look for the small foot-bridge. Cross it, continue down the path along the stream, and you will see the building at the end. Or, if you are feeling lazy, go directly to the mill at 6 Spring Street. For more information, call (508) 747–4544, or go to www.jenneygristmill.com. Sorry, but the complaint department isn't open today.

PLYMOUTH PEBBLE?
Plymouth

Anyone in the United States who has sat through coloring paper turkeys at Thanksgiving has heard of Plymouth Rock. But few know how lucky they are to see anything. First there is the question of what the rock actually was. According to the Pilgrim Hall Museum, none of the documents from that time mentioned a pebble, let alone a rock. The two books of the time written by participants said only that they had landed. It wasn't until a hundred years later that any written works mentioned Plymouth Rock, yet somehow a local legend became "fact." Okay; for the sake of grade school teachers everywhere we'll be nice and say that it was the stepping stone. However, that anything remains of the rock is a wonder. It was in the nineteenth century that people decided to make a monument of the rock, and the object of public affection barely survived. It had become embedded in a wharf, and attempts to move it with a team of oxen actually split Plymouth Rock into two pieces. So the people took the small piece from the top and placed it prominently in front of the town hall. At that point, all manner of people snuck in to chip away at the stone for a souvenir. The townsfolk decided to protect this remaining shard by carting it off to sit behind a fence at the Pilgrim Hall Museum. Whoops— the rock popped off the cart and cracked on the way. And at some point, someone carved the date *1620* into the rock. (Gee, we thought the Pilgrims found it that way.) It's just not easy being a legend.

*A local legend became fact when Plymouth Rock
was turned into a memorial.*
Photo by Erik Sherman

If you visit today, you'll find Plymouth Rock behind walls and under a fancy portico on Water Street, near the end of North Street. Or you could seek out the local hotel that advertises a hot tub with a plastic replica of the big stone—a regular chip off the old granite, and maybe even as authentic.

GENDER BENDER
Provincetown

Those with an aversion to the unusual in gender roles should avoid Provincetown in mid-October when the town hosts the Fantasia Fair, also known as TransGender week. An annual event since 1974, the Fair would more accurately be called a conference or convention. It is meant to help the transgendered live in the midst of regular society while providing "positive reinforcement and encouragement." Participants pay and register for either a half week or full week of sessions such as Daytime Makeup Tips, Trans in the Workplace, and Hormones 101. There is information for MTF (male-to-female) and FTM (female-to-male). Aside from information sessions, there are breakfasts, lunches, and dinners, and even a fashion show and musical review. This is not an occasion for gawkers, as the Fair costs a pretty penny. Those attending have paid hundreds of dollars for the full week or a discounted rate for four days and three nights, not counting lodging. Many bring partners and spouses, who pay a lower rate to take part. If you aren't part of the scene, then remember that October is past the summer season and a great time to visit a beautiful part of Cape Cod in relative quiet. Just try not to get rattled and use the wrong public restroom. For more information, see www.fantasiafair.org.

WHY? WHYDAH NOT?
Provincetown

Some people climb mountains, some swim the English Channel, and some seek shipwrecks. There is nothing else that can describe the drive that Barry Clifford has when it comes to finding boats that sank in the ocean. What can only be called an obsession of Clifford's with the pirate ship *Whydah* started when he heard stories in his youth. As an adult, he put together an expedition that had one of the great "in the nick of time" endings. After almost two years of searching, and down to his last dollar and tank of fuel, Clifford's group found the famous pirate ship, whose sunken fortunes raised Clifford's. Since then he has found the remains of one of Captain Kidd's ships, as well as a French fleet. Now Clifford thinks that he's found the *Santa Maria*—the flagship of Christopher Columbus.

At the time of this writing, there is nothing definite about the identification of Clifford's latest find, but you can visit the museum that commemorates his most famous discovery to date. The Expedition *Whydah* Sea Lab and Learning Center at 16 MacMillan Wharf features some of the 200,000 artifacts that Clifford's team brought up. Also take time to learn more about the ship, the lives of pirates, and the methods that put the jolly back in the roger. Call (508) 487-8899 or visit www.whydah .com for hours and other information.

G RUDGE   G RANITE
P r o v i n c e t o w n

T he words *Pilgrim* and *Plymouth* have a historic alliterative
American accent. Yet before the *Mayflower* neared the
famous P-rock, it stopped at the very end of Cape Cod, at what
would eventually become P-town. (They must have been the
first Provincetown summer tourists.) They even managed to
sign the Mayflower Compact during their brief stop on their
way to Plymouth. Not that you would know it from the way
history is taught in schools. To almost everyone, the first, last,
and only stop the Pilgrims made was north of the Cape. This
must have left the good folks of Provincetown feeling slighted.
To make sure that they got their due, the townspeople erected
the Pilgrim Monument. Work began in 1907 and ended three
years later.

The Pilgrim Monument is the tallest granite monument in
the country, at 252 feet 7 inches. The design was copied from
the Torre Del Mangia in Siena, Italy. Okay, so maybe someone
was confusing the England of the Puritans with the Italy of
Columbus. No matter: The view from the top can be spectacular, with Cape Cod Bay, Provincetown Harbor, and the sand
dunes of the Cape Cod National Seashore visible. On a clear
day, you can even see Boston. To get to that lofty sight, however, you must gain the lofty height, climbing 116 stairs and
sixty ramps. After all that work, you might want to take a
brief rest, which you can do in the museum while enjoying the
current exhibition and remembering not to take the first Pilgrim landing spot for granite. It's not open year-round, so
check http://pilgrim-monument.org or call (508) 487–1310 for
information. Then drive to One High Pole Hill Road.

The Pilgrim Monument, the highest point in Provincetown,
celebrates the area's highest point in American history.
Photo by Erik Sherman

A TALE OF TWO PRESIDENTS
Quincy

Like father, like son? There is a long tradition of offspring following parents into a line of work, except when it comes to being president of the United States. The Bushes have managed it, but before them the only case was that of John Adams

---

❧ *KILROY WAS IN QUINCY*

Anyone whose parents lived through World War II has likely heard of Kilroy. Like an armed forces Mary and her lamb, anywhere the military went, the mysterious man was sure to go. But unlike the nursery rhyme, Kilroy was a pioneer, not a follower. Wherever GIs went, the bet was more than even money that they would find written on a wall, a monument, or even a latrine that "Kilroy was here," often accompanied by a cartoon face peering over a wall. It got to be a race among soldiers and sailors to see if they could chalk the presence in a spot before others.

What might have surprised most of those GIs was that there actually was a Kilroy: James J. Kilroy, to be exact. The man worked at the Fore River Shipyard in Quincy, once a major building facility. He was an inspector, seeing how many holes riveters would fill in a day. To avoid double-counting by some worker trying to make the job rosier, Kilroy would mark his passage by writing "Kilroy was here" with a yellow crayon. Once a

and his son, John Quincy Adams. There are a number of similarities, such as both the fathers serving only one term and the sons taking office after losing the popular vote in a disputed election. But the presidents Adams were far closer, at least physically, in their origins and ends. Both were born within 75 yards of each other in the same house, and both are buried at the United First Parish in Quincy, also called the Church of the Presidents, along with their wives. The church keeps the Adams crypt open to visitors and is actually part of the Adams National Historical Park, although it receives no public funding. The rest of the park includes the birthplace of the

ship was finished and sent overseas, the expansive presence of Kilroy continued as it sailed around the world. However, no one bothered to explain the cryptic notation to the troops on the ships. Kilroy eventually got around in a big way: The name has supposedly been found on Mount Everest, the torch of the Statue of Liberty, the underside of the Arc de Triomphe, a girder on the George Washington Bridge, and in the dust on the moon. According to one probably-apocryphal story, during the Potsdam Conference, in which the United States, Great Britain, and the Soviet Union set the surrender demands for Japan, Stalin was the first to use an outhouse built for the occasion. Upon exiting, the leader reportedly turned to his aide and asked, "Who is Kilroy?" He was just this guy in Quincy. Chalk it up to a triumph of international relations. Although Kilroy is no longer there, you can see the shipyard and the United States Naval Shipbuilding Museum, which is housed on the old USS Salem, at 739 Washington Street. For information and hours, call (617) 479–7900 or visit www.uss-salem.org.

presidents as well as the Stone Library, which includes the entire book collection of John Quincy Adams. During the season, April 19 to November 10, there are guided tours of the homes. Go to the visitor center in the Galleria at Presidents Place for the first-come, first-served, first in the hearts of their—sorry, wrong president—tours. There is validated parking and a free trolley between the center and the historic homes about every thirty minutes on the quarter hour. For more information, call (617) 770–1175 or visit www.nps.gov/adam.

WILL THE REAL PETER PLEASE HOP UP?
Sandwich

K now the name Thornton W. Burgess? This native of Sandwich may not sound familiar, but chances are that you know some of his creations: Peter Rabbit, Hooty Owl, Grandfather Skunk, and Jimmy Skunk. Naturalist and author Burgess wrote more than 170 books and some 15,000 stories—enough to keep a child out of trouble for at least part of the formative years. Now you too can avoid some trouble in two facilities: a museum and a nature center.

The Thornton W. Burgess Society runs a museum in a house once owned by Burgess's Aunt Arabella. It is filled with memorabilia, art, and other items of interest; an herb garden and pond are out back. (There is a nominal entrance fee during the open season of April through October.)

Yet while looking into the museum's history, we ran into a bit of a problem. One Burgess character was Peter Rabbit, as his books and the Society Web site show. Yet there is a different Peter Rabbit, written by author and animal lover Beatrix Potter. According to a bit of online snooping, it seems that Potter's first book, *The Tale of Peter Rabbit,* appeared in 1902. The Burgess Peter Rabbit was in part of a set of syndicated children's stories illustrated by Harrison Cady, which appeared in 1910 as newspaper columns. So the timing is close, but the two characters are different in age and temperament, and the two authors were separated by the Atlantic Ocean. We guess that Peter is a common enough name, even among rabbits.

One difference between the two animal worlds is that Burgess's Peter Rabbit lived in a briar patch. If the kids, or the kid-in-you, want to move around more, wander over to the Green Briar Nature Center, open all year and situated next to a briar patch—yes, the one in the stories. You can find workshops, natural history programs, and some pleasant walking trails in a fifty-seven-acre conservation area, all open to the public. And while you're there, take a peek into the Green Briar Jam Kitchen. Call ahead, and you may be able to catch a jam-making workshop. The Robert S. Swain Natural History Library, containing books, magazines, and other materials on the flora and fauna of the Northeast, rounds out the visit. For more information, visit the museum at 4 Water Street (Route 130; 508–888–4668) or the Green Briar Nature Center and Jam Kitchen, 6 Discovery Hill Road in East Sandwich (508–888-6870).

C o r n   H i l l
T r u r o

Pilgrims? Plymouth Rock. It's a match made in the history books. But that town wasn't the ship's only stopping place. Right before landing there, the immigrants stopped on Cape Cod in the areas that would become Eastham, Provincetown, and Truro. After making some sojourns for supplies and a break for washing clothes—inspiring, we are sure, the

REVOLUTIONARY FEMINIST FIGHTER

*W*hen we hear the phrase "daughters of the American revolution," the images that come to mind include petticoats, churning butter by hand, sewing clothes, and picking up the eggs for breakfast from under the hens. But Deborah Samson, descended from Gov. William Bradford of Mayflower *fame*, would tend to wearing trousers, shooting guns, and fighting. Blame it on poverty and a father who abandoned her, but this was a woman who could take care of herself. This native of Plympton also became the first woman to masquerade as a man and fight in the Revolutionary War.

Samson's father went to sea and her mother couldn't make ends meet, so Samson lived with relatives and, at age ten, became an indentured servant to a family of ten. She stayed in this position until she was eighteen. Hard labor developed her strength and she learned to shoot a musket as well as to spin, weave, and cook. In other words, this was a woman to be reckoned with. When two of the sons of the family that she lived with were killed, her fate was decided.

Samson borrowed clothes from a man named Samuel Leonard, disguised herself as a boy called Timothy Thayer, and joined the Continental Army. Then in 1782, at age twenty-one, she enlisted in the Fourth Massachusetts Regiment under the name of Robert Shurtleff. She was 5 foot 7 inches tall and she bound her breasts to look like a lad. Other soldiers assumed that "Robert" was too young to have started shaving. Good thing they didn't check her legs. Eventually an illness revealed the truth, and she had her honorable discharge personally handed to her by George Washington. Obviously he knew better than to make her mad.

Samson even received a pension eventually, thanks to the intercession of Paul Revere, and her husband was granted a widow's pension after her death at age sixty-six, to complete the tale of gender reversal. In 1983 she was named the official heroine of Massachusetts. A plaque honoring Samson is on the Plympton Town Green; go to 11 North Main Street in Sharon to see a statue of her.

Corn Hill was once the site of perfidious provisions pilfering.
Photo by Erik Sherman

Laundromat—a group of men went exploring. While tromping about, they stumbled upon some fields cleared for farming and a store of corn, as well as a metal kettle that looked as though it came from Europe. After taking as much corn as they could carry to plant later, they buried the rest in the kettle. We can hear the conversation now: "Jumping Jehoshaphat, Brother Ephraim, look at all this corn. Good thing there's nobody here that it belongs to. Let's scram." That corn was a literal life saver; roughly ten bushels provided a crop for the spring and a welcome source of food after a winter that would kill a frighteningly large percentage of the party. So the successful colonization of Massachusetts started with an act of larceny. Good thing there were no laws making it illegal.

The Pilgrims vowed to make restitution, having a sneaking suspicion that the corn belonged to someone. Eventually they put two and two together and realized that it was Indian corn. The restitution came in the form of the weeklong feast that we now commemorate as Thanksgiving (to say nothing of disease, war, and land-grabbing). You can see the historic spot, called Corn Hill, and a commemorative marker near Corn Hill Road off Route 6, which is a darned sight harder to find than the corn was. While you are there, enjoy the beach.

T O W E R I N G   T A L E N T
T r u r o

E very age has its superstars. Even before music videos, CDs, and movies, there were performers who could command enthusiastic mayhem. One of them was Jenny Lind, the soprano known as the "Swedish Nightingale." She started playing piano at age four and eventually attended the Royal Theater School to study music, dance, and acting. She had her first big opera role at age seventeen, and she soon became the leading singer in Europe. Taking into account the slower pace of communications and travel, it is difficult to appreciate the furor that could bubble up about Lind's performances. When she came to New York for a concert tour promoted by showman P. T. Barnum, nearly 40,000 suckers . . . ah, adoring fans . . . lured by the masterful publicity packed the docks to welcome her arrival by ship.

As part of her tour, Lind was scheduled to sing in Boston in 1850, but someone massively oversold the concert and many of the people who paid their money could not fit in the building. According to legend, which seems to be unsupported by newspaper accounts at the time, Lind climbed to the top of

The Jenny Lind Tower is visible from the
Highland Light Beach parking area.
Photo by Erik Sherman

an adjoining 55-foot tower to sing to the people in the street.
Perhaps another piece of Barnum's hokum? Could be. However, in 1927, the tower was slated for demolition. Harry M.
Aldrich, supposedly a serious Jenny Lind fan, bought the
structure. He had it moved, stone by stone, to North Truro by
train, and then by horse-drawn cart to its present location in
Truro. The building, which came to be known as the Jenny
Lind Tower, was deeded in 1961 to the Cape Cod National
Seashore by Aldrich's daughter-in-law. You can't get to the
tower without trespassing on private land, but you can drive
up Highland Road and park at the Highland Light Beach
parking lot to take a look and a bow.

A PLACE MADE FOR RADIO
Wellfleet

Guglielmo Marconi was the first person to make it big in radio. First he invented it; then he demonstrated the first transatlantic broadcast in 1901. Too bad that he couldn't have staged his demonstration in Wellfleet, and moved to Canada instead.

Cape Cod was Marconi's preferred location, and his team was erecting transmission equipment there in 1901. Unfortunately, the quality of construction left something to be desired. In August, just two months after building had started, a stiff breeze bent the heads of the antenna mast and the Italian inventor moved north, where men were men and radio towers were sturdy. It was the first case of cheaply made electronics equipment with no written warranty in sight. So much for history.

In the fall of 1901, the masts totally collapsed. It wouldn't be until January 18, 1903 that the station finally was put back into commission. A transmission occurred from the United States, with Pres. Theodore Roosevelt sending a message to King Edward VII of England. The Wellfleet station remained in operation until the U.S. Navy closed it in 1917 for safety reasons. (How surprising.) The area became a military camp and, eventually, part of the Cape Cod National Seashore. Today some tower footings and a bit of the station's foundation are all that is left. There is an informative display as well as a pleasant beach, which is good because you will probably tire of the placards even faster than the towers fell. Head over to Marconi Site Road and drive down, following the signs to the beach. For more information, call (508) 255-3421.

BELLY CONFUSING
Wellfleet

T he Wellfleet town clock confuses the uninitiated. When its bell rings four times, it is 6:00 in the morning . . . unless it is 10:00 A.M., 2:00 P.M., or the middle of the night. No, the mechanism is not broken. Wellfleet has the only town clock that rings on ship's time. It's a complex system in which the day is broken into watches and then subdivided into hours marked by anywhere from one to eight bells.

The story of how the clock ended up here is happily simpler. It was the brainchild of a town selectman in 1952, Lawrence Gardinier, who was a brilliant tinkerer without a formal education. Because of the maritime history of the area, he wanted a town ship's clock. After convincing others to go along with the idea,

The First Congregational Church in Wellfleet is believed to have the only town clock that rings on ship's time.
Photo by Erik Sherman

Gardinier proposed a budget of $500 to create a striking mechanism for the three-faced clock in the steeple of the First Congregational Church, which was just ornamental. Combining motors, relays, wire, mechanisms, and other bells and whistles, he rigged a device that would ring the church bell the proper number of times at the correct hours. His contraption was used for twenty years before it was replaced for the most part by an electronic system. However, on special occasions, the old bell system still delivers on time, every time. You can see and hear the time at 200 Main Street.

Letting the Chips Fall
Whitman

Most roads lead somewhere, and most signs are put in place to draw attention to something. But there is the odd dead end and at least one carefully tended sign advertising a business that has been gone since the mid-1980s.

The story of the phantom sign has a uniquely sweet beginning. Most cookies don't have the prominence to deserve a history. Not so the original chocolate chip cookie—the toll house—which really came about by accident. Kenneth and Ruth Wakefield ran the Toll House Inn in Whitman. The building had originally been a toll booth on the road between New Bedford and Boston. One day in 1930 Ruth was baking a batch of cookies for customers. She usually chopped up baker's chocolate for this particular recipe, and the dark chunks would melt into the dough. One day she ran out of her usual ingredient and instead turned to the next chocolate thing she had: a bar of Nestlé semi-sweet. But instead of melting in, the bits of chocolate kept their shape. The cookie became a hit, her recipe

Pay no attention to the pointing hand. You can't get there from here.
Photo by Erik Sherman

was published in some newspapers, and sales for the chocolate bar went through the roof. Ruth then approached Nestlé. She struck a deal with the company, and the recipe appeared on the candy bar wrapping. Sales continued to improve and the company eventually started scoring the bar and including a special chopper. In 1939 Nestlé finally created a bag of special chocolate pieces that worked well in the recipe, and smart business met culinary history.

The Toll House Inn went through several owners and
finally burned down on New Year's Eve in 1984. Ruth Wakefield died in 1977 and is buried in the Mayflower Cemetery at
774 Tremont Street (Route 3A) in Duxbury. However, you
might call the one remnant of the late Toll House Inn the marketing equivalent of a headstone. To this day, if you go to
Route 18, right near the intersection of Route 14, standing
proudly between two fast-food emporiums is the sign.

GOLF GRAVE
Yarmouth Port

W e come into the world alone and we leave alone—unless we
have company. Many old graveyards in Massachusetts are
filled with figures from politics, literature, and the arts. They
tend to be crowded, as free space is scarce. But in Yarmouth
Port on Cape Cod, there is a singular phenomenon: a cemetery
with a single gravestone sitting on a golf course. In December
1801, a sixty-four-year-old resident, John Hall, died. The cause
of his death was smallpox, which, although long controlled
now, was a scourge of the world at that time. It was contagious
and a killer. In those days, people figured that the safest thing
was to keep everyone, and every corpse, with the disease far
away from the uninfected. And so, John Hall had a solitary
grave in the woods, as happened in other towns on the Cape.

Eventually, someone decided to build the Kings Way Golf
Club in that same patch of woods. In clearing the trees, they
found Hall's final resting place. It was neither a natural hazard
nor something that could be moved, so it became part of the
scene. Was John Hall married, and if so, can we call the Widow
Hall the first literal golf widow in this country?

Protecting the grave is a low, heavy chain supported by

John Hall's compact abode rests behind a sand trap.
Photo by Erik Sherman

short pillars. We assume that should a ball stray onto the grave, it must be considered dead, with the player losing a stroke. Here's hoping that Mr. Hall continues to find peace—and maybe a mulligan or two. To pay your respects to the late Mr. Hall, and to any wayward golf balls, go to the course by taking King's Circuit off Route 6A. Follow the large circular drive around the course, look for the sign that says "13," take the side street, and look for the parking area on the right. The grave is past the trees, on the right-hand side of the green for the par-three hole.

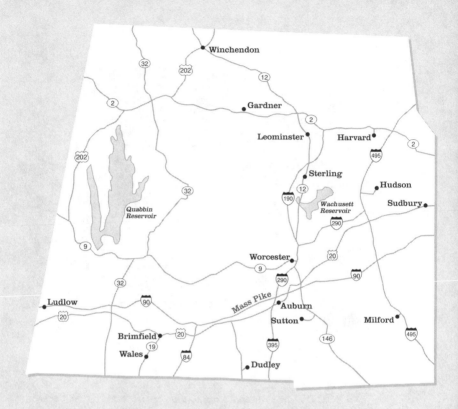

CENTRAL MASSACHUSETTS

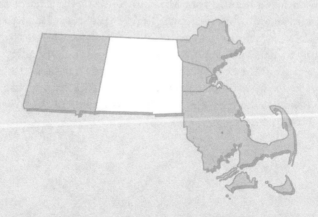

CENTRAL
MASSACHUSETTS

. . . *Seven, Six, Five, Fore!*
Auburn

Halfway between the tee and the green on the ninth fairway
of the Pakachoag Golf Course in the town of Auburn is a
unique hazard: a stone marker commemorating the flight of
the first successfully launched liquid-fueled rocket. Robert Goddard, a physics professor at nearby Worcester Polytechnic
Institute, set off his 10-foot rocket on March 16, 1926, on what
was then his aunt's farm. Goddard's gas- and liquid-oxygen
powered missile, nicknamed "Nell," soared 41 feet into the
heavens before landing in a frozen cabbage patch. The hometown newspaper's headline the next day read: "Moon rocket
misses target by 238,799½ miles."

The successful, if not stratosphere-breaking, launch earned
Goddard the title the "Father of Modern Rocketry," and today
road signs leading into Worcester proudly honor the hometown
scientist. Quite a different reception from the one the *New
York Times* gave Goddard in 1929. The prestigious newspaper
proclaimed him a crackpot who lacked "the knowledge ladled
out daily in high schools." Everyone knew, reported the *Times*,
that space travel as theorized by Goddard was impossible
because without atmosphere to push against, a rocket could
not move. Despite Goddard's certainty that Newton's law of
action and reaction was with him, the article sent the scientist

into a funk from which, despite his aeronautical achievements, he never really did recover. In 1969, after the first lunar landing, the *New York Times* published a correction.

Long after his death in 1945, Goddard posthumously received scores of honors, including the Congressional Medal and the National Inventors Hall of Fame Award. The awards are part of the extensive collection of Goddard memorabilia in the Goddard Library at Clark University. A time capsule containing a replica of a rocket Goddard built in 1940 and some dirt from his aunt's farm launch site is encased in concrete in the floor leading to the library. The rocket–time capsule is to be opened in 2466, five hundred years after it was dedicated by Vice Pres. Hubert Humphrey.

WORLD'S BIGGEST GARAGE SALE
Brimfield

A re you an inveterate collector? Is that being kind? Do friends and family more often use the term "pack rat"? If so, you will be in rat . . . uh, hog heaven three times a year at the Brimfield Fair. The fair is the work of a number of event producers, all of whom have their own staked-out spots. On a Tuesday through Sunday in late spring, summer, and early fall, 5,000 or more antiques dealers from all over the country converge here, lining a mile of Route 20. Add bargain-hunting crowds and you have something modern in the midst of the old treasures—a traffic jam.

Planning an outing through Brimfield on a show day is something like planning the Normandy invasion. If you are a serious shopper, do not—we repeat, do *not*—decide to "wing it."

Go to www.brimfield.com and check out the pre-show schedule. Also, come prepared. You'll want a backpack to carry your swag. And, another must, don't claim to be with the Internal Revenue Service; cash is by far the preferred currency. Another piece of advice: these dealers have paid good money to attend, and show organizers aren't inclined to offer refunds, no matter what the weather, so if it rains, quickly find an umbrella. Don't put off a trip until the last hours, as dealers often wrap up early. If you're so inclined, it's okay to buy some new things while you are there; they'll probably be antiques by the time you finally get out of traffic.

You Say It Your Way, I'll Say It Mine
Dudley

Lake Webster, in the town of Dudley, is also known as Lake Chargoggagoggmanchauggagoggchaubunagungamaugg. And contrary to popular opinion, the lake with the longest name in the United States does not mean "You fish on your side, I fish on my side, nobody fishes in the middle." The real meaning of the elongated word is derived from the local Indian name that means "Englishmen at Manchaug at the fishing place at the boundary." The Englishman in this particular instance was one Samuel Slater, who built a mill near the lake, near the village where the Monuhchogok Indians lived.

Lake Chargoggagoggmanchauggagoggchaubunagunga-maugg is more than 1,400 acres in size and composed of three lakes joined by narrow channels. You'll probably find wide-mouth bass there. Very wide-mouth bass.

SIT DOWN AND BE COUNTED
Gardner

They've been making chairs in Gardner since 1805. By 1837 they were turning out so many chairs that residents immodestly dubbed the place "Chair City of the World." Then in 1905 the town commemorated the one-hundredth anniversary of its chairmaking industry by building a 12-foot-tall mission chair. But the folks in Thomasville, North Carolina, the self-proclaimed "Furniture and Hosiery Capital of the World," weren't about to take a back seat to Gardner. So in 1928 they built a chair that was a foot and a half taller.

Over the next seventy-five years, other cities built increasingly larger chairs to lay claim to the throne as the king of chairdom. In Bennington, Vermont, they built a 19-foot 1-inch-tall ladderback. Again, Thomasville wasn't about to take this sitting down. They built a chair 5 inches taller. Morristown, Tennessee, got into the fray with a 20-foot-tall green sheet metal recliner. Then in 1976, for the bicentennial, Gardner defended the north's honor by building a 20-foot 7-inch-high job. The local Rotary Club in Gardner commissioned Leon W. Plante to design the mother of all chairs. His creation, 10 feet wide and 9 feet deep, stands (or sits, as the case may be) in front of the Helen Mae Sauter Elementary School at 130 Elm Street. However, Gardner sat tall in the saddle for just a year, when its chair was upstaged by a 24-foot 9-inch tall ladderback in Binghamton, New York.

In June 2002 rustic furniture maker Bim Willow of Michigan bent branches into a behemoth 55-footer and says he will build a 70-foot willow tree chair on request. It's left the competition weeping.

While you are in Gardner, you'll also see a 15-foot pretender to the throne on Route 2A.

*It may not be the largest chair in the world, but
Gardner's 20-foot 7-inch model is the biggest in
the Bay State.*
Photo courtesy of Yulia Govorushko

YE WITH LITTLE FAITH, THE WOR-SHIP
Hudson

Apparently the Rev. Louis Winthrop West was bored with retirement and wanted to do a little ministering. So in the summer of 1953, he began constructing a church on the front lawn of his house on Central Street in Hudson. By September he had put the finishing touches on his house of worship. It didn't take long to build because it wasn't very big. In fact, Reverend West's Union Church of All Faiths was the smallest church in the world. The mini-sanctuary measured just 5 feet wide, 11 feet deep, and 10 feet high. Inside, on the back wall, a 20-square-foot painting depicted a sailing ship grounded on rocks. Its title: *In the Cross of Christ I Glory.* The nautical theme was continued atop the church, where the steeple housed a bell from a Coast Guard vessel. Reverend West also placed a golf ball under the church's mini-weather vane.

Over the years more than 10,000 people have signed the tiny church's guest books. More than 600 weddings have taken place in the petite structure. Obviously Reverend West thought small was beautiful, because a few years later he built an even smaller church, measuring just 5 feet by 9 and a half feet at his summer home in Wiscasset, Maine. It was later dismantled.

When Reverend West died in 1966, his son, Horace, took over the micro-nondenominational church. The church was open 24/7 year-round until vandals broke two crosses and left beer bottles on the floor. Then in the fall of 1977, the tiny chapel was moved down the street to the rear of the First Federated Church, where it was rededicated but little used. Eventually the steeple fell off.

Vic Petkauskos, a contractor from Hyannis who grew up in Hudson in the 1950s, always remembered passing Reverend West's tiny church. In the spring of 2003, Petkauskos bought

The smallest church in the world was built by
Rev. Louis Winthrop West in Hudson.
Photo courtesy of the Hudson Historical Society

what remained of the building, hauled it to his garage on Cape
Cod, and began repairing "the whole shooting match." He
installed a new floor and even built a new steeple with stained-
glass windows. Petkauskos plans to place the church on a
barge, decorate it with flowers, and hold weddings afloat off
the coast of the Cape. The little church that could, still can.

THE SUNNY SIDE UP
Leominster

For years a giant frying pan that weighs 380 pounds, is 9 feet in diameter, and has an 8-foot-long handle, hung on the outside of Rob's Country Kitchen at 23 Sack Boulevard. Obviously, Rob couldn't stand the heat because in April 2004 he got out of the kitchen . . . and the restaurant biz. Today you will find Al Dente Pizzeria at the address. The giant pan still hangs outside, but now it holds several slices of very large pizza.

FEATHERSTONE'S FLAMINGOS
Leominster

Florida may have the real thing, but Massachusetts has the biggest flock of fake flamingos in the United States. Leominster is home to the plastic pink variety that have been produced by Union Products since 1957. The feather in the cap for the idea goes to Don Featherstone, who created the classic lawn ornament soon after he started working at the company. (His first design for the firm was an anatomically correct duck, but it didn't fly.) However, sales of the flightless 3-foot-tall birds immediately took off; more than 20 million of the Pepto-Bismol-colored birds have been sold.

In 1986 Featherstone's signature was added to the statue to guarantee authenticity, but when he retired from Union Products in 2000, the company removed his John Hancock. Traditionalists flocked together and caused quite a flap when they

Don and Nancy Featherstone hold
flightless fancy birds of his design.
Photo by Bruce Gellerman

heard the news, calling for a boycott against buying the statues sans his signature.

In the summer, to commemorate the year Featherstone created his first plastic fine-feathered friend, he and his wife, Nancy, place fifty-seven of the birds in their cement-covered backyard. In the winter they install a pair of "snomingos" (albino models of the birds).

Nancy and Don are a strange pair of birds themselves. Every day for the past twenty-six years, they have worn identical outfits she sews. Two years prior to that, before they were married, they wore the same outfits only on weekends.

SAY HELLO TO SOMEONE IN MASSACHUSETTS

*L*enny Gomulka is no Lawrence Welk, but he has penned a high-stepping polka worthy of the bubble master himself. His tune, "Say Hello to Someone in Massachusetts," is the official polka of the commonwealth. Lenny wrote the catchy little ditty in a moment of inspiration. He was driving near his home in Ludlow when the tune just came to him. He grabbed his handheld tape recorder and thankfully preserved the polka for posterity.

Despite the fact that it is really, really hard to come up with words that rhyme with Massachusetts, the state has more than its fair share of official songs. Arlo Guthrie's "Massachusetts" is the official state folk song. "The Road to Boston" is the official ceremonial march. The official patriotic song is "The Great State of Massachusetts," and let's not forget the official state ode, appropriately titled, "Ode to Massachusetts."

While we're on the subject, Massachusetts has a penchant for making things official. The cranberry, for example, is twice blessed. It's the state berry and the official beverage.

Johnny Appleseed of Leominster is the state folk hero, and Deborah Samson is the state heroine. (Samson dressed as a man and went by the name Robert Shurtleff to fight in the Revolutionary War.) The Boston terrier is the official bowser, the tabby is the official state cat, Boston cream pie (which is actually a cake) is the official dessert, and the titmouse is the official state bird. And, in case you were wondering, the ladybug became the state insect in 1974 after intense lobbying of the legislature by second-graders from Franklin, Massachusetts.

Syn(thetic) City, USA
Leominster

Fifteen years before Dustin Hoffman received unsolicited career advice in the 1967 movie *The Graduate,* Brownie Wise was cleaning up in plastics. Brownie Wise was a marketing genius who built an empire out of bowls that burped. Wise teamed up with Earl Silas Tupper, the inventor of the bowls that bear his name, and their work earned them a place in plastics history. Today a Tupperware party is held somewhere in the world every two and a half seconds, and 90 percent of American homes own at least one piece of the flexible containers.

The story of Tupperware is just one of the plastic fantastic tales told at the National Plastics Center and Museum in Leominster. From bulletproof "glass" and Styrofoam cups to Saran wrap and soda bottles, the past, present, and future of plastics is presented at the museum.

The museum that pays homage to plastics and polymers is aptly placed. In Leominster nearly half the companies are involved in the plastics industry. You could say the pioneering plastic city got its roots as the comb capital of the world. In 1770 Obidiah Hill moved to Leominster and began making combs by hand out of natural materials. By 1885 there were twenty-five comb companies in the city. As the demand increased and the supply of horn, tortoise shell, and ivory became scarce, the hunt for a replacement material began. A hundred years later, when celluloid (the first semi-synthetic material) was developed, one of its first uses was in making combs. Unfortunately, celluloid was highly flammable. For the next thirty years it caused many a bad hair day, until a safer plastic was invented.

Among those honored in the museum's Plastic Hall of Fame are John Wesley Hyatt, "the grandfather of plastics," and Roy

Plunkett, the inventor of Teflon. But you won't find Dustin Hoffman among the notables, even though he has made his career in celluloid. Inexplicably, another notable exclusion to the Plastic Hall of Fame is Don Featherstone, creator of the pink plastic flamingo.

The National Plastics Center and Museum is located on Derwin Street off Route 117. For the museum's hours of operation, call (978) 537–9529 or visit: www.plasticsmuseum.org/home .html.

A TOWERING ACCOMPLISHMENT, IN A ROUNDABOUT WAY
Milford

We've heard of keeping those native traditions when you travel, but this seems extreme. Ireland has round towers scattered about, erected at the time that the Vikings—the Scandinavian raiders, not the fancy kitchen stoves—were looting the coast of western Europe. To the Irish, the Vikings were technical wizards, with fast ships and tempered-steel swords, who also had an advantage with a degree of organization not available to the separate European tribes. They were also wizards at pillaging and burning. The latter was particularly problematic when what went into the fire were priceless illuminated manuscripts, often the only copy of works of learning. Dealing with the Dark Ages was bad enough, and no one likes to start over, especially when the job takes months, so the Irish monks responsible for the manuscripts began to build round towers, nearing 100 feet in height, with doors some 15 feet off the ground. When the Vikings came a-callin', they had a hard time a-knockin': The community would climb a rope ladder into the tower to seek refuge, then pull the ladder up behind them. A lookout floor at the tower's top allowed them to see when things were clear and they could leave. It was frustrating for the invading hordes and a relief to the monks, who must have figured that the privations of the early monastic life were ample hardship. Of the original one hundred towers, sixty-five still survive in Ireland. And a single one remains in North America, at St. Mary of the Assumption Cemetery (27 Pearl Street, Milford). It's shorter than its native brethren, rising only 65 feet. The cemetery, one of the first Catholic burial grounds in Massachusetts, was built around the turn of the twentieth century by Irish immigrant stone workers who decided to re-create one of the structures from their motherland. They must have had a tough time leaving work at the office. Did anyone tell them that while the Vikings did come to America, it was eight hundred or nine hundred years earlier?

N O W H E R E S V I L L E , *U S A*
P o d u n k

Yes, Virginia, there is a Podunk. The place, whose name is usually analogous with Nowheresville, is an unincorporated town of about 6 square miles located in East Brookfield, about 15 miles west of Worcester. About a hundred families live there. *Podunk* is the Indian word for bog or swamp. And this town is podunky.

The town includes the Podunk Gift Barn and the Podunk Cemetery. To visit Podunk, permanently or otherwise, from Route 9/West Main Street in East Brookfield (hey, we said it was Nowheresville), travel south on Philip Quinn Memorial Highway. The road turns into Podunk Pike. Where the Pike intersects Adams Street and Adams Road, just before the cemetery, a sign welcomes you to Podunk.

THE ONE AND ONLY EWE
Sterling and Sudbury

For the past two centuries, the towns of Sterling, Massachusetts, and Newport, New Hampshire, have been locking horns over a critical civic matter. Did Mary really have a little lamb, or are she and her mutton just a myth? At stake in the historic debate is a claim to fame, if not fortune.

Sterling says that in 1815, when Mary Sawyer Tyler lived in the town, she had a little lamb named Nathaniel and it did indeed follow her to school one day. A visitor from Harvard University reportedly witnessed the entire event and penned the poem.

Supporting Sterling's version of things are reports that seventy-three years later Ms. Tyler announced that she was *the* Mary. She used her fame to solicit donations to restore Boston's Old South Meeting House by selling wool from unraveled socks made from *the* lamb's fleece.

You can find a statue of the scholarly Nathaniel in the Sterling town square. There is also an entire room in the town's historical society dedicated to his memorable trip to school. Descendants of Ms. Mary Sawyer Tyler still dress up as Mary, and her lamb dutifully follows in the town's annual parade.

Folks 70 miles away in Newport, New Hampshire, say they have evidence that makes mincemeat out of Sterling's claim to Mary's fame. They say there was no Mary, no lamb, and no school. It seems that Newport poet and abolitionist Mary Hale made up the entire thing and published the catchy little ditty in 1830. Newport's claim is supported by the *Oxford Book of Nursery Rhymes,* which lists Hale as the author but notes the historical controversy.

To complicate the lamb's tale, the little red schoolhouse to which Mary allegedly went is in Sudbury, Massachusetts, not

The lamb statue in Sterling.
Photo by Bruce Gellerman

The red schoolhouse in Sudbury.
Photo by Bruce Gellerman

Sterling. Reportedly, Henry Ford discovered a barn built out of wood from the original school in Sterling, had it disassembled, and then rebuilt the one-room schoolhouse in Sudbury. Ewe figure it out.

A statue of Nathaniel, the lamb whose fleece was white as snow, can be found in Sterling's town square on Route 62.

The Little Red School House in Sudbury is located on Wayside Inn Road off Route 20 South. It's open from May 15 to October 15, Wednesday through Sunday, 11:30 A.M. to 5:00 P.M. But to make sure school is in session and you're not tardy, call (978) 443-1776.

Yes, Hell Does Freeze Over
Sutton

Purgatory Chasm State Reservation, in the southeastern part of central Massachusetts, is an immense, unique, and perplexing place. Nearly half a mile long and fifty feet wide, its perpendicular walls rise 70 feet high in some places. Scientists are at a loss to explain how the chasm was formed. Some believe it was created 14,000 years ago when an earth dam holding back melted glacial ice suddenly burst and eroded the granite rock. Others suggest it was formed only a few hundred years ago by an earthquake.

Whatever the cause, the area now offers a lot of hiking trails, places to climb, and caves, along with a number of interesting rock formations bearing quirky names such as the Coffin, Lover's Leap, and Fat Man's Misery.

Purgatory Chasm is open year-round, and good hiking shoes are a must, especially in the winter. Purgatory freezes over and the rocks are very slippery. For more information call Purgatory Chasm State Reservation at (508) 234-3733.

From the Mass Pike (Interstate 90), take exit 10A to Route 146 South and follow the signs to Purgatory Road.

His Name Is Danger — At Least, We Think It Is
Wales

There is a category of words called *eponyms*—that's when people's names convey their occupations or environmental conditions, such as Dr. Cutter, the surgeon, or a fisherman named Baiter. We don't know if Doug Danger is the name this daredevil was born with, but if the shoe fits, throw it over dozens of cars. Danger did this literally, all the while keeping his foot in the shoe. In 1990 he sent his motorcycle soaring and cleared either forty-two cars, parked side-by-side, for a total of 251 feet, or thirty-eight cars, depending on who is recounting the record. Either way, that's longer than the efforts of the more famous Evel Knievel.

You might think that a modicum of fame would satisfy someone, but apparently *danger* in some language translates to "insane undertaking." Some riders have actually died trying to break this record. Danger is still alive, but that is due only to luck and competent medical care. The year after setting the record, he missed an eleven-car jump and crashed, breaking seventeen bones and winding up in a month-long coma.

For most people, that would have been a sign to hang up the leather chaps. But unfortunately for Danger, he had complete memory loss as a result of an accompanying head injury, so even if he had learned a lesson, he forgot it. The man actually returned to jumping motorcycles, even though, as his own Web site (www.dougdanger.net) states, he had little memory of anything, including how to jump a motorcycle. Danger is a fast learner, though, because he has since managed to jump seventeen semi-trucks as well as an L–1011 jumbo jet, wing tip to wing tip. Hopefully it was on the ground at the time.

A FLY-BY-WEEKEND MUSEUM
Winchendon

T he Top Fun Aviation Toy Museum is all about the Wright stuff. It is the only museum in the world devoted to aviation-related toys. Its mission is to "give children's dreams the Wright wings." Here, on the first floor of the Old Murdock School, kids will find noteworthy (if not airworthy) toys, from hot air balloons to space craft. There are flying toys from around the world made with metal, plastic, and wood. There are cast-iron statues of Bugs Bunny in his plane, and Olive Oyl soars in a die-cast model. A helicopter and an airplane made by children in Burkina Faso were fashioned from Dutch milk tins. Covering the entire wall of one room is an "On-the-Wall Airport" offering a pilot's-eye view of the ground and the feeling that you're flying overhead.

The museum encourages kids to take flights of fantasy and test-fly their balsa and paper creations in the large, high-ceiling activity room. The Top Fun Aviation Toy Museum is at 22 Murdock Avenue, about an hour west of Boston as the crow flies. If you feel like winging it, the closest airport is in Gardner. For hours and directions, call (978) 297–4337 or visit www.topfunaviation.com/default.htm.

WATCH IT WITH THAT FORK, BUSTER!
Worcester

I n August business is slow at the Sole Proprietor in Worcester. So to inflate sales the proprietor of the seafood restaurant calls upon Buster the Crab to pump up the volume. Buster is the world's largest inflatable crab. He has a 75-foot claw span and, if he were real, he'd feed 200,000 people. Of course, according to his owners, that would require 35,116 pounds of butter, 45,447 lemons, and who-knows-how-many moist towelettes.

The Sole Proprietor is at 118 Highland Avenue, (508) 798–FISH. Tell 'em Buster sent you.

Buster the Crab presides over his favorite Worcester restaurant every August. Photo by Bruce Gellerman

SECOND FIRSTS

*I*n the 1970s Worcester residents affectionately began calling their city "Wormtown" because it was, well, lifeless and it spoofed Boston's "Beantown." More recently local boosters have started calling Worcester "the Paris of the 00s." While we wouldn't necessarily go that far, being the second largest city in Massachusetts (and in New England) does not mean that Worcester is an also-ran. Far from it.

According to administrators at the Hampton Inn in downtown Worcester, "the city is the center of the known universe." Notwithstanding Beantown's claim to that title, each of the hotel's five stories is a unique tribute to the second city's many firsts, featuring books, memorabilia, and photographs. The hotel employees have also been schooled in Worcester lore and are brimming with facts and figures.

Consider these noteworthy Worcester claims to fame:

- WORC–AM disc jockey Dick "the Derby" Smith was the first DJ to play a Beatles song in the United States. The grateful Fab Four gave him a gold record of "She Loves You" and signed it, "To the first true believer."

- America's first Nobel Prize went to Albert A. Michelson of Clark University (in 1902, for his measurement of light).

- In 1952 Frank A. Firoillo was the first to market a pizza pie mix; five years earlier he had the first pizza stand in Worcester.

- *The monkey wrench was invented in Worcester in 1840 by Loring and Aury Coes of the Coes Knife Company.*

- *Albert Tolman of Worcester built a "man-drawn lorry" for a missionary heading to South America in 1846. The rickshaw was an instant hit in Asia.*

- *Worcester was once "the shredded wheat capital of the world." Henry Perky of Worcester created the flaky breakfast biscuit in his Jackson Street factory.*

- *In 1833 Worcester State Hospital became the nation's first publicly financed insane asylum. That same year the Boston and West Worcester Rail Road became the first in the country to charge commuter fares.*

- *The first typewriter and ballpoint pen were both invented in Worcester.*

- *Last but not least, Worcester was the second city to celebrate First Night. (Boston was the first.)*

The Poop on Indoor Plumbing
Worcester

The curators of the American Sanitary Plumbing Museum have been the butt of countless jokes, so don't even try to pull their chain. Despite the obvious potty humor that goes along with the subject matter, the institution is a serious effort to pay tribute to the devices that made cities livable and prevented countless deaths from disease and plague. On display in the museum's two floors are toilets dating back to the nineteenth century, along with sinks, bathtubs, and tools of the toilet trade.

The museum also puts to rest many myths about sanitary plumbing. For example, you'll be relieved to know that Sir Thomas Crapper did not invent the toilet. (He did have a hand in making some of the innards of the tank.) As his name graced many a toilet, it became equated with its function.

When you've just gotta go, you'll find the museum at 39 Piedmont Street. You can take the toilet tour Tuesdays and Thursdays from 10:00 A.M. to 2:00 P.M. The museum is closed in July and August.

World Smile Day
Worcester

Commercial artist Harvey Ball believed that when you smile, the whole world smiles with you. He wanted to spread the message far and wide, and he succeeded beyond his wildest imagination. Today his Smiley design is one of the most recognized faces in the world and a universal symbol of good cheer.

On October 4. 2002, more than 750 people gathered on Worcester City
Hall Plaza to create the world's largest living smiley face, honoring
both Harvey Ball and World Smile Day IV.
Photo courtesy of Harvey Ball World Smile Corporation

In 1963 Ball, a native of Worcester, was asked by a local
insurance company to design something to boost worker
morale. The company had just merged with another firm and
employees were unhappy with the move. Ball created Smiley, a
face that was turned into pins and given to employees and
clients. Since then the face has been featured on everything
from underwear to yo-yos, stamps to T-shirts.

Although Harvey Ball was paid just $45 for his design, he
was proud that his creation became the international symbol of
good will. In 1999, when he felt his original message had
become lost in the commercialization of Smiley, he created
World Smile Day to restore the meaning of the symbol.

On the first Friday in October each year, World Smile Day is
dedicated to good works and good cheer. The catch phrase for
the day is, "Do an act of kindness. Help one person smile."

SURELY WE JOUST
Worcester

Fair maidens in *amour* and their knights in shining armor will feel right at home at the Higgins Armory Museum in Worcester, Massachusetts. The museum is the only institution in the Western Hemisphere dedicated solely to arms and armor, and it is available for wedding receptions as well as birthday party "OverKnights," when kids can suit up and really wreak havoc. It's all in good joust, of course.

Those who really want to take in the knight life can take lessons in medieval combat at the Higgins Armory Sword Guild. We're told it is the only organization of its kind in the world, and since they're armed and we're not, who are we to argue with them?

Receptions are held in the Great Hall of the museum, which is lined with scores of knights in armor and their steel-plated steeds, some dating back to ancient Rome. The collection of more than 4,000 artifacts includes swords, lances, maces, and various other instruments of Asian and medieval mayhem. There's even a hunting dog decked out in armor.

The Higgins collection also includes a real chastity belt, but it is not considered appropriate to display and is locked away.

The Armory Museum began once upon a time (1929 to be exact) when one of Worcester's leading industrialists, John Woodman Higgins, a man of steel (he owned a steel mill) built a four-story Gothic castle to house his personal collection of arms and armor. The Art Deco building is one of the earliest in the

*Hunting dogs were sometimes outfitted with body armor to protect
them from antlers and tusks of stag and boar.*
Courtesy of the Higgins Armory Museum, Worcester, Massachusetts

nation to have an exterior constructed exclusively of steel and
glass. It is on the National Register of Historic Places.

The Higgins Armory Museum is located at 100 Barber
Avenue. For directions call (508) 853–6015 or log on to
www.higgins.org.

PITCHER PERFECT

*B*ack *in 1880 baseball was a different game than the one we know today. Eight balls were a walk, the batter got to determine the strike zone, and the pitcher stood just 45 feet from the plate. And forget about eating sushi at the concession stands.*

Still, whatever the differences, the record books show on June 12, 1880, that John Lee Richmond of the Worcester Ruby Legs (sometimes called the Brown Stockings) pitched the first perfect game in major league baseball. He beat the Cleveland Blues one to nothing, in what by all accounts was a nail-biter, delayed by rain in the ninth inning.

What makes Richmond's historic feat even more remarkable is that his perfect game in Worcester was actually the second game of two Richmond pitched that day . . . in two different states.

At the time Richmond was a senior at Brown University in Rhode Island and just four days from graduation. As was the tradition of the time, he had been up all night celebrating and had taken part in the traditional senior class

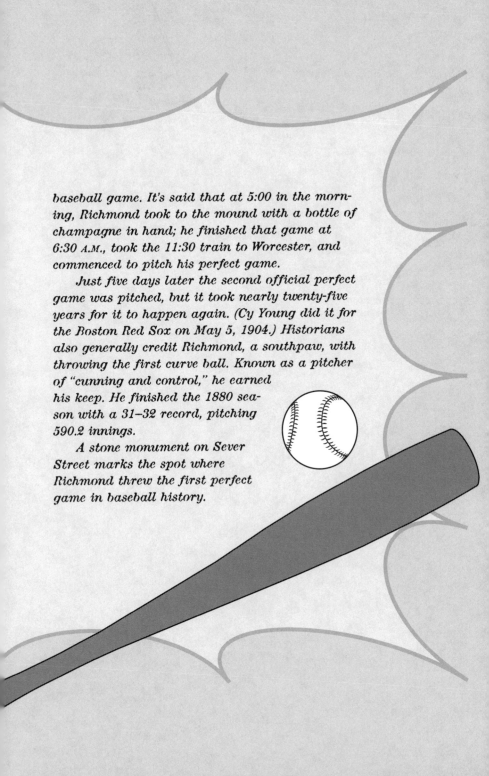

baseball game. It's said that at 5:00 in the morning, Richmond took to the mound with a bottle of champagne in hand; he finished that game at 6:30 A.M., took the 11:30 train to Worcester, and commenced to pitch his perfect game.

Just five days later the second official perfect game was pitched, but it took nearly twenty-five years for it to happen again. (Cy Young did it for the Boston Red Sox on May 5, 1904.) Historians also generally credit Richmond, a southpaw, with throwing the first curve ball. Known as a pitcher of "cunning and control," he earned his keep. He finished the 1880 season with a 31–32 record, pitching 590.2 innings.

A stone monument on Sever Street marks the spot where Richmond threw the first perfect game in baseball history.

WEST MASSACHUSETTS, THE CONNECTICUT RIVER VALLEY, AND THE BERKSHIRES

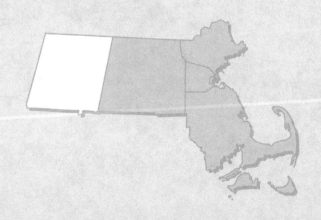

WEST MASSACHUSETTS, THE CONNECTICUT RIVER VALLEY, AND THE BERKSHIRES

BIG FEET
Amherst

Ever feel like you have two big left feet? Be glad that you weren't a dinosaur back in the Cretaceous period, when Tyrannosaurus Rex and other robust reptiles roamed. Imagine having one of those size-ninety-fives firmly planted on your toes while waltzing. But not all dinosaurs were that large. In the Jurassic age, no matter what the movies suggest, there's plenty of physical evidence that creatures were far smaller. To keep you in raptor attention, visit the Hitchcock Ichnology Collection in Amherst College's Pratt Museum. Ichnology, the study of fossilized footprints, is the focus of this especially fine group of more than 1,100 slabs. The collection, amassed by professor Edward Hitchcock, beginning in 1835, includes the world's most extensive series of dinosaur tracks, with examples ranging from 1 to 15 inches in length.

Why become the Imelda Marcos of the prehistoric set? Because footprints can reveal a wealth of information about the earth's early inhabitants, such as size, how quickly they moved, and even whether juveniles traveled by themselves. (The latter, presumably, would be proof of early malls.)

The museum is closed until sometime in 2006 because it's moving into a new building. But in the meantime, you can head over to the college's Frost Library, where the archives hold historical information about Hitchcock and the other academics associated with the collection. There's also an early catalog of the tracks and some photographs. Be sure to visit again when the facility reopens. After all, the fossils were millions of years in the making, so what is another year or two? For more information on the Pratt Museum, call (413) 542-2165 or visit www.amherst.edu/~pratt.

PICTURE PERFECT
Amherst

Some of us look at the latest bulging bestsellers and wish for simpler times, when men were men, women were women, and books were illustrated. Before moving on to Dostoyevsky, most people start their exposure to reading with picture books. These graphically evocative, deceptively simple tales pair a minimum of narration with engaging illustrations to help kids understand that, in the end, books are all about telling stories.

If you have a longing for less literature and more looking, then stop by the Eric Carle Museum of Picture Book Art. This is the first large museum—40,000 square feet, to be precise—devoted to kids' picture books. Carle's name may sound familiar if you've had young children in the last thirty years or so. He is a famous children's book illustrator, with such credits as *The Very Hungry Caterpillar* and *The Grouchy Ladybug*. (We wonder if, when in grade school, Carle submitted sheaves of drawings in lieu of book reports.) While there are Carle originals on display—what good is it if you can't exhibit at your own museum?—you can also take in the work of other noted American and international illustrators. The entrance fee is low, but don't plan to bring in food, drink, or pens and markers. (What, your parents never told you that you shouldn't scribble on the pictures?)

The museum is open year-round and even has free parking, a feature that is almost worth the trip in and of itself. For more information, call (413) 658-1100 or visit www.picturebookart .org. The museum is located at 125 West Bay Road.

O Y V E Y
A m h e r s t

I f you had to name a major center of Jewish culture outside the Middle East, what would you pick? If you said, "New York City," you would at least be in the right country. Given the subject of this book, you should certainly guess some place in Massachusetts. But the honor doesn't go to Boston or even Brockton or Sharon, all of which have a tradition of Jewish community. Instead, it goes to Amherst. What locked down the designation in 1997 was the opening of the 37,000-square-foot home for the National Yiddish Book Center.

The Center has become a big destination for Jewish tourists and claims to be visitor-friendly. No, the signs are not in Yiddish and English. Oy, our heads hurt from the thought. Maybe you don't know Yiddish (nor the Hebrew letters typically used for spelling), but it's worth some acquaintance. The sounds are

The National Yiddish Book Center hosts lectures, films, concerts, and live performances. Photo courtesy of Ned Gray

really intriguing. Yiddish is a language once shared by Jews all over Europe; it is derived from German, Hebrew, Aramaic, and several different Slavic and Romance languages. It is a language for schmoozing, a definite mish mash—a linguistic jumble. Yiddish is also probably the world's best language for cursing and lamenting the indignities of life.

The visitor center is free, open to the public, and offers gardens, exhibitions, and even an English-language bookstore. The Center also has research facilities.

To enjoy the National Yiddish Book Center, schlep over to Hampshire College at 893 West Street and ask for directions. To check whether you're trying to arrive on a Jewish holiday, or if you're *farblonzhet* (lost), call (413) 256–4900.

All in the Family
Charlemont

How are you going to keep them down on the farm after they've seen Paris? That doesn't seem to be a problem at Avery's general store, where five generations of the same family have been occupied since the business opened in 1861, with the sixth already hanging around. Do those Avery family members who stay at the store get chained in place?

The term *general store* does not do justice to this establishment—it's packed with almost every conceivable type of item, from custom-cut meats and organic maple syrup to hardware, paints, and clothing. The store, more officially called A. L. Avery and Son, brings everything to the town that the residents might want. A good thing, too, as few towns with a population under 1,500 can attract a mall. But Avery's offers a service you won't find at a mall: Every Friday there is a delivery run for homebound customers. You will find A. L. Avery and Son on 16 Main Street. Just don't bring pictures of Paris—you wouldn't want to tempt tradition.

The Cheese Whizzes
Cheshire

Cheshire was established by the first non-Puritans in the area—the founders were descended from followers of Roger Williams, who had headed off to Rhode Island in the mid-1600s in search of religious freedom. Perhaps they inherited his rebellious streak, for when a young United States of America voted for its third president, in 1800, Cheshire was the only town in that part of the state that sided with Thomas Jefferson—unanimously. Driven on by Elder John Ireland, the local preacher, the dissidents for once managed to align themselves with the winning party, and they wanted to celebrate. Fun back then wasn't quite the same as our current concept. The dissidents lived in dairy country, and someone had the bright idea of creating a giant wheel of cheese—Cheshire, to be precise. The town worked hard, gathering curds from every resident farmer and pressing them into a wheel totaling 4 feet across, 1½ feet thick, and 1,235 pounds in weight. It took six horses pulling a sled to bring the slab to a ship on the Hudson River, which then brought it to Washington, D.C. (Maybe the town fathers hoped to have their whey with the president.)

It took a few months for the appetizer to reach Jefferson. The president was duly impressed and put it on display in the East Room of the White House in January 1802, with Supreme Court justices, foreign diplomats, and Congress looking on. Federalist critics of Jefferson tried to make fun of the cheese as a trivial interest and not worthy of the country's attention. In doing so, they compared the big cheese to the recent unearthing of mastodon bones in New York. (The excavation, which had taken place with aid from the Jefferson administration, was another unworthy endeavor in the eyes of the critics.) These writers called the wheel the *mammoth cheese,* giving rise to a new adjective. (Never underestimate the power of cheese.) Jefferson, unfazed, responded to the town with a personal letter.

In the twentieth century, town residents decided to commemorate their earlier commemoration. In 1940 they created a monument, a concrete cheese press, in memory of "the big Cheshire cheese." You can see it for yourself near the intersection of School and Church Streets.

R ULING THE R OOST
C h e s h i r e

I n his time, FDR promised Americans a chicken in every pot. Today the people of Cheshire would be hard-pressed to find a pot that was big enough. Apparently the people in this town, who also have that memorial to a giant cheese, have an affinity for big food. Sitting atop the town's Country Charm restaurant is a statue of a rooster standing about 10 feet tall, according to staff. Over the years many small businesses have had the idea that creating some sort of unusual decoration would help attract business. What hatched this particular bird was the Chicken Stop, a restaurant that previously occupied the premises.

The rooster stood proudly on the grass in front of the Chicken Stop and then the Country Charm until college students abducted the mascot in the mid-1990s. Perhaps the whole lot of them were trying to fly the coop. But sanity—and the rooster—returned, the latter being relegated to the roof where a casual acquaintance could not easily turn into a pickup. To see the proud poultry, visit the Country Charm on Route 8. But if you're hungry, don't go before 11:00 A.M., as it doesn't serve breakfast. Apparently this particular rooster doesn't rise at the crack of dawn.

CHAMPIONSHIP CHILLING
Chicopee

K now that saying, "Save room for dessert"? Here's one treat that would have required, oh, about fifty-odd years of judicious eating. Many people have done some extreme and downright crazy things for an entry into the *Guinness Book of Records*. Owners of the Dairy Queen in Chicopee decided that it would only be natural to try for the title of largest blended dessert on July 1, 1999. This frozen feat was a mass of vanilla ice cream (or whatever it is that Dairy Queens serve) with a copious amount of crushed Oreo cookies. The sweet treat topped out at a walloping 5,316.6 pounds. And you thought that a brownie sundae at the local family restaurant was a challenge. Undoubtedly Jenny Craig is still having psychically induced nightmares from it.

Actually, "largest blended dessert" sounds a bit dull. We think that *Guinness* missed the banana-split boat by ignoring a more apt title: biggest brain freeze. The post-entrée entry was too large to host at the shop, so it made its debut at the nearby Riverside Amusement Park in Agawam, now part of the local Six Flags theme park. You can still see the shop that created the confection at 1535 Memorial Drive, or call (413) 535–3005. Don't be surprised, however, if service is slow; we are sure that some of the staff is still recovering.

BRIDGE OVER TROUBLED WATERS
Colrain

F ew bridges jump around the way the Arthur B. Smith covered bridge has. The peripatetic pathway started its history in the 1800s in one location. Then a reconfiguration of some roads made it unnecessary. Transportation's discard was the boon of farmer Arthur Smith, who had been driving his cows across an open bridge to pasture lands. But that structure had collapsed, giving his cattle what was probably their first and only bath.

The existing covered bridge was moved to aid Smith and served him well. Years later, when Smith was no longer in the agriculture business, a major local employer—a cider mill— needed a bridge to move its product across the river. Again the covered bridge was moved, taking Smith's name with it. (Are you feeling dislocated yet?)

The bridge enjoyed a relatively long period of stability until 1981, although it did suffer some deterioration. No surprise, as any of us would have worn down a bit after 150 years. Now on the National Register of Historic Places, the bridge could not simply be disassembled and turned into firewood. The Colrain Historical Society involved itself and the town worked hard, supporting an effort to raise $40,000 to repair and move the bridge yet again, this time to a corn field. A local logger donated his efforts and the state offered lumber from a nearby forest.

It was an example of civic efficiency—until the wood had been obtained. Then one delay after another occurred. Some residents claim that someone misappropriated a portion of the raised funds. The Historical Society opposed suggestions to make the structure a footbridge and insisted that the bridge be used for vehicle travel only. During all the arguing, the replacement wood, sitting under a tarp next to the bridge, eventually rotted.

Today there are still plans to renovate the bridge. But now that the Massachusetts Highway Department is involved, the project is estimated to run $1.2 billion. And there is still no way to cross the river at the spot that was to benefit from the restoration and relocation. Was it highway robbery? Or just the case of a bridge not far enough? You can usually see the bridge from Route 112, but if the corn is high, go to the end of Lydonville Road.

LONG MAY IT GLOW
Colrain

Neon artist Tony Palumbo moved to Colrain with his partner, Michael Collins, in 1994. As electrically charged art is not a major industry in this part of Massachusetts, the two opened a well-received upscale restaurant, the Green Emporium. But you know what they say about neon—it's in the blood, or tubes. No matter; Palumbo couldn't keep away from bending the light. So he kept producing art, with a number of galleries exhibiting his work. Fast forward to September 19, 2001, right after the attacks on the World Trade Center. Local farmer Kenny Shearer stopped to talk with Palumbo and the conversation turned to the recent tragic event. Palumbo, a native New Yorker, was feeling badly and Shearer said that he had thought of erecting a large flag on his own property. Suddenly the switch flipped on for Palumbo, who asked, "Why not neon?"

The two got to work, getting permission from town selectmen and obtaining a building permit. Shearer drew to scale what he had envisioned. Turns out that when he thinks, he thinks *big*. The flag he had envisioned was to be 28 feet wide and 16 feet high. More people got involved. Shearer enlisted his friends and family, and an electrician neighbor donated his time to do all the electrical wiring. Palumbo's assistant, Scott Hoffman, joined in. Neon tubing came from Palumbo's studio in Brooklyn, and he trucked the 350 feet of powdered tubing himself. The local electrical utility, WMECO, helped by donating the power cable, while E. W. Martin Electric dug the trench. Obviously the Colrain crew was charged up over the project. You might think that art, when political, is usually hypercritical, but this is one time when it was deeply moved by current events.

Palumbo's installation, *Glowing Glory,* was officially lighted on November 25, 2001. You can see the flag online at www.glowingglory.com. For the real thing, use Palumbo's directions: From exit 26 off Interstate 91, take Route 2 west for 3.5 miles, turn right (north) onto Colrain/Shelburne Road, drive 2 miles to the Colrain/Shelburne line, then look left at Coombs Hill Road. Keep your head up and you can't miss it. Want to take a bit of the flag with you? Chandler's General Store in Colrain, 7 Jacksonville Road, carries postcards. You don't even need a plug.

RAGS TO RICHES
Dalton

There are people who dream of wading through piles of money. We can relate, but short of either being employed by the U.S. Mint or being adopted by the likes of Bill Gates, the closest you might get is the Crane Museum of Papermaking. While you won't see the finished product, you can learn a great deal about the paper that our money is printed on. Crane sold paper to Paul Revere in 1775, who printed the first paper money in what was then the Colonies, and it has regularly provided stock for American currency since 1842. In 1844 Crane developed a technique for weaving silk threads in banknotes to

The Crane Museum of Papermaking traces the history
of American papermaking from rags to riches.
Photo courtesy of Crane & Co. Inc.

help deter counterfeiters; more recently it has patented the technique of putting in those identifying security threads. Even though the company knows where the money is, Crane also produces stationery and paper for digital printing.

Instead of using wood pulp like most mills, Crane continues to produce papers with high rag content for strength and beauty. And you thought cotton was just for blue jeans. You can learn about how the company has historically made paper and see old paper molds and other educational displays at the museum in Crane's Old Stone Mill, built in 1844 on 30 South Street (413–684–6481). Oh, and as for that banknote paper— sorry, but no samples.

KILLER BEAVERS

*B*eavers are known as the engineers of the animal world, not as predatory killers. At least, that's their reputation until you get out to parts of western Massachusetts, where Indian legends tell a different story. According to the Pocumtuck tribe of Deerfield, a giant beaver lived in a lake, now long gone, that was once in the area. Apparently the buck-toothed wonder, tired of wearing down its incisors chewing wood, would from time to time venture into the surrounding area and eat people.

This was not a habit to endear the creature to the Pocumtuck. According to their legends, the people requested the aid of another giant—the spirit Hobomock, who hunted the beaver and killed it. The beaver sank back into the lake, transforming from animal into rock. After the lake drained, over time, the carcass was left exposed. There are legends from some other nearby tribes that mirror the basic story, varying some details, such as what Hobomock used to smite the amphibious rodent.

These days, the beaver's body is what we call the Pocumtuck Range and the head is Mount Sugarloaf, now a popular ski resort.

TUNNEL TO NOWHERE
Goshen

U nexplained natural structures may be mysterious, but they are at least understandable in some remote, prehistoric way. It's when something unnatural is more recent, when you would think that there must be some record of the effort involved, that the unknown can be plain annoying. In those terms the Goshen Tunnel is extremely irritating and confusing.

In the nineteenth century, some hunters came upon a big hole in the ground, more than 3 feet in diameter. The opening runs straight down about 15 feet. At the bottom, two tunnels, about 2-feet tall, run parallel to the surface in two different directions. One of them is another 15 feet or so in length, while the other extends five times as far. Both end at cave-ins. It's a tidy hole, lined with rock and flagstones, so obviously someone spent considerable time and energy creating it.

But why? On that point, there is only conjecture. Recently people have started calling it the counterfeiter's den, because authorities once apprehended some practitioners of that art a few miles away. However, it is hard to imagine a counterfeiter creating such an elaborate hideaway with no light and little room to run a printing press. Others hypothesize that some settler in the area was trying to raise silkworms, or that someone in the Underground Railroad took the term too seriously. However, some research indicates that parts of the tunnels were dug about 10,000 years ago and that the stone ceiling was put into place around 3,000 B.C. Given the age, we think that the tunnels were actually an early relic of the Big Dig, the project that is (at this writing) still depressing the central artery of Boston underground—and depressing everyone who must put up with it. Any century now, the link between there and Goshen is bound to open up. In the meantime, to view the site (the entrance is usually blocked for safety), take a trip to the Goshen Cemetery off Williams Drive between Cape Street and Route 9.

GREEN POWER
Greenfield

I f you are convinced that one more visit to an enclosed educational enclave with meaningful content (a.k.a., a museum) will require medical professionals to drag you away kicking and screaming, it's time to run away and out into the open air at the Greenfield Energy Park. Whoever designed this place must have remembered what it was like to be a kid.

Kids blow off steam on a wooden play train.
Photo by Sandy Thomas/Courtesy of Greenfield Energy Park

Yes, it seems a bit politically correct to expect youngsters to frolic amid large solar panels and dance between the batteries. But don't be harsh. You'll soon be entranced by a sculpture of a train powered by an on-site electrical grid with figures that pop up and down on the hour. There's another sculpture that turns by wind energy, and custom tiles that identify trees and shrubs around the park. The amphitheater is made of recycled granite, and the transportation museum is housed in an old train caboose.

Perhaps the best attractions are the wooden play train and the butterfly garden, where your kids can blow off steam. To arrive for your day of fascination, take your favorite environmentally friendly transportation to the park on Bank Row, also on the Web at www.nesea.org/park.

G R A V E   R U B B E R S
Greenfield

Does history leave you cold? Not as cold as the subjects of this organization's focus. The Association for Gravestone Studies thinks that much of history is written in stone—headstones, to be specific. They see important information—from genealogy and religious history to changing fashions in art and literature—locked into the letters at the tops of burial sites.

Any of the association's 1,200 members can check with the central registry to get information on gravestone subjects. The association has a lending library of reference volumes and an online store with instructions on how to do research on the occupant of a particular grave. The association also offers cemetery guides, calendars, note cards with images of gravestones in the snow (be careful whom you send these to), and

This organization hopes to rub you the right way.
Photo by Robert Posson/Courtesy of the Association for
Gravestone Studies

even software for recording details of gravestones. Information kits give you the practical instructions on how to do everything from making gravestone rubbings to understanding symbols on the stones to learning techniques for analyzing cemetery data.

For more information, call (413) 772–0836 or go to www.gravestonestudies.org. The organization's headquarters are at 278 Main Street, Suite 207.

WHAT COMES DOWN MUST GO UP
Greenfield

I sn't it nice to know that some things don't change? For example, the trusty law of gravity is bound to bring things to their lowest point. Well, it will, *most* of the time. If you're the type who likes to know about exceptions to the rule, head over to Greenfield and take the exit off Route 91 for Gravity Hill. According to legend, a horrible accident happened there, involving a bus full of children going off the overpass, killing all the occupants. As the story goes, if you stop a car beneath the overpass and take it out of gear, the phantom children's hands will push the vehicle down the road a bit so that you won't get hurt.

Okay, so the story might seem a bit hard to believe. But many people who've tried it have found that their cars rolled at least a good 20 feet in a direction that seemed to be uphill. If you are interested in trying to bend gravity to somebody else's will, or just experiencing a good optical illusion, take Route 91 to exit 26. Turn so you can drive under the overpass, shift into neutral, and wait to see what happens.

ON BALANCE
Lanesborough

K eeping on your toes will be easy after a visit to Balance Rock. This massive piece of limestone, 25 feet by 15 feet by 10 feet weighing some 165 tons, perches delicately on another

SUPERNATURAL CITIZENS

For some reason, Hadley seems to have attracted the worst and the best of the supernatural. We have all heard someone describe a woman as a "witch" when what they are really thinking involves a simple substitute of the initial letter. We wonder whether that might be what provoked the denunciation of Mary Webster, the Witch of Hadley. She reputedly had an unpleasant temper under the best of conditions. After a life of poverty and social shunning, she had a tongue ready to attack those who drew her displeasure.

Some of Webster's neighbors decided that she must be a witch. They blamed her for scaring cattle and children, among other things. At a time when accusations were almost as good as proof, she was brought before a local court, sent on to Boston, and held over for further trial. Yet ultimately she was found not guilty by a jury. (Perhaps they thought they would be safer were she back from whence she came.)

Back in Hadley, Webster's neighbors disagreed with the judgment. A group of young men dragged her from her house, attempted to hang her, then tossed her in the snow. Being a tough old bird, she lived another eleven years and died of old age at around seventy. If they thought she was a witch before, we'd hate to see what she was like after.

Hadley also had an angel—William Goffe. He was one of the fifty-nine judges who signed the death warrant of Charles I of England, endearing none of them to Charles II. Both Goffe and fellow judge Edward Whaley had to flee to the New World in 1660 and go into hiding.

After a few years of moving about, the two were hidden by the Rev. John Russell for sixteen years. It is said that once, when a group of Indians were attacking the Colonists, an aged man, unknown to any of the group of fifty or so families, took charge. He repelled the braves and then vanished. The people said that it was an angel sent to protect them, but the legend claims that it was Goffe, who had left his hiding place to lend aid and then disappeared as soon as the fight was over. Unfortunately, later scholarship disputes that Indian forces ever approached the town and suggests that the "angel of Hadley" story started in the eighteenth century. We consider it a case of miraculous conscription.

rock 3 feet above the ground. You'd think it was a shaky position, and it is—touch the rock and it shivers—but it hasn't come down yet.

This wasn't some invention by a tipsy architect, but rather a natural result of glacial action. That might explain why stories about the boulder go back centuries. In the 1800s it was owned by the Hubert family, who welcomed those who came to gawk. Then a traveling band of rascals who asked to see the rock promptly set up shop and tried to charge others a dime each for the view. Grove Hubert, the family member in charge at the time, was angry enough to try to rock the rock. Luckily, he learned that oxen do little when it comes to moving large chunks of mineral.

Eventually the state purchased the property and planted tens of thousands of trees to make it an inviting park. There are some other interesting rocks here, too: a rock that looks like a whale, one with a series of cracks that look like a cross, and a pair of twin rocks.

On balance, we know it's only a rock that doesn't roll, but we like it. See the stone at Balance Rock State Park on Balance Rock Road in the northwest corner of Pittsfield State Forest. For more information, visit www.state.ma.us/dem/parks/pitt .htm.

Face Facts
Lanesborough

Ever had that funny feeling that someone is watching you? That is what happened to residents in northwest Massachusetts from May 10 through May 14, 1990. Heavy rains throughout that time finally sent earth, granite, and everything else tumbling down the side of nearby Mount Greylock, revealing the image of a face on the slope of this tallest peak in the state. In sort of a reverse face lift, the rough visage of an Indian appeared, staring down. People started calling the figure Chief Greylock, after a Waronoke Indian who spent a good part of his time in the early 1700s harassing English soldiers from a secret cave in the mountain. At one point, he had half his foot amputated after a run-in with an animal trap; little wonder that he gained the nickname "the frowning chief of the Waronokes." But apparently that didn't slow him down. He sided with the French during the French and Indian Wars and was never caught or defeated, although he did manage to humiliate English forces time and again.

You can find the Mount Greylock State Reservation on Rockwell Road in Lanesborough. Bascom Lodge, at the top, offers a place to stay overnight as well as food in the summer and fall. Call (413) 499–4262 for more information.

THIS IS THE CHURCH, THIS IS THE STEEPLE
Lee

Record-tall buildings are usually the province of corporations. But for some reason, the First Congregational Church in Lee has come out on top in the area of timber frame construction—that's where the skeleton of the building is a series of large posts and beams that interlock. It's a beautiful style of building to see because the frame is exposed on the interior, adding not only great strength but also aesthetic pleasure.

For the First Congregation Church building, the timber construction is in the 105-foot-tall spire. It is the highest structure in the country using this method of construction. But remember, we're talking about the steeple—the very top of the church, a needle point rising even above the church bells, which are above the four-faced clock (itself a curiosity because it is wound by hand and runs for seven days before needing another winding). Sitting atop the rest of the church, the steeple reaches 192 feet high. In other words, this is a part of the church that rarely receives visitors.

However, some people have had a look. Built in 1857, the steeple had been struck by lightning and by 1987 needed some repair. (What kind of makeover do you think *you* might need at the age of 150?) Besides other bits of maintenance, it seems that the tower was tilting a couple of feet. Over a period of two weeks, Dalton-based Hill-Engineers, Architects, Planners, Inc. used hydraulic jacks to move some columns up an eighth of an inch a day. Presumably, they wanted to avoid moving too quickly and causing a need to yell "timberrrrrrrrr." To see the no-longer-tipping tower, head to 25 Park Place.

ACTION MAN
North Adams

Norman Rockwell was known for his highly realistic style of illustrations of everyday life. No surprise that his son Jarvis was also drawn to the visual. But the younger Rockwell had a more playful attitude and the toys to prove it. Since 1979, Rockwell has been collecting toys—specifically, action figures ranging from an inch to a foot in height. We're talking enough toys to fill eight large containers in storage at a moving company, sixty or seventy used liquor boxes at a storage facility, and even more in the attic of his home. No one has counted how many there are, though Rockwell has started a list. So far, his list, complete with descriptions and locations, fills six looseleaf notebooks. "I think they're extraordinary," he

Jarvis Rockwell's action figures fill an 11-foot-high,
four-sided pyramid.
Photo by Robert B. Wyatt/Courtesy of Jarvis Rockwell

says of his toys. "They represent where we are, what we think as we go along. They're endlessly inventive. Even watching the way they change the Hulk figure—how big can you make him? I just keep buying them."

At one time in the past, Rockwell invited passersby off the street to come into his home and pick a toy to take with them. But that was unsatisfying, so he created a piece of conceptual art using thousands of the figures arranged around an 11-foot-high, four-sided pyramid. The sculpture is now in storage at the Massachusetts Museum of Contemporary Art. When the museum's sixth building is opened sometime in the next couple of years, the pyramid—called Maya, after the Hindu concept of the illusion of the world—will again be on exhibit.

Rockwell isn't getting any younger—he's in his early seventies at the time of this writing—and he'd like to do something
with many of the figures in storage. So don't be surprised if
you hear about him toying with more art.

THE BIG SHOW
North Adams

W here would you go for contemporary art? New York? L.A.?
Chicago? San Francisco? How about an old textile town in
northwest Massachusetts with a population hovering around
15,000? North Adams is home to the Massachusetts Museum of
Contemporary Art, or Mass MoCA—the largest American
museum devoted to the genre.

How such an institution found itself in an economically
depressed region of the commonwealth is an interesting story
that starts in 1988, when then-governor Michael Dukakis ear-
marked funds for the project. The idea was to provide an economic transfusion to the region. Then "the Duke" had his
picture taken while wearing a helmet and sitting in a tank,
and not long after, he lost his presidential bid. The Massachusetts economic "miracle" turned out to be a temporary turn of
events, money became tight, and gubernatorial successor
William Weld froze the funds. But in 1995 he finally approved
a large sum of money to begin converting old textile mills into
galleries and theaters. These days, Mass MoCA sprawls among
twenty-six nineteenth-century factory buildings on a thirteen-
acre campus and covers not only the visual arts, but electronic
media and the performing arts as well. Included amid the
100,000 square feet of exhibition space is a single gallery that
is as long as a football field; undoubtedly, some artist will bring
in two eleven-man teams and make the project interactive by
selling beer and hot dogs.

Natalie Jeremijenko's Tree Logic *greets visitors to Mass MoCA.*
Photo by Doug Bartow/Courtesy of Mass MoCA

It seems equivalent to finding a major league baseball stadium in the middle of a wheat field. But Mass MoCA seems to be thriving on the concept that "if you build it, they will come." With theaters, outdoor cinemas, workshops, and even companies subletting office and retail space, this is almost a mall-as-art project. You can see plays, hear music, dine at restaurants, and even bring the kids to a family gallery and studio space called Kidspace at Mass MoCA. You can probably even get lost and organize your own rescue expedition. Check the days and hours for Kidspace at www.massmoca.org/kidspace or at (413) 662–2111. You can get information on the parent organization by calling the same phone number or by visiting www.mass moca.org. To tour the main galleries, head to 87 Marshall Street; Kidspace is at 1032 Mass MoCA Way. Bring your own football helmet.

LOST ITS MARBLE
North Adams

I f you can take slang literally, then North Adams must be one of the craziest places in Massachusetts, having lost a lot of its marble. No, not *marbles*—we're talking about white marble, the stuff used in hearthstones and fireplace mantels and cemeteries. For more than a century, the area now called Natural Bridge State Park was the leading source for the material used throughout Massachusetts.

The famous author Nathaniel Hawthorne wrote in 1838 that parts of North Adams seemed gloomy and stern to him. Well, of course, Nat; we're talking the essence of fancy headstones here. The marble owes its quality in part to its chemical makeup: 98 percent calcium carbonate, otherwise known as limestone or natural chalk (or the antacid pills you might pop into your mouth after a bad burrito). Not only is the material beautiful and suited for building, but the dust and chips left after slicing slabs were also put into toothpaste, putty, and soap. How versatile: You can get your hands dirty cutting it, then wash with it afterward.

From 1837 to 1947 the mill literally ground out all these products, eventually shipping 400,000 pounds of stone a day. Then came a fire, putting the mill out of business and leaving the place as quiet as a mausoleum. A man by the name of Edward Elder purchased the upscale rock pit from the company that had owned it, and he ran it as a tourist attraction until his death in the mid-1980s. Shortly afterwards, his widow sold the site to the Massachusetts Department of Environmental Management, which turned it into a park.

One of the interesting features is a natural marble bridge. (Hence the name.) For more information, see www.berkshire web.com/mohawktrail/natbridge.html, or call either (413)

663–6392 (May to October) or (413) 663–6312 (November to April.) To cross to Natural Bridge State Park, drive north on Route 8 half a mile from downtown North Adams.

GETTING KIDDED
Northfield

A hoy, matey. *Ahhhrrrr,* you'd think that a pirate's story would take place on the ocean. Last map we checked, this part of Massachusetts is some 90 miles from the Atlantic. So why would anyone associate raiders of the high seas with Northfield? The legend goes that Captain Kidd actually sailed here up the Connecticut River, trying to find a hiding place for his loot. After all, even in the early eighteenth century, it was difficult to walk into a bank with chests of stolen goods to make a deposit.

So Kidd and some compatriots supposedly buried a chest of gold somewhere on Northfield's Clark's Island. That alone might sound suspicious, as the Connecticut River is often too shallow in spots for any boat, let along one carrying a chest of gold coins.

According to the stories from Temple and Sheldon's *History of Northfield, MA, 150 Years,* Kidd and a few of his crew managed to make their way to Clark's Island at a part called Pine Meadow. They supposedly buried a treasure chest and left. After the hangman's noose snagged Kidd, the treasure was left to be found. A legend grew that the only way to find the gold was to have three people dig soundlessly under a full moon that was directly overhead. In the 1800s a trio of men reportedly was digging about under these conditions, not even swatting the mosquitoes that were munching them (for fear of making noise), when they spotted a chest. Someone spoke in elation, at which point the money sank out of reach, never to be found again.

Feel the need to dig into the legend more? Maybe you will be the one who finds the treasure. At some point cartographers took the legend seriously enough to rechristen Clark's Island as Kidd's Island. It's roughly in the middle of the river alongside a spot about half a mile down from the northern start of Pine Meadow Road. Bring your own boat—and be very quiet. You're hunting treasure.

Derby Day
Pittsfield

Traditional 4-H fairs are a staple of rural areas, including much of western Massachusetts. Youths compete by exhibiting vegetables, flowers, and even livestock they have raised. But while the Berkshire County *4-H Fair Handbook for 2004* states how much cleanliness—both of animals and the areas in which they are kept—contributes to scores awarded by judges, there is a delicate lack of mention of the annual dung drop derby.

The derby is an annual fundraiser. Fair organizers and workers divide a field into a large grid. People purchase a square for $5.00, much as they might buy a raffle ticket. A cow is turned loose in the field, where it is welcome to stroll around, chew its cud . . . and drop a cow patty. The person who wagered on that square is the winner. It's not clear what happens if the deposit drops on the border between two grids.

Unfortunately, there have been times when the cow simply wouldn't cooperate, at which point another is brought in. It might seem udderly silly to you, but we have it on good authority that locals anticipate the event. To find the next derby, check the Massachusetts listings of agricultural fairs at www.state.ma.us/dfa/fairs/fair_list.htm. Go to the youth fairs section, then look for the Berkshire County 4-H Fair. You can also call (413) 448–8285 for more information. The fair itself runs one day, usually the third Saturday in August, and can be found at Utility Drive, which is off Holmes Road. Needless to say, don't wear your good clothes.

Sing, Sing, Sing
Sheffield

D o inveterate shower singers make you wish that the ring around the tub was a wringing of a neck? If you want to K-O people who start bellowing, "O-K-L-A-H-O-M-A . . . Okla-homa!" then by all means, be wary of Sheffield in the summer, when it hosts the Berkshire Choral Festival. Started in 1982 and running on the campus of the Berkshire School, the festi-val attracts 1,600 people from all over the world who have an insatiable desire to burst into song and want to spend a week doing nothing but that. They call it "the week that lasts a life-time," and we have a funny feeling that we would agree with them. Participants come from an even larger pool, and would-be choristers must enter a drawing by February to get a spot on the roster. Warning: This event is not over in seven days. Professional conductors switch off to provide a season that lasts for about five weeks.

If you'd like to sing classical works in intensive rehearsal periods under accomplished conductors, this place might be for you. Just make sure you are vocally in shape. The choral music is moderately difficult, and if you don't know how to keep to your part—whether soprano, alto, tenor, baritone, or bass—the music lovers around you may cease to be lovable. You have to study tapes and written music ahead of time, and if management thinks that your singing is not up to snuff, they reserve the right to kick you out on your andante. If you like singing but have a voice that depresses even the tone deaf, you can still attend . . . as a member of the audience. For more information, call (413) 229–8526 or visit www.chorus.org.

BRIDGE OVER TROUBLED LILACS
Shelburne Falls

There are people who will turn *anything* into a planter, but most are amateurs compared to the folks in Shelburne Falls. These gardening gurus took an old trolley bridge and transformed it into a garden. And this isn't some little stone structure adorned by a few gladioluses and petunias. The Bridge of Flowers runs some 400 feet, with 500 varieties of flowers that start blooming in April and end in October in a floral last hurrah of chrysanthemums. Originally built in 1908, this piece of civil engineering was as staid as any waterworks or highway overpass. It was the property of the Shelburne Falls and Colrain Street Railway and part of the route of the freight trolley that operated between this town and the mills in nearby Colrain.

But progress reared its ugly head as the automobile made way for its big brother, the truck. Suddenly it was cheaper and easier to make runs between the towns with individual vehicles and not maintain an entire train system; the rail company went out of business in 1928. Sure, there was no problem taking the cars off the tracks, pretending that the entire venture never existed, but a bridge is a hard thing to hide, especially when water mains run across it. To keep from being high and dry, the town bought the bridge in 1929. Some locals thought that there was no reason that something so utilitarian had to look seedy. If water was going to run over the bridge, they reasoned, they might as well sprinkle some *on* it. That year, the town raised money to transform the bridge into a public garden. (Undoubtedly, this was before the great stock market crash, which left few people with a pot to plant in.) Since then, donations and a largely volunteer effort have kept the bridge in bloom and the weeds at bay. Today the Shelburne Falls Women's Club does much of the work, along with a hired gardener. For more information, call (413) 625-2544 or just travel to the intersection of Water and Bridge Streets—how appropriate—to see the floral frenzy.

Prehistoric Potholes
Shelburne Falls

If you've ever made pothole jokes like, "Oh, this one is so big that it almost swallowed my car," take time to visit Shelburne Falls and see what real potholes are like. These aren't the measly little pits that dot pavements after a cold snap. The biggest of them ranks as the world's largest pothole, 39 feet across. Not only could you literally lose your car in this mother of all potholes, you could probably say goodbye to a good-sized truck.

Luckily for the residents, the potholes are not on the streets but down near a hydroelectric dam. It seems that during the time of the last glaciers melting, the region's level of high water was quite impressive and the Connecticut River greatly expanded its reach. Stones, trapped in a riverbed, were shaken about by the flow of water and acted as drills. They created the potholes near the dam.

You might think it strange for a town to look at a collection of old holes in the ground and consider it a tourist attraction.

Even stranger is that people actually *do* come by to see the potholes. Residents have even given them a name: the Glacial Potholes. (Better that than the Pits.) Go to the end of Deerfield Street and you will find an observation deck overlooking the potholes, as well as some local falls. Just get there before some zealous department of public works makes a pilgrimage and leaves a mass of asphalt.

SIMPLE OR SIMPLE-MINDED?
Shutesbury

Eugenics is the dubious pursuit of using genetics to argue for the supposed superiority of groups of people. Although it turned into a horror in World War II, before that it actually had proponents in the United States. And the evidence they waved about was actually garnered from Shutesbury, a sleepy town of under 2,000 that hasn't any stores. As explained in an interesting story in *Boston Magazine* (www.bostonmagazine .com/special1/eugenics_1202.shtml), the Shutesbury Study of 1928 was a deceptive inquiry into the personal, medical, and educational histories of the residents. It was used as evidence for the necessity of culling society's undesirables. Getting shameful support from leading academics from such schools as Harvard as well as others less "qualified" (the man who arranged the study, Leon Whitney, was actually a dog breeder), the movement gained attention for its views at the time. Much of the evidence came from field studies where people were supposedly trained to detect human character by appearance. One of the proponents, Walter Fernald, was the first resident superintendent of the Massachusetts School for the Feeble-Minded, an institution that would eventually take his name and go on to greater fame by feeding radioactive cereal to children in the 1950s as part of another experiment.

Yet Shutesbury seems to have survived it all. People still live there, the air is clean, the traffic is insignificant, and the surroundings are beautiful. When you come from a congested urban locale, it makes you wonder who the simple-minded people are after all.

FEE, FIE, FOE, FOOT
South Hadley

M any youngsters are interested in dinosaurs, and for a few, the fascination never ends. In the case of the Nash family, you might say that dinosaurs became an obsession that turned into a vocation. The business used to be called Nash Dino Land, but when the founder, Carlton Nash, died a few years ago, his son, Kornell, changed the name to the Nash Dinosaur Track Quarry.

Dinosaur tracks go back a long time in the area. (Okay, okay, they go back a long time *everywhere*.) But it was in 1802 that people found the first prehistoric footprints in the South Hadley area. For some reason, during the Jurassic period the roaming lizards were ill-bred, walking through the local mud flats and never wiping their feet. Such is the way of the world that one man's messy ground can be another man's living. Growing up in the area, Carlton Nash was fascinated with dinosaurs. Right after high school he began prowling through the local woods, hoping to unearth a cache of footprints. He found one in 1933, but it took him six years to save enough money to buy the property.

The elder Nash began working his track mine. It must have felt as though he was on a treadmill: At first he cut Christmas trees in the fall, worked for the electric company in the spring, and sold dinosaur prints in the summer. By 1950 he was able to make dinosaurs his business. His son eventually joined him, and now Kornell spends his time trying to update displays that are showing their ages. (Though after the first million years, who notices a decade or two?) Much of Kornell's living comes from selling two groups of actual fossil prints: one about 4 to 7 inches, and the other about 12 to 20 inches. Prices start at $50 and go to roughly $1,000, depending on the size of the track and the condition. It must be said that he prices by the foot.

Nash Dinosaur Track Quarry is just off Route 116, about 3 miles north of South Hadley Center. Look for the sign.

Seuss I Am
Springfield

That Dr. Seuss, that Dr. Seuss, you cannot fault that Dr. Seuss. Could he, would he illustrate? Books for kids would seem his fate. And his words were always pat. He could write about a cat. He could top the cat with a hat from the desk at which he sat. Kids would laugh and that was that.

Before he found his kids' book fame, young Ted Geisel's job was tame, marketing a corporate name. After this came work more rare, magazines requiring care: *Judge* and *Life* and *Vanity Fair*. Then he got to draw and write; publishers had seen his light, work that was a pure delight. Raves from critics it did woo: Emmys, Oscars, Pulitzer, too.

When he died, his hometown thought, "Celebrate," and so they sought something fun, not overwrought. Artist Lark Grey Dimond-Cates was called in, to craft bronze statues thick and thin. These show Dr. Seuss, cat in tow, Yertle Turtle, Grinch, and Max, Horton's Who and the Lorax. The author had watched the sculptress grow; he was her step-dad, you should know. So drive to State and Chestnut Streets to see some art that can't be beat.

Dr. Seuss and the Cat in the Hat sculpture.

E L D E R   R I D E R
S p r i n g f i e l d

H arley-Davidson was not the first major brand that came out
of the motorcycle industry; that distinction belongs to the
Indian Motorcycle Company, which started in Springfield. More
than a motorcycle, the Indian was a way of life. The makers
combined the top in technology with élan and a tradition of
making great bikes. But the brand was sold in 1999, and who
knows what will happen to the company. But if you want to
remember the original, head to the Indian Motorcycle Museum
and Hall of Fame to join the wild bunch that appreciates this
part of history.

Aside from Harley-Davidson, Indian was the only one of
more than two dozen American motorcycle companies that
made it through the Great Depression. But Indian was on
shaky ground and finally failed in the 1950s.

The museum includes the world's first Indian motorcycle,
as well as a bike made of wood; aircraft engines and boat
engines; the world's first snowmobile; products from other
famous manufacturers; and a load of toys. There is also a
replica of the first commercial motorcycle—not an Indian, but
an 1885 Daimler (the original is probably still out on a road
trip). To see the museum, saddle up and head to 33 Hendee
Street. For more information, call (413) 737–2624. Leather
jackets are optional.

Extra-Large Stack
Springfield

Most of the breakfast-going world divides into two camps: short and full stacks. Where you come down on the question is a matter of devotion and capacity because, let's face it, instead of soaring, those doughy flying saucers can pin you to the floor as efficiently as a professional wrestler. For some people, a mass of pancakes is something to avoid, while for others, it means a bigger sponge for sopping up the syrup. Do you find yourself asking, "May I have more?" If so, the answer is that you may—in May. Every May the city of Springfield hosts what it has come to call the world's largest pancake breakfast, in celebration of its anniversary. Forget any church or charity breakfast you have seen. This is the morning's first meal on a scale frightening to behold. The event takes place outside (there is no indoor venue that will do) along Main Street, from State to Bridge.

In the past few years, about 70,000 people have shown up for this feast each year, which is a huge jump from the estimated 40,000 in 1999. We are talking enough flapjacks to make a stack that is literally miles high. The Library of Congress has deemed this May-munching-madness a Local Legacy Event. Undoubtedly it happens only once a year so that the volunteers have a chance to wash all the dishes and pans in time for the next observance. If you want more information, call (413) 733-3800.

STATUESQUE
Stockbridge

We thought that artists were supposed to be perpetually hungry and ensconced in garrets. After learning about Chesterwood, we've come to the conclusion that such stories are nothing but aggressive public relations to convince tax authorities and debt collectors to forgo phone calls and write off any owed money as unobtainable. This 122-acre estate was not even the main residence of sculptor Daniel Chester French, but rather the man's summer home and studio. Oh, well, he was in his seventies when he acquired the property, so some allowance can be made for financial endurance.

While French's name may not be immediately familiar, his work is bound to be. It includes such memorials as the seated president in the Lincoln Memorial and the Minute Man statue in Concord. There are literally dozens of his statues tucked away in

The 1920s summer home of Daniel Chester French is open from May through October.
Photo by Ron Blunt/Courtesy of Chesterwood

various parts of Massachusetts. At Chesterwood you can see models of some of French's works, as well as paintings that he's created and others that he's collected, his tools, and even exhibitions of other artists' sculpture. Enjoy the spacious Italian gardens May through October, and remember, it was a summer residence, so don't expect to wander the grounds in the off season (although there are special programs at Christmas). For more information, call (413) 298–3579, or visit www.chesterwood.org. To reach Chesterwood, go to the west end of Main Street and follow the signs to the location on Williamsville Road.

NO WICKED WITCH HERE
Tyringham

Most of us grew up with fairy tales, including the story of Hansel and Gretel, who were enticed by the gingerbread house. They had troubles, but nothing that putting a little heat on the situation couldn't cure. Those visiting Tyringham, however, can feel as cool as a cucumber while visiting the gingerbread house of Sir Henry Kitson. The edifice, which he called Santarella, was his art studio. It featured a whimsical design that made visitors feel like they were in the middle of a storybook. But whimsy can be deceptive. The studio's wavy thatched roof is actually a carefully constructed sculpture, formed from sliced dyed asphalt roof shingles set in stacks more than 1½ feet thick. Heavy chestnut beams hold the estimated eighty tons of weight.

There is a certain degree of irony that Sir Henry, a Brit, was the sculptor of the Puritan Maid in Plymouth. He was also responsible for the Minute Man statue in Lexington, commemorating a war in which, to put it nicely, our side whooped his.

(The statue is not to be confused with the Minute Man in Concord, created by Daniel Chester French, whose former house is now a museum in Stockbridge.) Some of Kitson's other works include statues of Robert E. Lee and Jefferson Davis, so his subjects weren't always on the winning side.

Like French, Kitson built his getaway when he hit his seventies. Perhaps on a small scale, Kitson struck one for Britain, taking the money he made in statues of the political elite and in memorials and hiring workers from the United Kingdom to build his roof. But he was reputedly an incredibly difficult man to work for, so we wonder how many came to wish that the project's roof would just cave in.

Santarella is open from Memorial Day through the end of October and is at 75 Main Road. Not only can you visit the museum and gardens, but there are even overnight guest rooms to rent here—just make sure you have easy access to the oven. Call (413) 243–3260 for more information.

THE BIG SQUEEZE
Washington

If you have a taste for French cafes, Cajun two-stepping, Italian weddings, or just a lively polka band, we have an event for you. Something that all four have in common is the accordion—or squeeze box, to use the more down-home and eclectic title. The instrument has been the butt of humor for years, whether called a concertina or a button box. Yet to its devotees, there is nothing more endearing than the reedy, wheezy sound produced by this family of miniature, portable, wind-driven pianos. In Amherst there is a shop that specializes in the sales and repairs of accordions and concertinas. Obviously the management has a soft spot in their hearts (and, those who don't like the sound would say, in their heads) for the instruments and those who love them.

And so, to promote camaraderie (and presumably sales) the store, called the Button Box, began to organize and sponsor the Northeast Squeeze-In Festival in Washington. Every September it sports what is undoubtedly the largest collection of players who gather to do nothing but to press their own buttons, if not each other's. The gathering takes place at Bucksteep Manor, an estate on Washington Mountain Road. For more information, call (413) 549–0171 or visit www.buttonbox.com.

FORWARD INTO THE PAST
West Springfield

Have your kids seen any of the television programs in which modern families live in the setting of some earlier era— whether Edwardian, frontier time, or Pilgrim? They can actually have a taste of it themselves at Storrowton Village, a re-creation of a nineteenth-century New England community, complete with town green. Kids can spend a day or even a week dressed in period clothing, trying their hand at such crafts as candle dipping and tile mosaics, milking a cow, and spinning wool and weaving. If they are going for the day, the kids bring their own lunch. (What, there was a time without Big Macs?) For longer visits, meals are provided.

We bet that no matter how good the program, your children won't return ready to haul the water or feed the pigs. But at least you'll have a few days of relative quiet. For more information, call (413) 205–5051, or visit www.thebige.com/ storrowton.html to check programs and events.

A NOSE FOR BUSINESS
West Stockbridge

When things go well, most businesspeople would not say that they smell. But a heavy aroma is a good sign at Charles H. Baldwin and Sons, a shop established in 1888 and dedicated to the proposition that not all vanillas are created equal. The store is a major source of upscale vanilla extract—a distillation of the fruit of tropical orchids. And here the dismissive phrase "plain vanilla" is a euphemism for "unbelievably expensive." Baldwin's uses only Madagascar Bourbon vanilla beans distilled in a copper apparatus that is over sixty-five years old. They then age it in hundred-year-old oak barrels to add to the flavoring and color. When Charles Baldwin started his business, he went by horse and buggy from door to door. Today orders come in from chefs and demanding amateur cooks from around the world over the Web site (www.baldwinextracts.com). But as good as vanilla is, the current owners, the Moffatt family, have branched out to such flavors as lemon, almond, and peppermint. They also have a Worcestershire sauce and a maple syrup with walnuts and (what else?) vanilla, both from old recipes the Moffatts found in the store.

Years ago many women used a dab of vanilla instead of perfume. Men who might feel a bit uncomfortable doing the same can pick up a bottle of Baldwin's bay rum. Accept no substitutes, as you'll "nose" the difference. The shop is at 1 Center Street, (413) 232–7785.

INDEX

ABOUT THE AUTHORS

Bruce Gellerman is an international award-winning journalist with more than twenty years' experience in radio, print, and television, including creating and hosting the popular public radio show *Here & Now*. Journalist **Erik Sherman**'s writing and photographs have appeared in many national publications, and he is the author of *Geocaching: Hike and Seek with Your GPS*.